The Missing Link

An Introduction to Web Development and Programming

by Michael G. Mendez

Open SUNY Textbooks

2014

ISBN: 978-1502447968

Published by Open SUNY Textbooks, Milne Library (IITG PI)

State University of New York at Geneseo,
Geneseo, NY 14454

Licensing

*To my family and friends, for supporting, encouraging,
and challenging me over the years.*

About the Textbook

Web development is an evolving amalgamation of languages that work in concert to receive, modify, and deliver information between parties using the Internet as a mechanism of delivery. While it is easy to describe conceptually, implementation is accompanied by an overwhelming variety of languages, platforms, templates, frameworks, guidelines, and standards. Navigating a project from concept to completion often requires more than mastery of one or two complementing languages, meaning today's developers need both breadth, and depth, of knowledge to be effective.

This text provides the developer with an understanding of the various elements of web development by focusing on the concepts and fundamentals through the examples within, providing a foundation that allows easier transition to other languages and a better understanding of how to approach their work. The reader will be introduced to topics in a manner that follows most project development methods, from initial conceptualization and design through front end development, back end development, and introducing additional concepts like accessibility and security, while focusing on responsive design techniques. Each section of the text includes opportunities to practice the material and assess increased knowledge after examining the topics.

About the Author

Michael Mendez, M.S., is a professional web developer and professor with a master's degree received after studying computer science, business, and communications at the State University of New York, University at Fredonia. Having worked in the information technology field for over 12 years, he has provided the small to medium business market and public sector agencies with services in hardware and network installation and support, web development, systems support and maintenance, and solutions design and implementation. These experiences have involved academic, media, emergency management, non-profit, business to business, and business to consumer organizations.

Reviewer's Notes

It is always a challenge to teach a course in web design or web programming. Systems that run on the World Wide Web must necessarily change with the emergence of any sort of new computer technology, creating a rapidly evolving landscape. The students that enroll in web development courses are a particularly diverse group; the subject attracts strong programmers with weak aesthetic design skills as well as those who are more aesthetically inclined with little knowledge of programming. Finally, the visibility and mission criticality of web platforms makes the design and security of these systems paramount.

The Missing Link attempts to bridge the gap between these conflicting educational demands. While most web development texts opt to delve deeply into one or two of the tools in the belt of a web programmer, the author of this text takes a broad approach to teaching web programming and development. The result is a single resource that integrates good design practices, modern technologies, and all of the programming tools that one would need to build a successful, dynamic web site.

Unlike many texts, this one begins by giving the readers a solid foundation in the technology that runs the Internet along with a sense of what technology is currently coming of age. This is followed by both a process and pattern-oriented slant on web design that focuses on the Model-View-Controller structure which underlies the rest of the text. HTML and CSS covered for the development of web interfaces. The PHP and JavaScript sections enable readers to develop the controllers for those interfaces. Finally, a concise introduction to databases and SQL allows for the development of robust data models.

In addition to the unique combination of content found in this book, the tone is also one of practicality. The author doesn't mince words and gets right to the point with examples meant to be referenced quickly and often. Although this directness may put off some readers who prefer to read texts cover to cover, all software developers know that this is how texts are used in the real world.

In the end, the broad approach that *The Missing Link* takes to web design and programming combined with the text's concise presentation of information makes this a web programming text unlike any other.

Robert Olson, M.S.

Professor Robert Olson is a Visiting Instructor of Computer & Information Sciences at the State University of New York at Fredonia where he teaches courses in computer programming, computer security, mathematics, and artificial intelligence. He also teaches Microcomputer Applications at Jamestown Community College. Professor Olson received a Master of Science in Management Information Systems from SUNY Fredonia on May 2007.

About Open SUNY Textbooks

Open SUNY Textbooks is an open access textbook publishing initiative established by State University of New York libraries and supported by SUNY Innovative Instruction Technology Grants. This initiative publishes high-quality, cost-effective course resources by engaging faculty as authors and peer-reviewers, and libraries as publishing infrastructure.

The pilot launched in 2012, providing an editorial framework and service to authors, students and faculty, and establishing a community of practice among libraries. The first pilot is publishing 15 titles in 2013-2014, with a second pilot to follow that will add more textbooks and participating libraries.

Participating libraries in the 2012-2013 pilot include SUNY Geneseo, College at Brockport, College of Environmental Science and Forestry, SUNY Fredonia, Upstate Medical University, and University at Buffalo, with support from other SUNY libraries and SUNY Press.

For more information, please see http://opensuny.org.

Table of Contents

Table of Figures

Table of Tables

Preface

When I began creating course materials of my own, I carried with me an acute awareness of several things. First, the volume of free, online reference materials including video tutorials, community groups, and books (now including this text) is so far greater than what a single printed volume could handle, that the idea of creating a comprehensive source seemed laughably redundant. Second, many of the texts that march across my desk for review each semester focus primarily on the underpinnings of a particular language, while spending little time introducing or reinforcing the methodology and general practice of the language in question. While this allows those authors to delve deeper into limited topics, I have found that focusing on how languages relate and intertwine is often more beneficial, especially when just beginning to study web development. Studying languages independent of one another does little to prepare a programmer for complex systems involving multiple languages.

This text is meant to reduce the confusion brought about by integrating multiple languages into one site while at the same time providing an overview of the entire development process. Within, you will find information on a variety of topics involved in the overall process of planning, designing, and finally creating a website; this background will help you understand how these pieces fit together, so you are better able to understand and contribute to a project and work with others on your team.

As this is an introductory level text, the goal is not to exhaust the covered topics. Instead we will focus on familiarizing ourselves with each language's abilities and how to fuse those languages and methods together to create a responsive, well-developed site. You will frequently find links and keywords throughout the text, which you can use as a starting point to further research topics that interest you.

We will examine web development in a full stack approach; the premise behind the phrase "full stack developer" is that the person has an understanding of all of the elements necessary to create and run a website. The topics included below all lend themselves towards this goal by touching each aspect of the process.

Section 1: Web Development

A brief history of the development of the Internet along with current trends and emerging technologies such as virtualization, botnets, internet of things, and more.

Web Servers: Analysis of the components of servers from both a hardware and software perspective with introduction to LAMP software and alternative solutions. Introduction to basic networking topics to provide an understanding of device addressing and URL translation.

Design: Techniques useful in the design of web projects including site maps, wireframes, storyboarding and more.

Development: Introduction to development models and best practices. Includes APIs, developing with or without others, and practices like pseudo code, code formatting, and variable naming conventions.

Section 2: Document Markup

HTML5: Introduction to HTML including features from the current specifications for HTML5. Covers tags and attributes, layout elements, forms, canvas, and more.

CSS: Introduction to CSS3 including selectors and rules, classes, responsive styling, positioning, and more.

Section 3: Scripting Languages

PHP: Introduction to PHP including debugging, arrays, email, file interaction, logic and control structure, and more.

JavaScript: A brief contrast of JavaScript to PHP, use of jQuery, and the document object model. Demonstration of how to complete basic page manipulation using JavaScript.

Section 4: Data Storage

MySQL: Primary and foreign keys, normalization and design, query design, and more.

Section 5: Tying It Together

Security: An introduction to risk management and examples of basic methods of securing elements of a site.

Advanced Examples: Examples of site features and methods, which combine the languages and topics in the text.

Finishing Touches: Integration of common website elements that complete the user experience including search optimization, analytics, and important information.

Learning Features

Colored blocks of text provide additional notes, important reminders, or highlight useful features of a language.

ADDITIONAL NOTES

IMPORTANT REMINDERS

USEFUL FEATURES

Words found in **bolded red** are links that connect to definitions in the glossary.

Examples are interspersed throughout the entire text that you can try out as you follow the material. Each major section of the text also contains questions and assignments at the end to give you an opportunity to test your understanding of the material. Assessments include several small to medium sized assignments, discussion questions, and multiple-choice questions. Discussion questions are meant to encourage deeper examination of topics and will frequently require effort to find additional information beyond this text (hint: start with the following feature).

Select topics are followed by a "Learn More" box (shown below), which identifies vocabulary and other sources you can use to delve deeper into the topic. Whenever possible, these external sources will also be openly published, free material.

LEARN MORE

Keywords, search terms:

Resource Name: Location

Acknowledgments

I would like to thank my colleague and friend Robert Olson for his efforts in editing this work. I would also like to thank the Department of Computer and Information Sciences at SUNY Fredonia who not only served as my instructors, but also welcomed me back as a colleague. I would also like to thank Drs. Dan Berggren and Charles Telly whose infectious passion for academics has kept myself and countless others engaged in the field.

Finally, I would like to thank those students who participated in reviewing and commenting on drafts of this text:

Dennis Adey

Ankit Ahuja

Julian Anjorin

Brandon Artymowycz

Michael Barry

Selin Bora

James Fefes

Marissa Forward

Melissa Grove

Jenna Hume

John Iburg

Marcello Miceli

James Morrissey

Brett Mueller

Zachary Murray

Jarrett Parow

Erik Pokornowski

Jordan Shelton

Joseph Steinbrenner

Jonathan Wdowiasz

Section 1:

Web Development

Section Contents

Brief History of the Internet
Current Trends
Web Servers
Network Basics
Website Design
Development

Learning Objectives

By the end of this section, you should be able to demonstrate:

- A basic understanding of the development of the Internet
- Awareness of current trends in web development
- An understanding of the components of a server
- Awareness of networking basics
- The ability to plan and design basic websites
- An awareness of different methods and approaches to development
- An understanding of types of tools that can assist development

Chapter 1

Brief History of the Internet

As far back as the early stirrings of the Cold War, the concept of a network connecting computers was under development by both government and university researchers looking for a better means to communicate and share research. The military at the time relied in part on microwave transmission technology for communications. An unexpected attack on some of these towers demonstrated how susceptible the technology was to failure of even small portions of the transmission path. This led the military to seek a method of communicating that could withstand attack. At the same time, university researchers were trying to share their work between campuses, and were struggling with similar problems when their transmissions suffered drops in signal. Parties from both groups ended up at the same conference with presentations, and decided to collaborate in order to further their work.

At the time, computers were far from what we know them as today. A single computer was a large, immobile assortment of equipment that took up an entire room. Data entry was done by using punched cards of paper, or the newest method of the time, magnetic tapes. Interacting with the computer meant reserving time on the equipment and traveling to where it was. Most machines were owned by universities, large corporations, or government organizations due to the staffing demands, size, and cost to acquire and maintain them. The image below depicts the UNIVAC 1, a system used by the United States Census Bureau and other large organizations like universities. One of the fastest machines at the time, it could perform roughly 1000 calculations per second.

US Army, Public Domain, via Wikimedia

Figure 1 UNIVAC Computer System

In comparison, the K computer, a super computer produced in 2012 by the Japanese company Fujitsu, was capable of 10 petaflops per second when it was launched. Before you reach for your dictionary or calculator, we will break that down. FLOPS stands for floating point operations per second, or in basic terms, the number of calculations the system can finish in one second. A petaflop is a numerical indicator of how many 10^{15} (10 with 15 zeroes after it) calculations are completed per second. So, 10 petaflops means the K computer can complete 10^{15} calculations ten times in one second. If we fed the UNIVAC 1 just a single petaflop of data the day it was turned on, it would still be working on the problem today. In fact, it would barely be getting started, just a mere 60+ years into a roughly 317,098-year task!

ADDITIONAL NOTES

You may have heard of **Moore's Law**, commonly defined as the tendency of technology's capability to double every two years. Moore's actual prediction was that this would apply to transistors, an element of circuits, and that it would continue for ten years after seeing its trend from 1958 to 1964. His prediction has shown to be applicable to memory capacity, speed, storage space as well as other factors and is commonly used as a bench mark for future growth.

As cold war tensions grew and Sputnik was launched, the United States Department of Defense (DoD) began to seek additional methods of transmitting information to supplement existing methods. They sought something that was decentralized, allowing better resiliency in case of attack, where damage at one point would not necessarily disrupt communication. Their network, Arpanet, connected the DoD and participating universities together for the first time. In order to standardize the way networked systems communicated, the Transfer Control Protocol/Internetwork Protocol (TCP/IP) was created. As various network systems migrated to this standard, they could then communicate with any network using the protocol. The Internet was born.

Email was soon to follow, as users of the networks were interested in the timely transmission and notification of messages. This form of messaging fit one of their initial goals. As time progressed, additional protocols were developed to address particular tasks, like FTP for file transfers and UDP for time-sensitive, error-resistant tasks.

Ongoing improvements in our ability to move more information, and move it faster, between systems progressed at a rate similar to the calculative power of the computers we saw earlier. This brings us to where we are today; able to watch full-length movies, streamed in high quality right to our phones and computers, even while riding in a car.

LEARN MORE

Keywords, search terms: History of the Internet, Arpanet

A Brief History of NSF and the Internet: http://www.nsf.gov/od/lpa/news/03/fsnsf_internet.htm

How the Internet Came to Be: http://www.netvalley.com/archives/mirrors/cerf-how-inet.html

Chapter 2

Current Trends

As important as it is to know how we reached where we are today, it is also important to stay current in web development. New products and innovations can greatly affect the landscape in a short amount of time. We can look to the rapid rise in Facebook, Twitter, and the myriad of Google services now relied upon around the world as examples of how fast new technology is embraced.

Cloud Computing

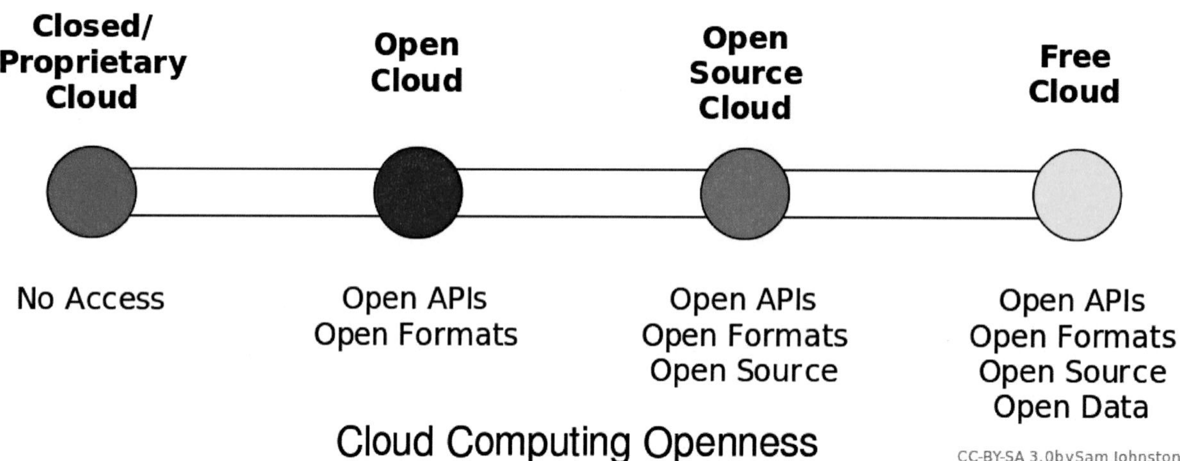

Figure 2 Cloud Computing Styles

Cloud computing can be loosely defined as the allocation of hardware and/or software under a service model (resources are assigned and consumed as needed). Typically, what we hear today referred to as cloud computing is the concept of business-to-business commerce revolving around "Company A" selling or renting their services to "Company B" over the Internet. A cloud can be public (hosted on a public internet, shared among consumers) or private (cloud concepts of provisioning and storage are applied to servers within a fire wall or internal network that is privately managed), and can also fall into some smaller subsets in between, as depicted in the graphic above.

Under Infrastructure as a Service (IaaS) computing model, which is what is most commonly associated with the term cloud computing, one or more servers with significant amounts of processing power, capacity, and memory, are configured through hardware and/

or software methods to act as though they are multiple smaller systems that add up to their capacity. This is referred to as virtualizing, or virtual servers. These systems can be "right sized" where they only consume the resources they need on average, meaning many systems needing little resources can reside on one piece of hardware. When processing demands of one system expand or contract, resources from that server can be added or removed to account for the change. This is an alternative to multiple physical servers, where each would need the ability to serve not only the average but expected peak needs of system resources.

Software as a Service, Platform as a Service, and the ever-expanding list of "as-a-service" models follow the same basic pattern of balancing time and effort. Platforms as a service allow central control of end user profiles, and software as a service allows simplified (and/or automated) updating of programs and configurations. Storage as a service can replace the need to manually process backups and file server maintenance. Effectively, each "as-a-service" strives to provide the end user with an "as-good-if-not-better" alternative to managing a system themselves, all while trying to keep the cost of their services less than a self-managed solution.

ADDITIONAL NOTES

One of the best methods to keep current is by following trade magazines, industry leader blogs, and simply browsing the internet looking for new items or site features you have not noticed before. Content aggregators like Zite, Feedly, and Slashdot are some of my favorites.

As a micro-scale example, imagine you and four friends are all starting small businesses. Faced with the costs of buying servers and software for data storage, web hosting, and office programs, each of you would invest funds into equipment and the staff to maintain it, even though much of it may get little use in the early stages of your company. This high initial investment reduces available funding that may have been used elsewhere, and your return on investment becomes longer. Instead, each of you would create an account with Amazon's cloud services for file storage and website hosting, which are private to you, but physically stored on servers shared by other users. Since these services are managed offsite by Amazon staff, none of you need to hire IT staff to manage these servers, nor do you have to invest in the equipment itself. Just by not needing to hire a system administrator (estimated at $40,000 salary) you can pay for just over 3 years of Amazon service (calculated using Amazon's pricing calculator[1] for basic web services and file storage). When you combine the savings of that employee's fringe costs like health care, along with those of not purchasing your own hardware, this approach can make your initial investment last longer.

These lowered costs are attractive to small businesses and startups for obvious reasons, but are also attractive to large companies with highly fluctuating levels of need. For example, a football team's website sees far more traffic on game days than the off-season. They do not need the ability to serve the same amount of users all the time. Some tangible examples of "as-a-service" tools you may already be using are file hosting services like Dropbox[2] or Google Drive.[3] Your files are kept on servers along with those from other users that you do not see (unless you share with them intentionally) and you can add or remove extra space

[1] http://calculator.s3.amazonaws.com/index.html
[2] http://www.dropbox.com
[3] http://drive.google.com

to your account whenever you like. Similarly, services like Amazon Web Services[4] offer the ability to host your files, applications, and more to both home consumers and commercial clients.

Virtualization

Server virtualization is the act of running multiple operating systems and other software on the same physical hardware at the same time, as we discussed in Cloud Computing. A hardware and/or software element is responsible for managing the physical system resources at a layer in between each of the operating systems and the hardware itself. Doing so allows the consolidation of physical equipment into fewer devices, and is most beneficial when the servers sharing the hardware are unlikely to demand resources at the same time, or when the hardware is powerful enough to serve all of the installations simultaneously.

The act of virtualizing is not just for use in cloud environments, but can be used to decrease the "server sprawl," or overabundance of physical servers, that can occur when physical hardware is installed on a one-to-one (or few-to-one) scale to applications and sites being served. Special hardware and/or software is used to create a new layer in between the physical resources of your computer and the operating system(s) running on it. This layer manages what each system sees as being the hardware available to it, and manages allocation of resources and the settings for all virtualized systems. Hardware virtualization, or the stand alone approach, sets limits for each operating system and allows them to operate independent of one another. Since hardware virtualization does not require a separate operating system to manage the virtualized system(s), it has the potential to operate faster and consume fewer resources than software virtualization. Software virtualization, or the host-guest approach, requires the virtualizing software to run on an operating system already in use, allowing simpler management to occur from the initial operating system and virtualizing program, but can be more demanding on system resources even when the primary operating system is not being used.

Ultimately, you can think of virtualization like juggling. In this analogy, your hands are the servers, and the balls you juggle are your operating systems. The traditional approach of hosting one application on one server is like holding one ball in each hand. If your hands are both "busy" holding a ball, you cannot interact with anything else without putting a ball down. If you juggle them, however, you can "hold" three or more balls at the same time. Each time your hand touches a ball is akin to a virtualized system needing resources, and having those resources allocated by the virtualization layer (the juggler) assigning resources (a hand), and then reallocating for the next system that needs them.

---

[4] http://aws.amazon.com

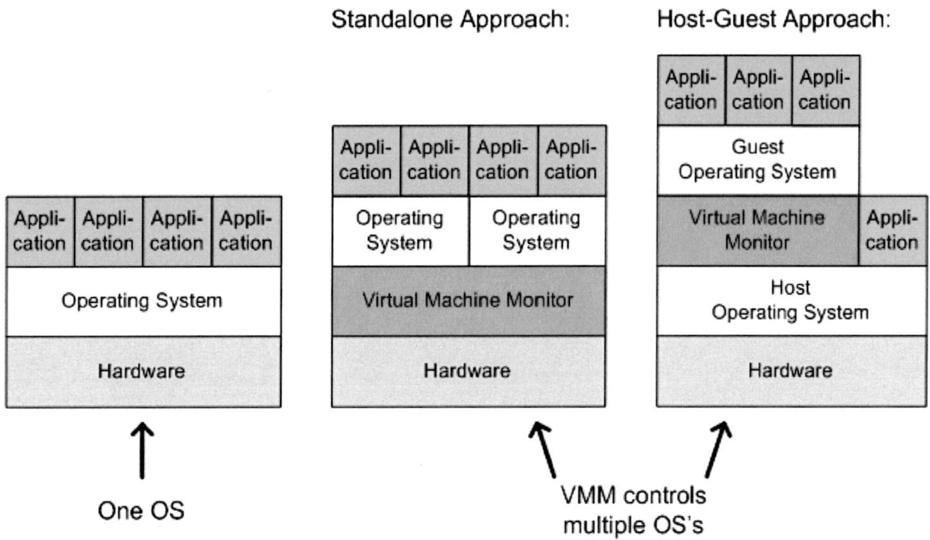

By Daniel Hirschbach [CC-BY-SA-2.0 Germany] via Wikimedia

Figure 3 Virtualization Styles

The addition of a virtual machine as shown above allows the hardware or software to see the virtual machine as part of the regular system. The monitor itself divides the resources allocated to it into subsets that act as their own computers.

Net Neutrality

This topic is commonly misconstrued as a desire for all Internet content to be free of cost and without restrictions based on its nature. In fact, net neutrality is better defined as efforts to ensure that all content (regardless of form or topic) and the means to access it, are protected as equal. This means Internet Service Providers (ISPs) like your cable or telephone company cannot determine priority of one site over another, resulting in a "premium" Internet experience for those able to pay extra. Additional concerns are that without a universal agreement, a government may elect to restrict access to materials by its citizens (see North Korea censorship[5]), and similarly that corporations controlling the physical connections would be able to extort higher prices for privileged access or pay providers to deny equal access to their competitors.

USEFUL FEATURES

Legislation continues to change regarding what is and is not legal or acceptable content on the internet. Laws change over time as well as across jurisdictions and can greatly differ. Just because material is legal in your area does not mean it is in others and you may still be in violation of laws applicable in the location of your server.

Existing laws vary around the world, some protecting the providers, some protecting the user. The United States received considerable attention in 2012 for anti-piracy bills

[5] https://www.google.com/search?q=north+korea+internet+censorship

that were highly protested both with physical rallies and online petitions. Each bill drew debate over what affects the stipulations would have not only within the United States, but over the Internet as a whole. Even though SOPA[6] (introduced by the House) and PIPA[7] (introduced by the Senate after the failure of COICA[8] in 2010) were not ultimately ratified, The United States and other countries had at that point already signed ACTA[9] in 2011, which contained provisions that placed the burden on ISPs to police their users regardless of sovereign laws in the user's location.

LEARN MORE

Keywords, search terms: Cloud computing, virtualization, virtual machines (VMs), software virtualization, hardware virtualization

Xen and the Art of Virtualization: http://li8-68.members.linode.com/~caker/xen/2003-xensosp.pdf

Virtualization News and Community: http://www.virtualization.net

Cloud Computing Risk Assessment: http://www.enisa.europa.eu/activities/risk-management/files/deliverables/cloud-computing-risk-assessment

Without formal legislation, judges and juries are placed in positions where they establish precedence by ruling on these issues, while having little guidance from existing law. As recently as March 2012 a file sharing case from 2007 reached the Supreme Court, where the defendant was challenging the constitutionality of a $222,000 USD fine for illegally sharing 24 songs on file sharing service Kazaa. This was the first case for such a lawsuit heard by a jury in the United States. Similar trials have varied in penalties up to $1.92 million US dollars, highlighting a lack of understanding of how to monetize damages. The Supreme Court denied hearing the Kazaa case, which means the existing verdict will stand for now. Many judges are now dismissing similar cases that are being brought by groups like the Recording Industry Association of America (RIAA[10]), as these actions are more often being seen as the prosecution using the courts as a means to generate revenue and not recover significant, demonstrable damages.

As these cases continue to move through courts and legislation continues to develop at the federal level, those decisions will have an impact on what actions are considered within the constructs of the law, and may have an effect on the contents or location of your site.

Cyber Warfare

Intentional, unauthorized intrusion of systems has existed about as long as computers have. While organized, coordinated attacks are not new, carrying them out in response to geopolitical issues is now emerging, as was found in the brief 2008 war between Russia and Georgia. Whether the attacks on each country's infrastructures were government sanc-

---

6 http://thomas.loc.gov/cgi-bin/bdquery/z?d112:h.r.3261:
7 http://www.opencongress.org/bill/112-s968/show
8 http://www.govtrack.us/congress/bills/111/s3804/text
9 http://www.ustr.gov/acta
10 http://www.riaa.com

tioned or not is contested, but largely irrelevant. What is relevant is that these attacks will only continue, and likely worsen, in future disputes.

In the United States and other countries, equipment that controls aging infrastructure for utilities is increasingly connected, with control computers at facilities for electric, water, gas, and more being placed online to better facilitate monitoring and maintenance. However, many of these systems were not developed with this level of connectivity in mind, therefore security weaknesses inherent in the older equipment can result in exploits that allow Hackers to cause real, permanent damage to physical equipment, potentially disrupting the utilities we rely on every day.

Tehran's uranium enrichment development facilities were targeted in late 2010 by a custom-created virus that focused on equipment used in the refining of nuclear material. The virus would randomly raise or lower the speed of the equipment in a manner that would not create alarms, but enough to strain the equipment. This would lead to equipment failures, after which the replacement hardware would be similarly infected. Eventually discovered, the virus had been running for many months, delaying the project and increasing its costs. This virus was intentionally designed to run in that particular environment and was based on the specific SCADA hardware involved, and in this case was such a sophisticated attack that it is widely believed to have been facilitated by the United States and Israel.

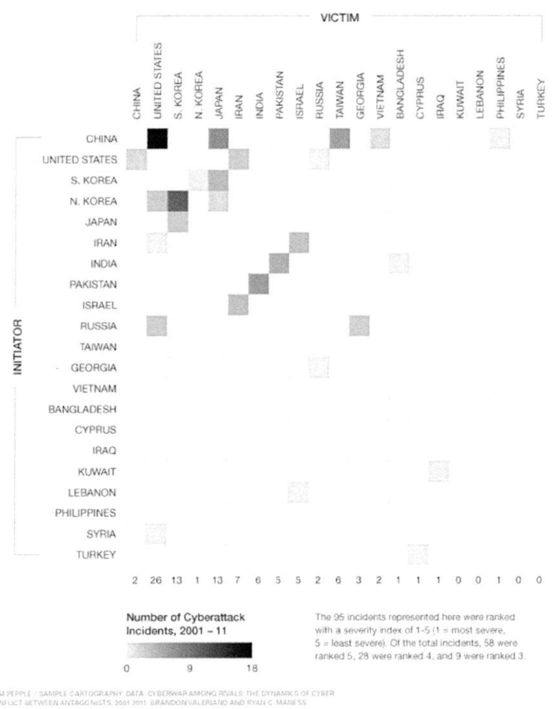

Figure 4 10 Years of Known Cyber Attacks

The graph above, from foreignaffairs.com, provides an idea of how prevalent government to government attacks are becoming. We should keep in mind that the ninety-five incidents depicted are only the known, reported incidents, and the true number is likely higher.

Botnets

Botnets are not exactly a new threat to the Internet, but they remain one of the most persistent threats to the average user and their computer. The word botnet, an amalgamation of the words robot and network, is an accurate description of what it entails. Botnets are programs that use a network connection to communicate with each other to coordinate and perform tasks. Originally, botnets were created as part of programs for Internet Relay Chat (IRC) to help establish and control channels people would log into to talk to each other. They are still in frequent use today for a number of legitimate, non-malicious tasks.

We have also seen a rise in malicious botnets, designed to work undetected in the background of your computer. The controller (typically referred to as the command and control server) uses the infected machines to complete tasks that require large amounts of processing power and/or bandwidth to complete, like finding or exploiting weaknesses in networks or websites, or to "mine" infected systems for personal data such as credentials, credit card numbers, and other information that can then be used or sold to others.

ADDITIONAL NOTES

It did not take long for the first virus to enter the internet. Just two years after the first systems were connected, The Creeper (a self-replicating script) was created in 1971, which did no harm but displayed "I'm the creeper, catch me if you can" on infected machines. It was immediately followed by The Reaper, the first anti-virus program, which too self-replicated, removing the Creeper wherever it was found.

Some botnet controllers have grown so large and organized that they act as businesses in competition, typically "renting" their botnet out as a service or tool to others for agreed upon rates. Efforts by security researchers to detect and analyze botnets often involve close coordination with government agencies and law enforcement as the size of an average botnet typically involves computers from multiple countries. Simply shutting down or attempting to remove the malicious files from infected systems could cause unintended damage to the machines, further complicating the process of eliminating a botnet.

By Tom-B [CC-BY-SA-3.0], via Wikimedia

Figure 5 Botnets

LEARN MORE

Keywords, search terms: Botnets, command and control system, malware, network security

Build Your Own Botnet: http://howto.wired.com/wiki/Build_your_own_botnet_with_open_source_software

Honeynet Project: http://www.honeynet.org/papers/bots/

Internet of Things

In much the same vein of the connection of older equipment to the networks of the modern world, the newest devices emerging into the market can also be a bit more non-traditional. This results in an internet that is soon to be awash with live connections from everything from cars to ovens and refrigerators, an explosion of devices no longer focused on delivering information to the masses as much as aggregating many data sources of interest to a small set of recipients. Some cars now include the ability for consumer service companies to perform tasks like remotely shutting down your car if stolen; coordinating use of these tools with law enforcement allows them to stop a vehicle before or during a pursuit. While these are innovative tools with positive uses, they also add new vectors for a malicious person to attack. Instead of the thief being thwarted, he might use a device to shut your car down at an intersection, eliminating your ability to simply drive away when he approaches. The very tool intended to stop him afforded him a means to gain access to your vehicle. This is not merely waxing philosophically, either. It has been demonstrated as a proof of concept[11] backed by researchers funded by DARPA.

As more devices are introduced to the Internet, the amount of interaction with things as simple as small appliances is increasing. Comments like "We have to stop by the store on the way home, the toaster report said we will need at least one loaf of bread for the week" seem silly to us now, but could eventually exist in the same breath as "The fridge called, it ordered our groceries for the week." For about $2,700 USD, Samsung already offers a fridge with interactive features similar to these ideas.

Items embedded with **RFID** tags contribute to the Internet of Things, as they can be tracked and provide information that can be aggregated and applied to processes. Shipping crates with RFID expedite taking inventory as their tags can be scanned automatically in transit. Access cards not only allow privileged access to restricted areas but also let us know where people (or, at least their cards) are located and where they have been. Home automa-tion systems allow lights, locks, cameras, and alarms to be managed by your smart phone to the extent that your lights can come on, doors unlocked, and garage door opened, when it detects that your phone has entered the driveway. All of these are items—not people—in-teracting with the Internet to fulfill a task, and are part of the emerging Internet of Things.

Proliferation of Devices

As reliance on the Internet and the drive for constant connection proliferate through our societies, and technology becomes more affordable and adaptable, we have not only left the age of one computer per home, but meandered even past the point where everyone in the house has their own device, and now the average consumer has multiple devices. The proliferation allows us to adjust technology to fit where we need it in our lives. I use my desktop for hardware intensive applications at home, or for doing research and web development where multiple monitors eases my need to view several sources at once. Out of the house, my tablet allows me to consume information and is easily slid into a keyboard attachment that allows it to operate as a laptop, turning it into a content creation device by reducing the difficulty of interacting by adding back a keyboard and mouse.

Improvements in software both in efficiency and ease of use allow older hardware to get second lives. My laptop, though ten years old, is still running happily (albeit without a useful battery life) and is still capable of browsing the internet and being used as a word processor due to a lightweight Linux operating system that leaves enough of its aging resources available for me to complete these tasks. When the average lifespan of a laptop is typically considered to be only three years, many older devices like mine have not left operation, and are still finding regular use in our growing set of tech tools.

[11] http://www.forbes.com/sites/andygreenberg/2013/07/24/hackers-reveal-nasty-new-car-attacks-with-me-behind-the-wheel-video/

Chapter 3

Web Servers

While we could simply focus on how to create web pages and websites, none of this is possible without the underlying hardware and software components that support the pages we create. Examining what these components are and how they interact helps us understand what our server is capable of.

The diagram below represents the basic elements of a web server. Hardware, an operating system, and an http server comprise the bare necessities. The addition of a database and scripting language extend a server's capabilities and are utilized in most servers as well.

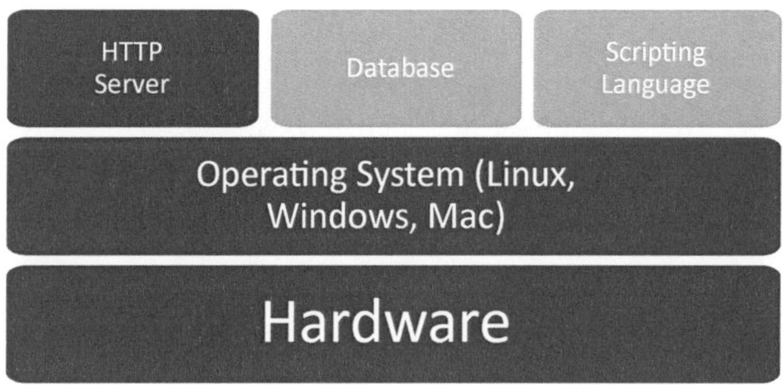

Figure 6 Web Server Software Structure

Hardware

The mention of phrases like data center, hosting provider, or even big name companies like Microsoft and Google can invoke mental images of large, sterile rooms full of tall racks of hardware with blinking lights and a maze of wires. Those more familiar with such rooms will also know the chill resulting from the heavily air conditioned atmosphere and droning whir of fans that typically accompany them. This, however, is not a requirement nor an accurate portrayal of a great deal of servers connected to the Internet. With the addition of the right software (assuming you are consuming this text digitally), the device you are using to read this with could become an internet connected server. While it would not sustain the demands made of domains like Amazon.com or MSN.com, you would be able to perform the basic actions of a server with most of today's devices.

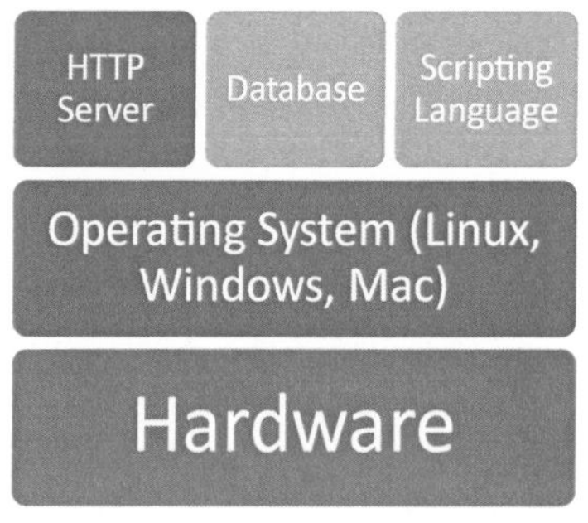

Even though we have reached this point, it is difficult to forget the mental picture conjured by the thoughts of the data center. In the current "traditional" model, thin, physically compact servers are stacked vertically. These are referred to as rack mount hardware. Many rack mount systems today contain hardware similar to what we have in our desktops, despite the difference in appearance.

A number of companies, including Google, Yahoo, and Facebook, are looking to re-invent this concept. Google for instance has already used custom-built servers in parts of its network in an effort to improve efficiency and reduce costs. One implementation they have tried proved so efficient that they were able to eliminate large power backup units by placing a 9 volt battery in each server—giving it enough emergency power to keep running until the building's backup power source could kick in. They have also experimented with alternative cooling methods like using water from retention ponds, or placing datacenters where they can take advantage of natural resources like sea water for cooling or wind and solar for energy.

ADDITIONAL NOTES

Take note! While all of the programs we refer to in our LAMP stack have free, open source versions, not all uses may be covered by those licenses (using them for study and research purposes is covered).

Even small, low powered devices are finding demand as servers in part to enable the Internet of Things. Devices like the Raspberry Pi[12] and an explosion of similar products like "android sticks" can be purchased for as little as $25 USD. These small, "just-enough-power" devices are used to connect data from the environment or other devices to the Internet, leaving the data center behind and living instead at the source of the data itself.

Software

A typical web server today contains four elements in addition to the physical hardware. These are the operating system, web server, a database and a scripting language. One of the most popular combinations of these systems has been abbreviated to LAMP, standing for Linux, Apache, MySQL, and PHP, named in the same order. There are many combinations of solutions that meet these features, resulting in a number of variations of the acronym, such as WAMP for Windows, Apache, MySQL, PHP or MAMP, identical with exception of Mac (or, rightfully, a Macintosh developed operating system). Among the plethora of combinations, the use of LAMP prevails as the catch all reference to a server with these types of services.

All that is ultimately required to convey static pages to an end user are the operating system and HTTP server, the first half of the WAMP acronym. The balance adds the capability for interactivity and for the information to change based on the result of user interactions.

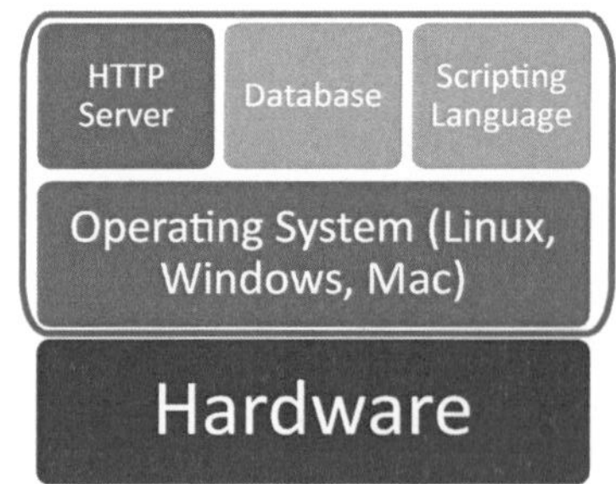

[12] http://www.raspberrypi.org

Operating System—Linux

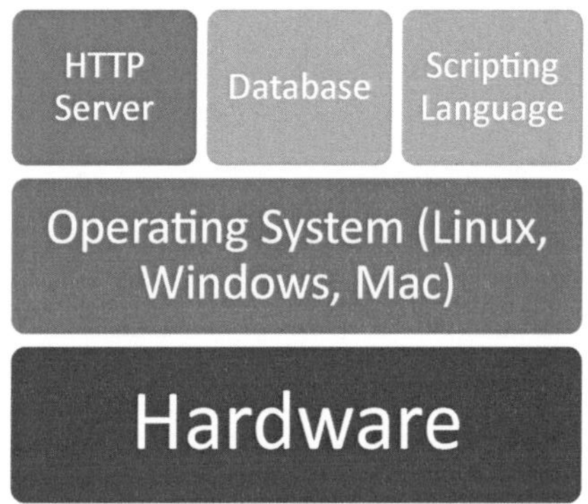

Your operating system is what allows you to interact with the applications and hardware that make up your computer. It facilitates resource allocation to your applications, and communication between hardware and software. Typically, operating systems for servers fall under three categories: Linux-based, Windows-based, and Mac-based. Within each of these categories are more options, such as various version of Mac and Windows operating systems, and the wide variety of Linux operating systems. We will utilize Linux, the predominant choice.

Developed by Linus Torvalds in the early 1990s while he was a student, Linux was created so Linus could access UNIX systems at his university without relying on an operating system. As his project became more robust, he decided to share it with others, seeking input but believing it would remain a more personal endeavor. What he could not have predicted was the community that would come together and participate in helping shape it into what is today. As the basis of a large number of Linux-based operating systems (or "flavors" of Linux), the Linux core can be found around the world, even in the server rooms of its competitors like Microsoft.

HTTP Server—Apache

Apache is an open source web server originally developed for UNIX systems. Now supported on most platforms including UNIX, Linux, Windows, and Mac, Apache is one of the most utilized server applications. First developed in 1995, Apache follows a similar open source approach as Linux, allowing users to expand on the software and contribute to the community of users. The user group around Apache developed The Apache Foundation, which maintains a library of solutions for web services.

In a web server, Apache serves as the HTTP component, which compiles the results from scripting languages, databases, and HTML files to generate content that is sent to the user. Apache (or any web service) will track which files on the server do and do not belong to the website, and also controls what options are available to the end user through its configuration files.

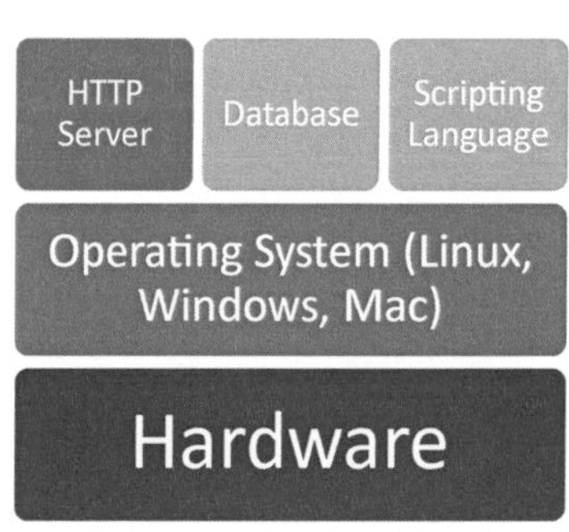

Apache and other HTTP servers allow us to share our webpages, scripts, and files with our end users. Any output from our database and scripting languages is turned into HTML output that the client's browser displays as our webpage. While we can view HTML and

JavaScript files on a computer that is not a webserver, we need an http server to view them as a destination on a network.

Configuration Files

When we create a new system, settings may not be exactly as we want them, or the time may come where we want to add, remove, or change something about our server. To do this, we will need to edit the configuration files that control the different pieces of our system. Our actual web server config file is called httpd.conf. For PHP settings, we need to refer to php.ini, and for MySQL we refer to my.cnf. These files may be located in different places depending on the operating system, and the version in use, so it is best to use your system's file search tools to find where they are on your machine. Configuration (or setting) files are typically a plain text format file with one setting on each line with comments near each value describing the setting's use. These files will also use the same commenting delimiter for their notes to enable or disable individual settings. Typically the delimiter used is a semi colon ; or pound sign #.

If you want to change settings about your server itself such as the port it listens on, what folder it looks for files in, its name, or other related features, look to the httpd.conf file. From the php.in file you can control elements like which modules are installed and enabled for your system, how much data scripts are allowed to consume, and more. Similarly your MySQL config file determines what port it listens on, which user it runs as on your server, what your admin account's credentials are, and more.

Changes to these files typically require you to restart your web server (in our case, for apache or PHP changes), or at least the service that you are changing (in our case, MySQL changes). This can be done using the control panel if you are using a combination program like Wamp 2, or by using your operating system's service tools or by using system commands at a command prompt. Restarting Wamp 2 in a GUI operating system like Windows can be done be right clicking on Wamp's icon in the tray. In a Cent OS server, the same effect can be achieved by typing "service httpd restart." If all else fails, you can always physically restart the machine (referred to as "bouncing"), but this is something you will want to avoid on a live system as it will cause a much longer period of down time.

If you use installer packages, or a combo installer like Wamp 2, you will probably get by initially without making any changes to these files. Binary installers however will not know where or how to make changes to config files and you will need to follow the instructions to edit these files by hand to integrate all of your elements.

Why would I use a combination other than Linux, Apache, My SQL, and PHP?

Given the popularity of this particular combination of four, it is easy to wonder why it has not simply become *the* system. However, needs and preferences may change why a particular approach is selected. Perhaps you are in an all Windows environment and feel more comfortable with a Windows operating system. Maybe your data is already available in a flat file or XML format and you want a database that can use XML files, like MongoDB.[13]

[13] http://www.mongodb.org/

Or, you might prefer the approach and packages available in Python to those found in PHP. Each system has its particular strengths and weaknesses, and should be chosen based on the needs of the project.

Open Source

At this point, you have come across many references to terms like free, free to edit, and open source throughout the text. In fact, all of the elements in our example LAMP are free, open source solutions. Open source means the provider of the software allows the end user access to the actual code of their software, allowing the end user to make changes anywhere in the program.

This differs from traditional software where you own a copy or license to use the program, but cannot extend or change elements of the program beyond what the developer allows. An executable in Windows for example is closed source. You cannot open the executable to read its code or make changes. If you wanted to change the program, the developer would have to provide you with the files used to create it (called source code) so you could make changes and compile your own, modified, executable program.

Open source is growing in popularity but the concept has existed for quite some time. Recently, larger governments have begun to embrace free, open source solutions as a means to reduce costs and achieve modifications that customize programs to fit their needs. Historically open source was viewed as a security risk as anyone could submit changes to the project, and it was feared that vulnerabilities or malicious code would be inserted. In fact, with so many users able to view and modify the files, it has actually made those with malicious intent less able to hide their modifications (sometimes called the "many eyes" approach to reliability). Development time has also been reduced as the community of developers on a popular open source project can greatly exceed that of a closed source solution with limited development staff.

A popular acronym referring to these projects is FOSS—Free, Open Source Software. As not all open source programs are free in terms of purchasing or licensing, FOSS indicates solutions that are free of costs as well as free to change. These solutions may be developed entirely by a community of volunteers, or may come from a commercial company with developers dedicated to the project. While it is odd to think of a company giving away its creation for free, these companies generate revenue by building advertising into their software or offering premium services such as product support or contracting with clients to customize the product. Many companies will also offer only some tools as open source alongside other products they sell, or offer a "freemium" model where the open sourced platform contains most of the features of their software. Here, additional features or add-ons beyond the open source package carry additional licensing and costs.

FTP

While not included in LAMP acronyms, another important element to note is the existence of a file transfer protocol (FTP) server. As you typically will want to perform development activities on private server before editing your live server, you will need a mechanism that allows you to move files between the two. FTP is designed for moving files between systems, allowing you to synchronize items when you are ready. In addition to an FTP server, you will also likely want an FTP client application for the machine(s) that contain the files you want to move. The client allows you to see files in both locations and interact with them to determine which file is moved to which machine. There are a number of free file transfer programs available, some of which can even be integrated into browsers like Chrome by using browser extensions.

Chapter 4

Network Basics

IP Addresses

An IP (Internet Protocol) address is a unique code that identifies a piece of equipment connected to a network. These addresses are used in messages between network devices like the network or wireless card in your computer, the equipment from your ISP (internet service provider), and all pieces of equipment between your machine and the one your computer needs to talk to.

IP Addresses live in the network layer, which is one of seven layers in the protocol suite defined in the OSI Model. The OSI model stands for Open Systems Interconnection, and was created by the International Organization for Standardization, an international non-governmental group of professionals who strive to establish standards and best practices in a variety of fields. The OSI Model for networking breaks the system of transmitting data into the layers show below in an attempt to delineate where certain actions should take place.

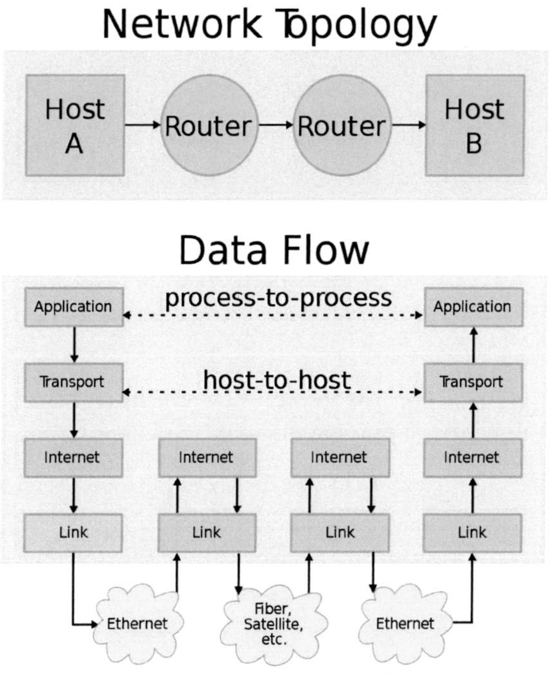

By User:Kbrose [CC-BY-SA-3.0] via Wikimedia

Figure 7 Network Topology

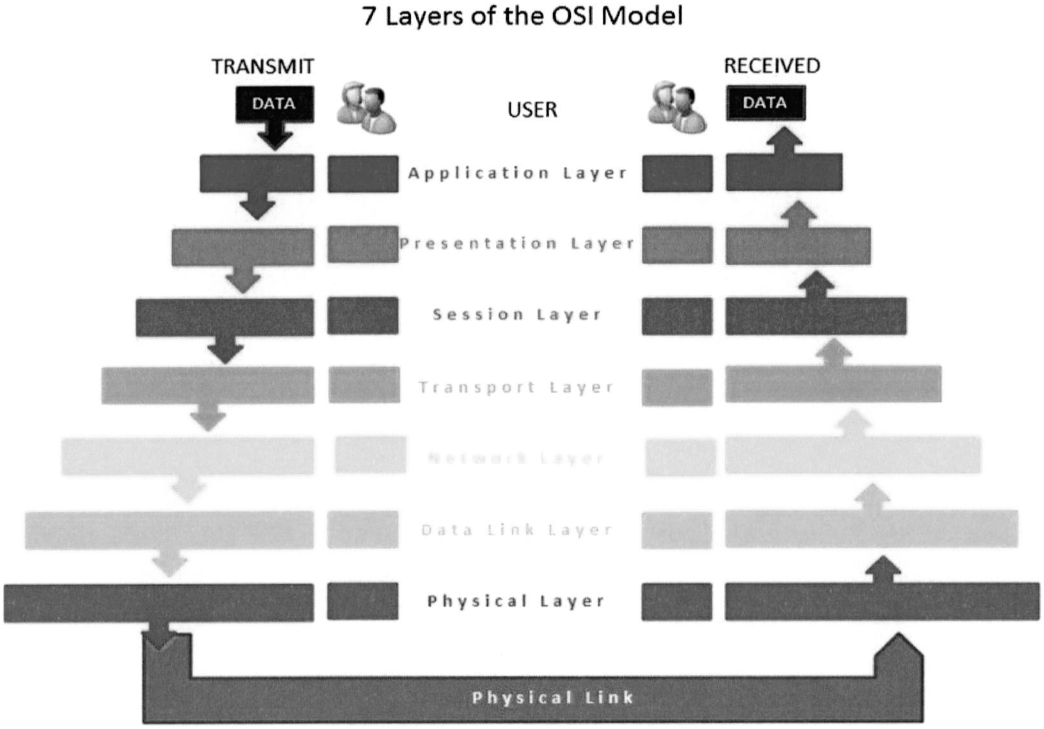

By MrsValdry [CC-By-SA 3.0] via Wikimedia

Figure 8 OSI 7 Layer Model

The seven layers depicted above make up the OSI body's recommended protocol suite. In the diagram, transmission of data crosses two routers and over the Internet to reach its destination. By following the data along the arrows, we see it pass through various layers of communication and processing as it crosses the internal network, through the first router, across the public network (internet connection), into the recipient's router, and then is reassembled into its original form.

Until recently, most network equipment has operated on IPv4, the fourth standard released for IP addresses, which has been in place for about thirty years. Addresses in this format are typically represented as a pattern of four blocks of up to three digits separated by periods, with no block of numbers exceeding 255 such as 127.0.0.1 or 24.38.1.251. This is referred to as dot-decimal representation, and although it is not the only way to express an IPv4 address it is the most recognized form. Segments of the addresses within the ranges of 192.168.xxx.xxx, 172.16.xxx.xxx to 172.31.xxx.xxx, and 10.0.xxx.xxx to 10.255.xxx.xxx are reserved for private networks, meaning they are used within a network in your house, at work, or anywhere else where a group of computers share a connection to the internet.

Each of these networks uses one or more of these blocks of numbers for devices on that network. Only the equipment connecting that local network to the Internet needs a unique address from the rest of the world. That equipment will track which computer inside the network to send data to and from by reading packets—the individual pieces of messages that are sent across networks. This means your computer might be 192.168.1.25 at home, and so might your computer at work, according to your home and work networks. The connection between your house and office thought still have a different, unique number assigned to them.

This separation of networks was done to reduce the speed at which unique addresses were consumed. Although this scheme allows for almost 4.3 billion (accurately, 2^{32}) addresses, the last one was officially assigned on February 4th, 2012. To sustain today's growing number of devices, IPv6 was created, which is depicted as eight blocks of four hexadecimal digits now separated by colons. These new addresses might look like 2001:0db8:85a3:0042:1000:8a2e:0370:7334, and can support roughly 4 billion unique addresses. Since the new range is so staggeringly large, additional protocols were created that specify when certain values or ranges are used in addresses. This allows additional information about the device to be conveyed just from the address.

The actual messages sent between machines are broken down into multiple pieces. These pieces, called packets, are sent piece by piece from sender to recipient. Each packet is sent the fastest way possible, which means some packets may take different routes—picture a short cut, or getting off a congested road to take a different one. This helps to ensure that the message gets from sender to receiver as fast as possible, but also means packets may arrive in a different order than they were sent.

ADDITIONAL NOTES

Hexadecimal is a number scheme that allows 0 through 9 and A through F as unique values, which means we can count to 15 with one character.

To account for this, each piece of the message, or payload, is wrapped in a header—additional information that describes how many other pieces there are, what protocol is being used, where the packet came from and is headed to, along with some other related information.

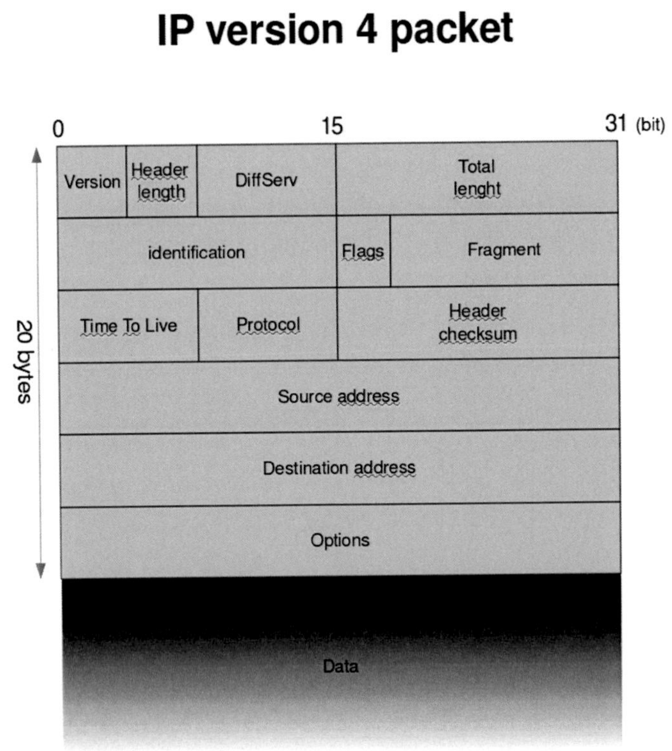

IP version 4 packet

0 15 31 (bit)

Version
Header length
DiffServ
Total lenght
identification
Flags
Fragment
Time To Live
Protocol
Header checksum
Source address
Destination address
Options
Data
20 bytes

By Nicolargo [CC-BY-SA-3.0-2.5-2.0-1.0] via Wikimedia Commons

Figure 9 IP 4 Packet

After the packets are reassembled, the receiving computer sends any necessary responses, and the process repeats. This all takes place in fractions of a second, beginning with the "hello," or handshake packet to announce a communication request, to the last piece of the packet.

URL

Seeing as most of us would have a hard time remembering what IP address is needed to get to, say, Facebook (173.252.100.16) or the Weather Channel (96.8.80.132) we instead use URLs, universal resource locators. This allows us to use www.facebook.com and www.weather.com to get to where we want to go without referring to a long list of IP addresses. Specialized servers (called name servers) all around the world are responsible for responding to requests from computers for this information. When you type facebook.com into your address bar, if your router does not have a note of its own as to where that is, it will "ask" a name server, which will look it up in its records and reply.

There are three parts to a network address: the protocol, name, and resource id. The protocol represents how we want to send and receive messages, for example we can use http:// for accessing websites and ftp:// for moving files. The name is what we associate with the site, like www.facebook.com, and the resource id, or URI, is everything after that, which points to the particular file we want to see.

Ports

While an IP address and a URL will bring you to a particular web server, there may be more than one way you want to interact with it, or more than one thing you want it to do. Maybe you also want the server to provide email services, or you want to use FTP to update your files. These ports act as different doors into your server, so different applications can communicate without getting in each other's way. Certain ports are typically used for certain activities, for example port 80 is the standard port for web traffic (your browser viewing a page), as opposed to ftp, which typically uses port 21. Using standard ports is not a rule, as applications can be configured to use any available port number, but it is recommended in most cases as firewalls and other security devices may require additional configuring to keep them from blocking wanted traffic because it is arriving at an unusual, fire walled, or "locked" port.

Hosting Facilities

If you are using a server that is not under your physical care, and is managed by an off-site third party, then you likely have an agreement with a hosting facility. Hosting facilities are typically for-profit companies that manage the physical equipment necessary to provide access to websites for a number of clients. Many offer web development and management services as well, but if you are still reading, then that tidbit is probably of little interest as you are here to build it yourself.

ADDITIONAL NOTES

Up Time is the average amount of time that all services on a server are operational and accessible to end users. It is a typical measurement of a hosting company's ability to provide the services they promise.

The benefit of using a hosting service falls under the same principles as other cloud computing services. You are paying to rent equipment and/or services in place of investing in equipment and managing the server and Internet connection yourself. Additionally, hosting facilities are equipped with backup power sources as well as redundant connections to the internet, and may even have multiple facilities that are physically dispersed, ensuring their clients have the best up time as possible. Ads like the one below are common to these services and often emphasize their best features. Price competition makes for relatively affordable hosting for those who are not looking for dedicated servers and are comfortable with sharing their (virtual) server resources with other customers.

Domain Registrar

Domain registrars coordinate the name servers that turn URLs into the IP addresses that get us to our destinations. These companies are where you register available names in order to allow others to find your site. One of the most recognized registrars right now is GoDaddy—you may know them from their ads, which feature racecar driver Danica Patrick. Like many registrars, GoDaddy also offers other services like web and email hosting as well as web development in an effort to solve all of your website needs.

LEARN MORE

Keywords, search terms: Networking, network topology, OSI, network architecture

Cisco Networking Example: http://docwiki.cisco.com/wiki/Internetworking_Basics

List and description of all top level domains: http://www.icann.org/en/resources/registries/tlds

Ongoing comparison of hosting providers: http://www.findmyhosting.com/

Chapter 5

Website Design

Website design is a topic of study often neglected until after a programming background has been developed. Worse, it may be entirely ignored or missed by computer science students when courses covering the topic are in other programs like graphic arts or media. This results in programmers trying to understand how to write code meant for layout and design elements without understanding design. By studying these elements first, we can develop a better knowledge of the concepts of web design before we write code. Progressing through the topics in this section during your site design will greatly ease your development efforts in the future, allowing stakeholders to understand the project and provide feedback early on, reducing (re)development time.

A number of factors affect design in web development, complicating what would otherwise appear to the end user to be a relatively simple process of displaying a picture or document. In truth, the development process involves not only the HTML and multimedia that make up the visual aspects of the page but also considerations of software engineering, human-computer interaction, quality assurance and testing, project management, information and requirement engineering, modeling, and system analysis and design.

Today's sites are now becoming more application centered than traditional sites. This further complicates our projects as we integrate with legacy software and databases, strive to meet real-time data demands, address security vulnerabilities inherent to the environment we are working in, and ongoing support and maintenance typical of robust software applications.

In response to these advances in complexity and capability, web development has grown to embrace many of the same development processes of software development. We will consider some of these processes below, which you may wish to use depending on the size and complexity of a given project.

Planning Cycle

Web development is best achieved as a linear process, but is usually completed asynchronously. The planning process described is intended to build upon itself to refine project requirements, look and feel, and development plans. However, limitations in timelines, mid-project revisions, and the extensive time that can be invested into the early stages of design lead many programmers to begin development while a project is still in design.

Starting early with programming during design planning can accelerate a project when the elements created early on are unlikely to be affected by later changes in the scope. When done carefully, early programming also allows an opportunity to test concepts before investing time into an idea that may not work. It is important to avoid aspects that are assumed to change, like visual layout or particular pieces of content, instead focusing on data structure, frameworks, and other components that are easily adapted to design changes.

While you are planning, keep an eye out for indicators that things are going off-track. Some of the more important flags that should be resolved include:

1. Vaguely defined use cases and inadequate project requirements
2. Overly broad or undefined scope of features
3. Unresolved disputes between stakeholders about project features
4. Unrealistic time table, budget, or inadequate resources

When considering your milestones, tasks, objectives, or whatever label you or your team place on objectives, a handy acronym to reference is SMART. SMART stands for Specific, Measurable, Attainable, Realistic, and Timely. The idea is to check all of your objectives against these criteria to determine if they are appropriate and well developed. By ensuring all of your objectives meet the SMART criteria, you will have a better chance of keeping your project on time and well planned.

Specific:

Is your objective specific enough to convey its full scope? While you do not want to specify implementation of the objective, you should convey enough specific information that the person assigned to the objective can begin their portion of implementation.

Good Example: Deliver our standard proposal with adjusted price quotes to reflect customer's discount rate of 15%.

Bad Example: Deliver a proposal to the customer.

Measurable:

Your objective should have a clear indicator of when it is complete.

Good Example: Complete the first 15 pages identified in the site plan.

Bad Example: Complete the first 20% of the site.

Attainable:

Is it possible, at all, to complete the objective?

Good Example: Get the server to a FedEx store by close of business on delivery date.

Bad Example: Drive the server from New York to California within 24 hours.

Realistic:

Is it possible to complete the objective given the timeline and resources on hand?

Good Example: Have Team A (staff of 20) complete 10 pages by tomorrow.

Bad Example: Have Bob the Intern complete 10 pages by tomorrow.

Timely:

Will the objective be useful if it is completed at (not near or before) its deadline?

Assuming a proposal deadline of Friday morning:

Good Example: Have draft sitemap completed by the end of Wednesday to include in the proposal.

Bad Example: Have draft sitemap completed by the end of Friday to include in the proposal.

"But, wait, Attainable and Realistic sound like the same thing!" Well, yes they are quite similar. However the difference lies in what else you know about the project, timeline, resources and objectives. In our Realistic example this is highlighted by specifying the resources available for the objective. While our example company could assign sufficient resources to complete 10 pages in a day, it could never drive a server from New York to California in a day no matter how many people it has or how fast their car is given current speed limits. In the same vein, the objective of creating 10 pages in a day is perfectly attainable for our example company, but is not realistic if your company lacks enough manpower to complete the task.

While we broke these examples down to highlight the particulars of each element of our litmus test, real world objectives would contain all of these together in up to two or three brief sentences:

Team A will complete the customer's proposal using our standard forms including their discount and a sample site plan by the 15th for delivery the 20th.

Now we need to test it. Is the objective specific? Yes. We are not left needing basic questions asked before we could work on the objective. Is it Measurable? Yes. We have a deadline of the 15th of the month for a specific list of items. Is it Attainable? Yes. With appropriate resources there is nothing impossible about the objective. Is it Realistic? Assuming Team A has enough time and manpower to complete the task by the deadline, yes. Is it Timely? The work is due 5 days before delivery, allowing time for review, changes, or delays, and its deadline does not extend beyond its useful life, so yes, we have a SMART objective.

How do we come up with our objectives? We extract them as the "big things" that need to be done from the customer's request, the mission statement, or other sources of information that define the scope of your project.

What do we do with our objectives? The individual(s) tasked to the objective will break it into actionable tasks, or individual items that need to be completed. For example, our hypothetical objective of ten pages in a day could be broken down into ten tasks, one for each page. Helpful Hint: SMART can be applied to tasks, too (really any future planning/goal).

Why bother with any of this? Why even create a scope document in the first place if we know things will change? Well, we do it because things will change. New ideas will crop up, problems might be found, or something might be forgotten in the mix. The planning stage will define for us and our client exactly what we are going to do, and what our price, time, terms, etc. are meant to cover. As a project is in progress, especially if iterative meetings are held with the client, new requests will come into play. These may be great ideas. They may be terrible. They may derail the project's success if they are not completed. However, each of them will affect your timeline and resources. The tendency to squeeze in "one more idea" over and over again is called Feature Creep, as it creeps into your project and eventually eats away at your resources and profit.

LEARN MORE

Keywords, search terms: Website planning, web development plan, planning templates, project management

Good Planning Worksheet: http://www.goodworkmarketing.com/docs/WebsitePlanningGuide.pdf

BusinessBalls.com Guide to Project Management: http://www.businessballs.com/project.htm

The Fold

As we begin to develop our pages, we need to begin to consider where we want to place pieces of our content. If you look at newspapers, you will find that the most attractive story of the day (as decided, at least, by the publisher) is emblazoned in large letters near the middle or top of the front page, surrounded by the name of the paper, the date, and other pieces of information that quickly lend to your decision of whether or not to purchase a given paper. This is done intentionally, to make the paper attract your attention and get you to buy their edition over their competitors. In the printed news industry, the prime retail space in the paper is the top half of the front page, or what you see when the newspaper is folded normally at a newsstand. This is referred to as "above the fold," and is crucial to getting their audience's attention. This also applies to websites, except in our case, our "above the fold" is what the user sees on the landing page for our site, without having to scroll down or use any links.

What you typically find here is the name and or logo of the company, and what they feel is most important for you to see first. As you begin to analyze web pages in this light, you will find it very easy to determine what kind of site they are, or what they want or expect from you as their guest. News sites will typically follow a similar setting to a printed paper, leading with headlines and links to other sections. Companies will lead with a featured product or sale to attract your attention, and search engines will make the search bar prominent, usually with ad space close by to increase their revenue streams.

The concept of "The Fold" is another of the many highly argued concepts in web development. Proponents are quick to point out the same example I used of traditional print media methods, while detractors will argue that if it were true, scrolling would never have

been created, or users would lose interest in following links. While I endorse "The Fold" as a useful approach to landing pages, I do not mean to imply that all of your pages should fit on only one, non-scrolling screen.

Recent trends on sites like Facebook and LinkedIn show us there are in fact places for scrolling. Indefinitely, as it were. Both sites now feature status pages where older content is continuously appended each time you near the bottom of the page. This is quite similar to the concept of paging, but instead of clicking a link to the next page, the content is simply written in at the bottom creating a never-ending feel to the page. Ultimately, your design phase will help identify where following "The Fold" is not really an option, or if there is enough content to warrant indefinite scrolling, and all other ranges in between.

Typography

Typography is the study of font. While an important topic in media arts, it has until recently received little attention in web development. Utilizing unusual fonts used to be a complicated process that required the end user to have your font(s) installed in order to see the site as you intended. Now, advances in CSS allow us to use unusual fonts by connecting to them through our styling. This allows us to use a tremendous variety of fonts in our sites to add to our look and feel, adding an aspect that has unlocked new approaches to design. Some of the elements of typography include the study of features like readability, conveying meaning or emotion through impression, and the artistic effect of mixing styles.

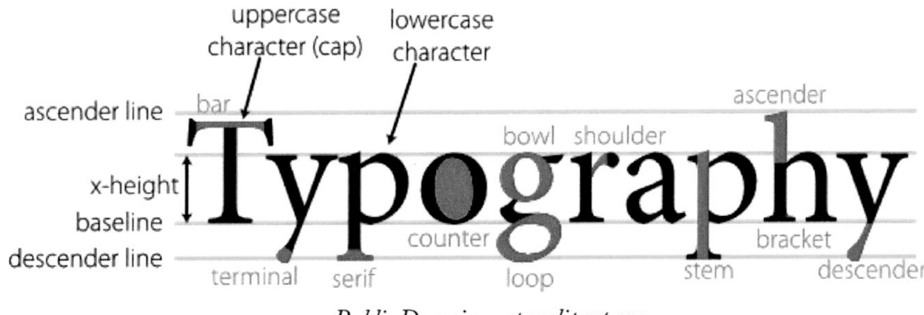

Public Domain—openclipart.org

Figure 10 Typography

For ease of reading and to avoid a cluttered appearance, most sites keep to two or three fonts when creating their design. One for text, and one or two for headings, titles, and distinguishing marks. All of these should be kept in the same family for a more congruous experience, and each unusual font defined in your site should include fallback definitions in case there are problems loading your primary style (we will see this in examples later on). You may want to set your regular text as one of the standards supported by all browsers as users are most familiar and usually comfortable with that set.

Web Fonts

To tap into this aspect of design, a great place to start is with the Google Fonts[14] website. This site is a repository of character sets for a great variety of fonts that you can link to or

[14] http://www.google.com/fonts/

download and include in your own site's files. We will look at connecting to these later, but browsing the site now will give you an initial look at the amount of variety that is available for design.

Site Maps

A site map is a file that contains a master list of links to the pages on your site, and can provide information about those pages like how often they are updated, how pages connect to each other, and how important it is relative to the other pages. It can be a reference tool to both Bots that index your site for search engines, as well as your visitors trying to find particular content. Site map files are XML documents arranged in hierarchical format that bots read to gain understanding of your site layout, page relevance, and organization. The file may also be a human readable page that diagrams how pages relate to one another, and serve as a master list of the pages in your site. Site maps are best kept in the root of your website, at the same level as your initial index page.

While a complete site map cannot be finalized until after your site is ready to be published, I include site maps under development methods because laying out your site's organization on paper will help with developing your menu system, logically organizing content, and in defining the scope and purpose of your site. The more content or pages you can define at the beginning of the process will reveal information that will help during your design phase.

To create a site map, you can start by creating a running list of all the content you wish to have on your site. Anyone involved in the production or validation of content should be in room! In each of these steps, it is important to identify your stakeholders. As you are creating your running list, it is often helpful to use index cards so you can determine by card color or pile where a particular piece of content should be. This will help you discover your menu system, as you create names for piles of cards as your menu title. After, as you diagram what cards are with what pile and where that pile is relative to others, your site map will begin to take shape.

Samples: Detailed Sitemap

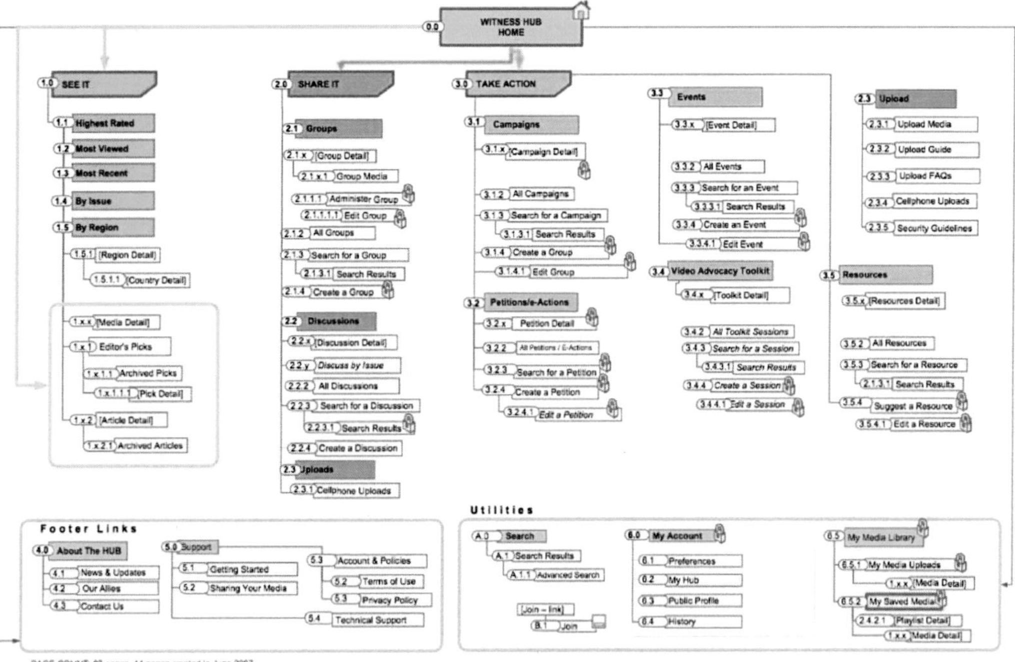

Creative Commons 2.0 Licensed by Kent Bye

Figure 11 Site Map

If you are rebuilding an existing site, you may wish to adapt the existing menu system or scrap it entirely and start new. Larger sites or those with a large number of stakeholders involved will need more time to complete this step. To break larger projects down, you may wish to begin by defining what type(s) of content you do *not* want on your site. For example, if your target audience is casual shoppers looking for in-home plants, you can eliminate information on plants not suited for indoor living, or restrict the amount of information provided to basic care and maintenance, as opposed to the greater detail professional landscapers will look for. Distributing the process of identifying what material needs to be published into several groups of stakeholders who share interests in certain categories will also help streamline this process.

Photo by Jonas Maaløe Jespersen (CC BY-SA 2.0)

Figure 12 Website Planning

The sitemap you create should follow the URL standards RFC-3986[15] (notably the use of entity escape codes) and the standards for XML.[16] Your character encoding must also be in UTF-8, which means some special characters and markings beyond those traditionally used in text will not be available. Once your sitemap is complete and uploaded, you can add it to your robots.txt file as:

```
Sitemap: http://www.yourwebsite.com/yourfilename.xml
```

You can also submit your site (and sitemap) for crawling directly to the search engines. While this may not happen immediately, it lets them know that your site is new or has changed. Some engines, like Google[17] provide tools and reporting for a comprehensive experience while others like Bing[18] have quick entry forms that only require your site's main URL and a confirmation that you are, in fact, human (which seems amusing when you consider the point of what you are doing is to trigger a bot).

Let us plan a small site of just a few links: our index page, a contact page, an information page, and publications and research pages off of our information page. As an XML file, our visual sitemap above would be expressed as the following:

```
<?xml version="1.0" encoding="UTF-8"?>
<urlset xmlns=http://www.sitemaps.org/schemas/sitemap/0.9>
<url>
   <loc>http://www.oursite.com/</loc>
   <lastmod>2013-01-13</lastmod>
```

15 http://asg.web.cmu.edu/rfc/rfc3986.php
16 http://www.w3.org/TR/REC-xml/
17 https://www.google.com/webmasters/tool
18 http://www.bing.com/toolbox/submit-site-url

```
      <priority>0.8</priority>
   <url>
   <url>
      <loc>http://www.oursite.com/contact.htm</loc>
      <lastmod>2013-01-13</lastmod>
      <priority>0.9</priority>
   <url>
   <url>
      <loc>http://www.oursite.com/publications.htm</loc>
      <lastmod>2013-01-13</lastmod>
      <priority>0.5</priority>
      <changefreq>monthly</changefreq>
   <url>
   <url>
      <loc>http://www.oursite.com/information.htm</loc>
      <lastmod>2013-01-13</lastmod>
      <priority>0.5</priority>
   <url>
   <url>
      <loc>http://www.oursite.com/research.html</loc>
      <lastmod>2013-01-13</lastmod>
      <priority>0.7</priority>
   <url>
      </urlset>
```

As we are focusing on the sitemap aspects of this example at the moment (we will learn more about XML later), just take note that the <loc>, <url>, and <urlset> tags for location are required. Everything else is optional, but adds more information for site crawlers. You will also note that in this example you cannot deduce the menu or hierarchy that we saw in our visual diagram—indexing services do not care about this. For a site visitor, we would style this page differently or create a sitemap optimized for our visitors to read.

Robots.txt

Robots are automated scripts typically used to index, or take inventory, of the content in a website for use in things like web searching sites or collecting statistics. A robots file is a basic text file kept in the root folder of your website that instructs these robots on what sections or types of content in your site you do or do not want them to index. Legitimate robots will read this file when they first arrive on your site to honor your request. Keep in mind this is an enforceable act, and malicious or less-than-reputable robots are still perfectly capable of reading through all non-privileged (i.e. no login required) content on your site.

The simplest robots.txt file involves only two lines:

```
User-agent: *
Disallow: /
```

The first specifies that the rules below apply to all robots that read the file. The second adds that nothing is allowed below (meaning deeper, or all the files and folders inside of) the root folder (/ represents the main folder of the site). If we wanted to be more specific about what sections we want to keep bots out of, we can identify them individually instead of the whole site:

```
User-agent: *
Disallow: /pictures/reserved/
Disallow: /index.php
Disallow: /media
Disallow: /scripts
```

To distinguish cases where a particular bot has a different set of permissions, we can use the bot's name in place of our "all" wildcard:

```
User-agent: BadBot
Allow: /About/robot-policy.html
Disallow: /
User-agent: *
Disallow: /pictures/reserved/
Disallow: /index.php
Disallow: /media
Disallow: /scripts
```

The above settings tell BadBot that it is allowed to see the policy file, but nothing else. It still specifies the blocked paths for the rest of the bots that might visit.

Wireframes

Wireframes in the web development world are not exactly their literal three dimensional counterparts in the real world, but they bear a similar purpose. A wireframe may include things like location and size of elements such as a login button, where banners and content sections will sit, and provide an overall idea of how a site will operate. When wire framing a website, the idea is to create a mockup of one or more designs that portray how the interface might appear to the user. By the end of your wire framing process, you should have an idea of how the site will operate, and have resolved questions over where users will find particular features and elements.

Wireframes typically do not include color, actual content, or advanced design decisions like typography. Some of these considerations will have been at least partly addressed when creating your site map, and the rest will come once we begin storyboarding.

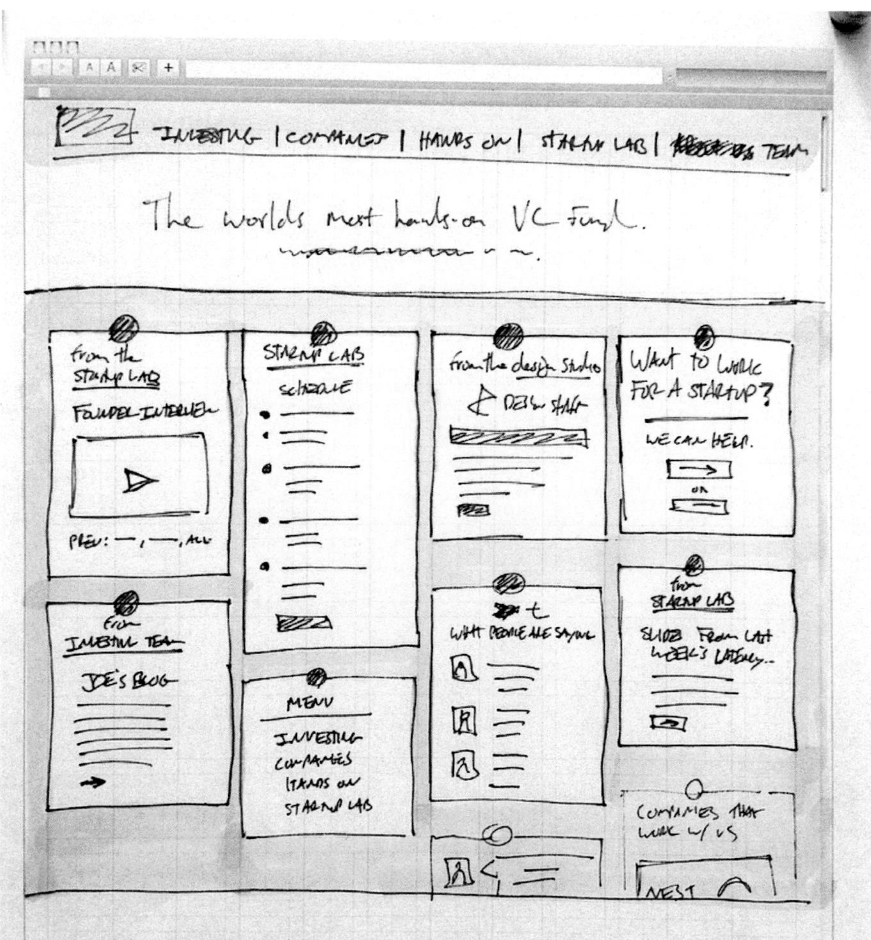

Creative Commons 2.0 Braden Kowitz

Figure 13 Wireframe

Storyboarding

Storyboarding a website is quite similar to storyboarding a TV show, comic, or other forms of media. Using our wireframes, we can begin to add color, font, and rough images to our documents. Keep in mind at this point we are probably still in a graphics editor or document style program like PowerPoint, Photoshop, etc. Real code is coming soon, but we can do more mock-ups faster without taking the time to make it function.

As you storyboard, you will create separate pages, or panels, for the screen a user would see as they complete the most important processes on your site. If you are selling something, for example, your storyboard may include examples of product pages, adding items to their cart, logging in, and completing their purchase.

By paging through these panels, you can see how the user experience will progress and identify potential problems like a confusing check out process, or you may discover that your shopping cart block from wire framing may be better off in a different, more predominant location. This process may be repeated several times until a final version is accepted by everyone in the decision process.

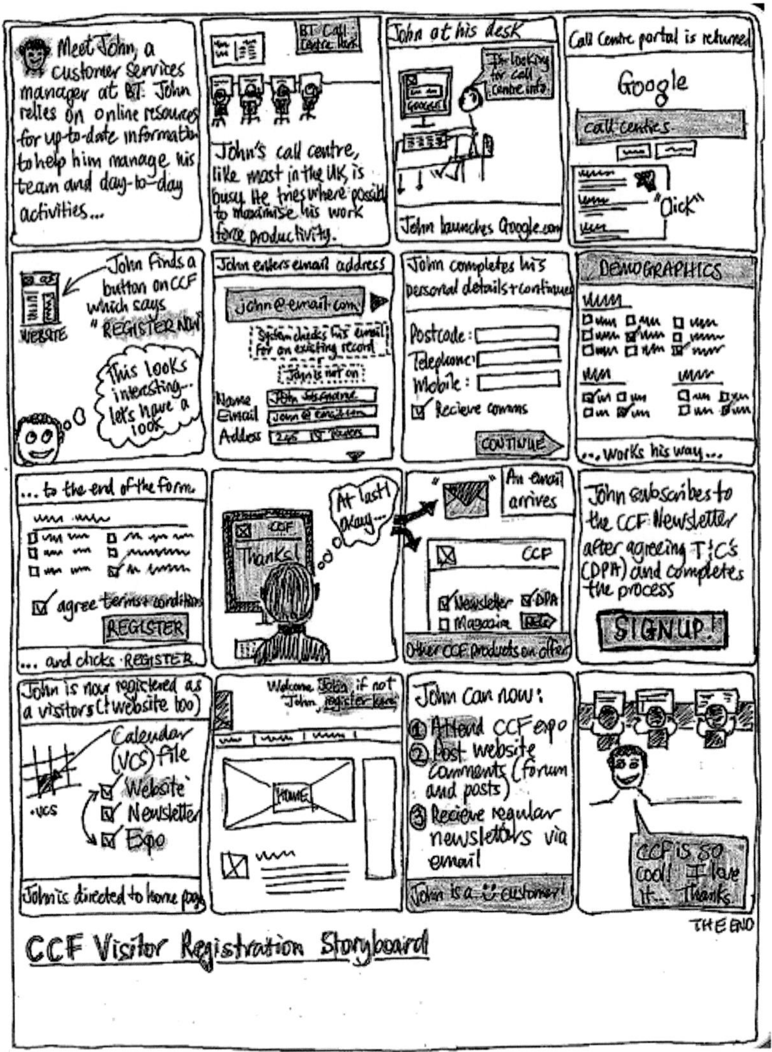

Creative Commons 2.0 Rob Enslin

Figure 14 Storyboarding

Color Schemes

The process of determining the color(s) involved in your site could fill a book. In fact, it does.[19] Regardless of the varying opinions of what emotions colors instill, or represent, the quickest way to alienate a user is to give them a visual experience that is unappealing. The layout, appearance, and cohesiveness of your site are something that are immediately judged when a user first visits. These elements influence everything from their impression of what the site represents, its reputability, and even its trustworthiness as an ecommerce option. If your site appears to be disorganized, dated and out of style, or seems too "busy" or complicated, you can lose users in less than ten seconds.[20]

You can address this issue (even without an artistic eye) by following the techniques we discussed earlier to plan out a simple, intuitive interface, and by using tools to help you

[19] https://www.google.com/search?q=website+visual+design

[20] http://www.nngroup.com/articles/how-long-do-users-stay-on-web-pages/

select and compare color schemes like http://colorschemedesigner.com/ or http://www.colorsontheweb.com/colorwizard.asp.

Whether you choose to study other books on the subject or not, a great way to keep current is to get ideas from what others are doing by following sites that list or rate sites by appearance such as the annual Times review[21] and http://www.thebestdesigns.com/.

LEARN MORE

Keywords, search terms: Web design, aesthetics, graphics, typography

Web Style Guide 3rd Edition: http://webstyleguide.com/wsg3/8-typography/index.html

TypeCulture: http://www.typeculture.com/academic_resource/

[21] http://techland.time.com/2013/05/06/50-best-websites-2013

Chapter 6

Development

Below are just a few examples of different methods of programming found in the workplace. This is not an exhaustive list, but is meant to induce some personal analysis of what approaches might be effective for you. We will look at examples of styles based on the number of programmers—one, two, or many—to demonstrate how programming can be approached as team sizes change.

Staffing Styles

Single Developer

Also called The Lone Cowboy or Lone Wolf. Typically found in small companies, benefits of being a single developer are that you are intimately familiar with the entire code base (at least while you are writing it—we will get to that under Good Practices), do not have to agree on coding styles, branching, or integrating code, and your functions and classes are built to what you specify.

Downfalls however are also large. A second pair of eyes or fresh mind can help find bugs faster, the workload burden is entirely yours, and any security issues or bugs you are not aware of are likely to be found the hard way, by an end user or malicious visitor.

Paired Programming

Sometimes referred to as Holmes and Watson programming, paired programming is the practice of assigning two programmers to the same task, and having them (quite literally) work side by side. This allows one person to write while the other contemplates code interactions, watches for bugs, and keeps track of tasks. By altering which programmer in the pair is the lead at different intervals both programmers are able to contribute and learn from each other. Proponents of this model will highlight studies that show decreases in bugs, increased performance (it is, after all, harder to sneak in that Facebook post when co-workers are regularly using your screen), increased knowledge across staff members, and less distraction.

This approach may or may not work well depending on the culture present, and paying two staff members to complete one task can be more expensive, possibly offsetting reduced programming time. Poor pairing decisions (e.g., two programmers with little experience) and other factors like addressing sick time and vacations that interrupt teams can also reduce the potential benefits of this approach.

Team Development

Team development allows the work involved in a project to be dispersed among a group of individuals (a necessary step for most large scale projects) and reduces overall development time. A team with well-defined divisions of labor who adhere to an agreed upon set of methods can be a highly effective group.

Detractors are found where agreements on labor or method are ill defined or not adhered to. They can also arise from personal issues or conflicts of personality, and physically dispersed teams may find issues with time zone differences, limitations of communication methods, and increased "lag" time caused by not being face-to-face for immediate communication.

Project Management Methods

Once you move beyond programming alone and into groups, or have multiple parties working on the same project, a management approach will be needed to determine pace, goals, deadlines, and to maintain order and understanding of the project. There are a great deal of approaches to this problem, and we will take a quick look at some of the currently popular solutions.

Agile

While some of the principles of agile development go against the planning process we examined above, it can be effective in instances where fast turnaround is necessary and a highly iterative release process is acceptable. Some of its tenets are frequent communication between parties, self-organized groups motivated for the project, and requirements that are changed as ideas progress through the project. Changing requirements are driven by what is revealed through the iterative releases, and this fluidity is one of the strengths to be found in this approach.

Ultimately, the guiding principle here is to work in the mindset where you get the best people, trust in them, and focus more on the customer's wishes and the project itself than length contracts, internal processes, and bureaucracy. You are most likely to run into this approach in start-ups that are not burned by an internal bureaucracy and heavily structured atmosphere.

The twelve principles of agile development, according to a published manifesto[22] by seventeen software developers are as follows:

1. Our highest priority is to satisfy the customer through early and continuous delivery of valuable software.
2. Welcome changing requirements, even late in development. Agile processes harness change for the customer's competitive advantage.
3. Deliver working software frequently, from a couple of weeks to a couple of

[22] http://www.agilemanifesto.org/

months, with a preference to the shorter timescale.

4. Business people and developers must work together daily throughout the project.
5. Build projects around motivated individuals. Give them the environment and support they need, and trust them to get the job done.
6. The most efficient and effective method of conveying information to and within a development team is face-to-face conversation.
7. Working software is the primary measure of progress.
8. Agile processes promote sustainable development. The sponsors, developers, and users should be able to maintain a constant pace indefinitely.
9. Continuous attention to technical excellence and good design enhances agility.
10. Simplicity—the art of maximizing the amount of work not done—is essential.
11. The best architectures, requirements, and designs emerge from self-organizing teams.
12. At regular intervals, the team reflects on how to become more effective, then tunes and adjusts its behavior accordingly.

Scrum

The Scrum process is a more focused and organized approach than agile development. The Scrum process maintains the defined roles of team members while pursuing the fast-paced development goals of agile. Daily meetings are held at the same time/place, and are typically held standing, to encourage shorter meetings. Core team members lead the 15-minute meeting by briefly reporting on what they did since the last meeting, their plans for the day, and any obstacles they have come across. Stumbling blocks brought up in these reports are addressed by the Scrum Masters, who address obstacles in order to keep the rest of the team on task.

Scrum goals are organize into Sprints, blocks of time usually shorter than 30 days, in which certain tasks of the project should be completed. Sprints are kicked off with planning meetings, and the goal is to have those portions of the project in full working order by the Sprint's completion.

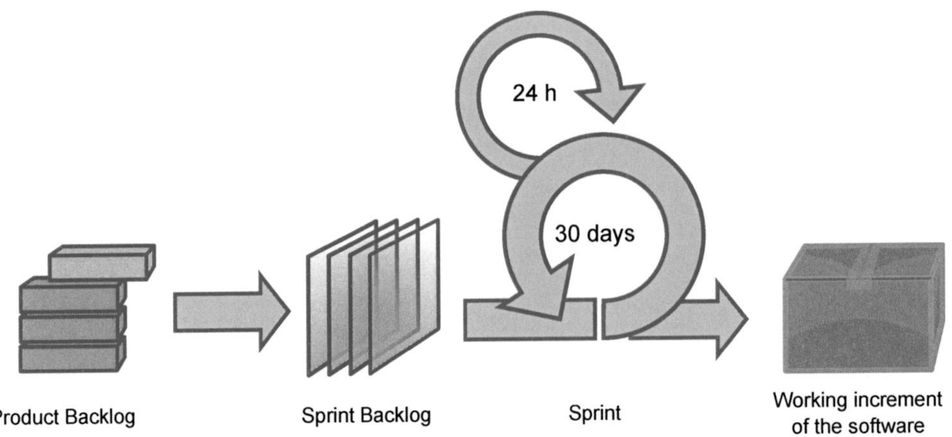

By Lakeworks [CC-BY-SA-3.0-2.5-2.0-1.0], via Wikimedia Commons

Figure 15 Scrum

Waterfall

The Waterfall approach to project management recognizes the projects are typically cyclical, and builds that recognition into its five stage approach to management:

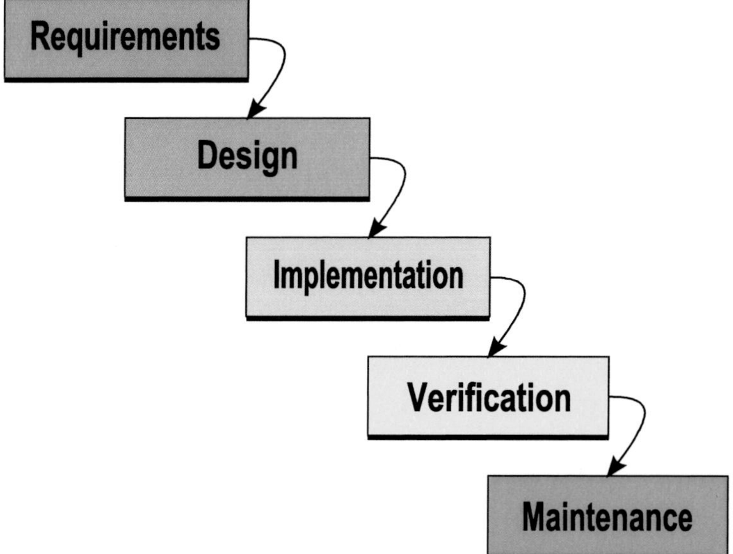

Paulsmith99 at en.wikipedia CC-BY-3.0, via Wikimedia Commons

Figure 16 Waterfall Diagram

Requirements

Requirement gathering can be interactions with your users that generate feature requests, initial project definition like its scope, or discovery of other important information during the planning phase of a project.

Design

Development of pseudo-code, storyboards, wireframes, or any other materials necessary to depict what will be implemented to satisfy the requirements. See sections: Pseudo-Code First!, Storyboarding, and Wireframes.

Implementation

The actual programming and development phase to generate the working solution.

Verification

Testing and debugging the solution to ensure it meets the requirements and works as intended.

Maintenance

Ongoing tasks such as database maintenance, modifications to support changing requirements, or new tasks created by the discovery of bugs.

Items discovered in this phase trigger the process to begin again in order to address them. Eliminating a bug, for example, requires determining how to fix the problem, after which the bug resolution will move through the rest of the steps just like the project did initially. New ideas or feature requests will also trigger the requirements stage to begin. As these events will not occur at the same time, the waterfall effect occurs as individual items in the project will be in different phases as the cycle continues.

Structural Patterns

More decisions! Now that we have our team(s), and an approach for managing the project as a whole, we need to determine how to manage the development of the code as well. How the code is organized contributes to how easy or difficult change management becomes, how flexible the system is, and how portable it is. The options of how to approach organizing the actual code are called Architectural Patterns.

Model View Controller

In the MVC approach, we create three distinct concepts in our code. The image below depicts a de-coupled approach to MVC, where the model and view have no direct communication.

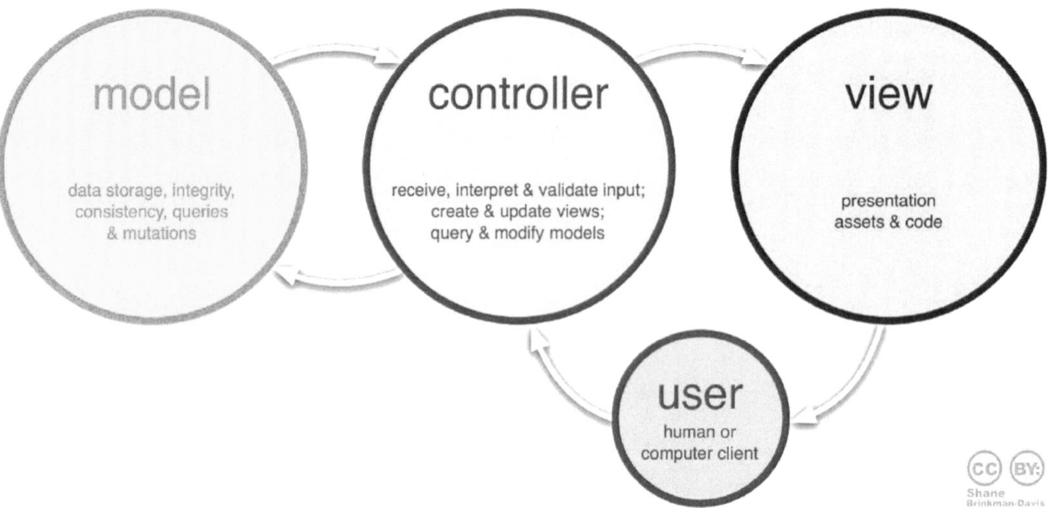

Shane Brinkman-Davis, December 2012 CC-A 3.0

Figure 17 Model View Controller

Models

Our models contain the logic, functions, and rules that manipulate our data. A model is the only piece of the system that should interact directly with your data source. It should also respond to a request with a consistently formatted reply, and not simply return messages from the data source. This allows you to utilize multiple different sources for your data, or easily change how it is stored, as you would only need to edit your model's interactions and connections instead of adjusting code throughout your entire site.

Views

Views generate the output that is presented to the user. They request, or are given, the data needed to complete the page by the model. In some interpretations of MVC, the controller may also act as a mediator between the model and view—the important fact is that you should not see code in a view section that completes any actions other than formatting and presenting output. The view contains the images, tables, styling, and page formatting that make up the site itself. By keeping these items isolated from the models and controllers, we can easily duplicate our site's appearance somewhere else, or "skin" several sites differently, but have them all use the same data and models for interaction.

Controllers

Controllers recognize changes and events, such as user interaction and results of model responses that drive other actions. The controller will then call the appropriate model(s) to interact with data, and the appropriate view(s) to reflect the changes made. When controllers also manage passing data from the model to the view, the system is considered passive, or de-coupled, as the models and views have no awareness of each other.

Variations

MVC was originally developed as a method for traditional software development. Migrating it to web development is not a simple task, as the concepts become muddled when interacting with multiple languages, and a client-server model of communication. Other approaches to interpreting the MVC method for web development such as model/view/presenter, model/view/adapter, and presentation/abstraction/control attempt to resolve and clarify implementing this approach online.

Service-Oriented Architecture

SOA is a modular style approach to interaction. It is used in web services and Cloud Computing (APIs) as a method of providing tools, actions, and information to other systems that allows for larger and/or multiple systems to integrate into. Each item in an SOA approach is oblivious to the actions of other services. It only knows how to request information or actions contained in other services as they are needed.

By building in this approach, the programmers can specify and limit what actions are available and under what conditions (end user's authentication level, nature of data, etc.) all while keeping the actual systems removed from direct interaction with the consumer. This helps protect internal systems by limiting access to raw data and intellectual property while still providing an organized platform from which developers can retrieve what they need.

Larger companies might develop an API that provides information from multiple data sources from one place. By creating the common platform, their developers can connect to the data from other applications or websites without having to connect to each data source. These companies might also allow their partners to access their API in order to provide automate communication between companies, create other add-on tools, or to contribute their own information. Walgreens recently opened a portion of their internal API for just this reason. By allowing third parties access, outside vendors were able to create applications like printing from Instagram right at your local store, or refilling prescriptions from a mobile device.

Unit Testing

Unit testing is an exercise in writing each element of your software to meet very specific requirements. By reducing your project to its smallest testable component, each part can be tested individually. These modules are then connected together to form the larger whole. It is included under methods instead of practices as it is an important approach that needs to be followed by each team member if it is to be used at all. Testing these units before including them in the software should reduce debugging, and more readily allows for testing components before a full implementation has been assembled. This technique can also be combined with other methods because it is more of a coding practice than an approach to project implementation.

Unit testing is frequently used in fast paced approaches like Scrum to help ensure a less error prone product. Keep in mind that this is not a perfect solution. While individual units may test fine, logical problems can still be created as these modules are combined. Continued testing of the results of not only single units but also units working in combination will help in addressing this potential point of failure.

LEARN MORE

Keywords, search terms: Project management, programming architecture, software planning and development

Architectural Blueprints—The "4+1" View Model of Software Architecture http://www.cs.ubc.ca/~gregor/teaching/papers/4+1view-architecture.pdf

Project Management Advisor http://www.pma.doit.wisc.edu/index.html

Good Practices

File Organization

As we begin to create more and more files to complete our website, keeping everything in one folder will quickly grow cluttered. To address this, we can create folders just like we do when sorting files in My Documents. Traditionally you can find folders for images, scripts, pages or files, or for different sections of content or tasks, like an admin folder or ecommerce store. How and why these folders are created varies to personal taste or group determinations, and in some cases is done to maintain a particular method of writing code such as model-view-controller.

Pseudo-Code First!

Whiteboards, notepads, and napkins are your friends. Writing out how you plan to tackle a particular problem will help you identify logic problems before you are halfway through coding them, and will help you keep track of what you need to work on as you progress. Creating pseudo-code is the process of writing out in loosely structured sentences what needs to be done. For example, if my task is to look at each element in an array and tell the user if it is true or false, we might draft the following:

```
foreach(thing in array){
      if(thing / 2 is 0) then show Even
      else show Odd
}
```

Imagine that while writing this example out we realize that we want to store the responses for use again later, not just show them to the user. So, let us update our pseudo-code to take that use case into mind:

```
foreach(thing in array){
      if(thing / 2 is 0) then add to even array
      else add to odd array
      send arrays back in an array
}
```

Reviewing what we have now, not much looks different, but so far we have not had to rewrite any code either. After some thought, it might occur to us that creating two additional arrays could be more memory intensive and less efficient than editing the one we already have. So, to simplify things and possibly improve performance, we might try this:

```
foreach(thing in array){
      if(thing / 2 is 0) then add it to even array, delete
         from this array
      send arrays back in an array
}
```

Finally, since we are now editing our existing array, we need to make sure we reference it (ensuring our changes are reflected after the foreach completes), which also means we only have to pass back our even array:

```
foreach(reference! Thing in array){
      if(thing / 2 is 0) then add it to even array, delete
         from this array
      send even array back
}
```

While none of the above examples would work (they are just pseudo-code), we were able to edit a conceptual version of our program four times. Alternatively we would have spent time creating and revising actual lines of code three times, only to keep finding an issue, backing up, and make lots of changes.

Comments

To quote Eagleson's Law, "Any code you have not looked at for six or more months might as well have been written by someone else." This is not to say that your style or approach will change drastically over time, but that your immediate memory of what variables mean, why certain exceptions were made, or what the code, ultimately, was meant to address may not be as apparent as when you last worked on the file. It is natural for us to feel that we will remember these details as they are so obvious when we are creating them. The need for good commenting becomes immediately apparent when reviewing someone else's work, and you are wallowing in frustration trying to figure out what that person was trying to do.

This is not meant to endorse comments that are obvious to the reader from the line, like:

```
$int = 2 + 2 //we added 2 and 2 together
```

Rather, comments are best suited to explaining why agreed upon methods were not used or what difficult to understand code might be doing, like:

```
// This block of code checks each text file in the folder for
the given date and deletes it
// This is legacy code from when Frank M. worked here. If we
change anything, payroll breaks
```

Order of Assignment

Many scripting languages distinguish between assignment statements and logical tests based on the number of equal signs used in the statement. For example, giving the variable $temp the value of 10 (also called "setting" or "assigning" the variable) can be expressed as *$temp = 10,* while checking the value would look like *if($temp == 10).* It is very easy to forget the extra = when writing logic statements, since we are so conditioned to using it in singular form.

This creates issues as a logic test written as *if($temp = 10)* will always be true. First, we are executing what is in the parenthesis—in this case, setting temp equal to 10. When this occurs, the system returns returns a result of "true" to the script—the request has been completed. This is like asking if true is true—it always is! Since this does not cause a problem that stops the program from running, we will not get any errors before running it. The errors will be discovered only when the program does not behave as intended, and depending on the nature of the logic statement we wanted, that might be a rare case, making for some frustrating debugging. These are called logical errors, as the compiler or engine can run the code we gave it, and the error lies between expected execution and what the system is actually programmed to do. We will look at this further in Chapter 27.

To protect ourselves from this, we can invert our logic statements to put our values first. Since we cannot assign a variable to a number, writing *10 = $temp* would be considered invalid, as 10 does not represent a place in system memory. Neither variables nor constants can start with a number, even $10 is invalid. However, *if(10 == $temp)* is still valid, as the system compares both sides of the equation to each other, and is indifferent to the order.

By placing values first in our logic statements, if we forget to use the correct number of =, we will get an error from the engine early on that we can immediately find and fix. Otherwise we are left with a logic error that needs to be traced through our program later when we discover it is not working correctly.

Read Me

Closely connected with the concept of good commenting is the ubiquitous readme file—familiar to many users as the basic text file no one ever reads despite its title's quiet plea. The readme file's continued prevalence in such an antiquated file format is done to ensure it is legible on the widest variety of operating systems, and is still considered the best delivery format.

Within your readme file should be notes targeting your end users. Unless you release open source code, they would not be able to read your comments. These notes should tell the user what the application's requirements are, how to install it, how to get help, and if you like, what notable changes are in the version they are looking at compared to its predecessor(s). Typically, the most common location to put a readme file is in the root folder of your files, or in a sub folder in which the readme notes apply to.

Spacing

Just as we use spacing in documents to convey that a topic change is occurring, we can break up longer string of commands by putting spaces around lines that are grouped together to complete a particular task, signifying that the next set of lines is for another task.

Brackets

Some languages require the programmer to use a combination of parenthesis and brackets to identify what pieces of code belong together. This allows the engine or compiler to delineate between the code that should be tested as a logic statement, code that gets executed if that statement is true, and code that belongs to functions or classes.

As we write our code and reach instances where we need these elements, it is good practice to immediately enter both the starting and ending marker first, then create space between them to enter your code. This will help ensure that you do not forget to close brackets later, or close them in the wrong places when nesting code. Depending on your text editor, it may assist you by automatically adding closing brackets and helping you identify which opening and closing brackets go together.

Indentation

To make your code easier to read, you can use indentation to give the reader an idea of what lines of code belong to different sections. This is typically done inside functions, classes, and control structures. When we nest code, extra indentations are added for each layer within, moving those blocks of text further right to visually distinguish. As we finish the contents of a loop or function, our closing bracket is lined up with our function definition or logic statement to show that the section of code belonging to it is complete.

While our program will run just fine without indentation, it makes it easier to see where you are in your program and where the line you are looking at is intended to be in the logic flow.

```
<html>
 <?php
  spacing
   function(){
      echo "Hello World";     // Outputs to screen
   }  indentation                commenting
 ?>
</html>
 tags
```

Figure 18 Code Formatting Examples

Meaningful Variable Names

When you create variables and functions, try to create names that will have meaning not only to you, but to others who may read your code. While it can be tempting to use a lot of short variable names while writing your code, it will be more difficult later to follow what the variable is supposed to represent. You might decide to use short names like queryResult or query_result or something longer like numberOfResumesReceived. While the latter takes longer to type while coding, the name is very clear on what it represents. As spaces are generally prohibited in variable names, these examples show us a few ways to approach longer names. The method you use is up to you, but should be used consistently throughout your code to reduce confusion. Differences in how and where you use capitalization or underscores can be used to represent different types of variables like classes or groups of variables.

Short variable names like a simple x or generic name like temp may have their places in your code, but are best reserved for when they identify a small variable or one which will have a very short shelf life in your code.

Versioning

This is the process of creating multiple versions of your software, instead of continuously overwriting your sole edition of code. By creating different copies of your program as you create new features, you can preserve working copies or even create different versions of your program. This allows you to "roll back" or restore previous versions if unforeseen errors are created in new code, or to allow different features to be tried and discarded over time. Naming conventions for different versions of your code might involve numbers, letters, release stages (i.e. alpha, beta, release candidate, and release) a combination of all of these, or just "development" and "live."

GitHub

A popular tool for collaborating on projects right now is GitHub.[23] Focusing on open source projects, GitHub is a cloud service with locally installed application options that focuses on branching. Branching facilitates multiple working versions with varying features to co-exist in the same project space, giving the developers the ability to selectively merge

23 http://www.github.com

new code into their project's official repository. The platform supports code sharing, generating branches, and includes discussion boards, bugs, and feature request areas.

Development Tools

The following tools can be very useful in accelerating project development by reducing repetitive tasks and providing collections of tools to help you write your code. I would encourage you to refrain from using them until you have at least mastered the material in this text, otherwise, you may complicate your debugging tasks or not fully understand what those tools are doing.

Frameworks

Frameworks are compilations of code that you can use to quickly start a site with a collection of features already in place. In a home building analogy, it would be akin to ordering parts of your house already completed, and having special tools in your toolbox for putting the pre-built pieces together.

A typical framework is a set of files that come with their own instructions, and can be so extensive that they take on a life and syntax beyond the language they are written in. They extend the features normally found in the language they are written in by adding their own classes, functions, and capabilities. The goal is that by giving the framework a few commands, we can create much larger processes like a menu system or complete color scheme. Some frameworks focus on the automation of repetitive tasks like generating forms and pages based on tables in a database, or applying in depth style and structure across a website.

Multiple frameworks can be combined in a single project in order to add a combination of features, for example using one framework for the site layout and another for generating database interactions. Each framework will require some time learning how to use its features, just like learning a programming language. This may be an important factor when deciding when and how many to use in your work.

Smarty[24]

The Smarty template engine targets the separation of application logic and presentation. While it creates delineations between the code necessary to generate the content and the code to present the content, it is not a full model-view-controller design. A smarty template page supports special tags and commands that are part of the smarty engine. These elements help to generate what the end product will look like, after generating the PHP necessary to build the page. Smarty also uses a template caching approach to facilitate delivering pages faster, only updating cached templates when changes to a smarty file or its dependencies are detected.

[24] http://www.smarty.net

Yii Framework[25]

The Yii framework focuses on reducing SQL statement writing, follows Model View Controller methods, and helps create themes, web services, and integration with other platforms. It also includes security, authentication, and unit-based approaches to development.

Zend Framework[26]

The Zend framework is focused heavily on modularity, performance, and maintaining an extensible approach to allow continued integration. This framework is popular at the enterprise level, and includes some of the original creators of PHP on staff. Zend itself is a full service PHP company, providing training, development services, and the continued refinement of the PHP language itself.

Templates

Similar to the idea behind frameworks, templates are sets of files that dictate the basic structure that provides a layout to your site. Templates typically create a grid format you can select from, like two or three columns, fixed or relative width and height, etc. If you are starting a site fresh and putting it into an empty template, there may be some placeholder content and styling as well. Templates are useful for getting the look and feel of a site up and running fast and there is little concern about the particulars of appearance, or whenever the template meets your needs well. When inserting your content dynamically, multiple templates can be used for one site to change the look and feel quickly based on which one is applied. This might be determined by what type of device your guest is using, or what type of authentication they are using.

Templates can be both freestanding, or can be an extension of a content management system or framework.

Bootstrap[27]

Bootstrap was created by Twitter in order to help them manage their extremely popular service. As it matured, they made it open source to allow others to utilize the toolset. Their framework provides tools for styling, interaction elements like forms and buttons, and navigation elements including drop downs, alert boxes, and more. Using this frame work involves little more than linking to the appropriate JavaScript and CSS files and then referencing the appropriate style classes in your code.

Foundation[28]

The Foundation system focuses on front end design and follows the principles of responsive web design (see next section). Their approach uses a grid layout to allow flexibility, accelerate prototyping and wire framing, and provides integrated support for multi-platform designs.

---

[25] http://www.yiiframework.com

[26] http://framework.zend.com/

[27] http://twitter.github.io/bootstrap/

[28] http://foundation.zurb.com/

Responsive Web Design

As often as possible, this text will focus on coding methods that support responsive web design. This approach replaces the practice of developing several version of your site in order to support different devices. An example of this is when you come across sites with a regular site, a mobile site (for example m.yoursite.com) and then provide an app for each of the tablet platforms, or force tablet users into their mobile or desktop experience.

Instead, we will create one set of files that changes its own layout and appearance based on what we know. By using information made available in the initial http request to our site, we can determine the features the user's browser supports, width and height of their screen, and more. We can use this information to instruct our CSS files on what rules to apply when styling the page, how much or little to resize elements on our page, what we want to eliminate or hide on smaller screens, and more.

While this approach is still not a perfect solution, it gives us a much-improved ability to support a wide variety of devices without managing several code bases and developing across multiple proprietary platforms.

Integrated Development Environments

This list is by no means comprehensive. These editors are sufficient to get you started. If you wish to continue in web programming, you may elect to invest in a development platform like Adobe Dreamweaver or another professional product that supports more advanced design, or try any number of other IDEs available that focus on a variety of different languages.

You might consider the following programs to help you write your code (listed in no particular order). Each of these has features particular for web development and should be sufficiently capable to get you through the examples in this text.

Jedit[29]

A free editor based around Java. Works on multiple platforms (Windows, Mac and Linux) and includes syntax highlighting.

Notepad++[30]

Notepad++ is a source code text editor with syntax highlighting, multiple document handling using tabs, auto-completion of keywords (customizable), regular expressions in the search and replace function, macro recording and playback, brace and indent highlighting, collapsing and expanding of sections of code, and more.

[29] http://jedit.org

[30] http://notepad-plus.sourceforge.net/

Bluefish[31]

Supports many programming and markup languages. An open source development project, multi-platform, and runs on Linux, FreeBSD, MacOS-X, Windows, OpenBSD and Solaris.

TextWrangler[32]

This editor is related to BBEdit. It does not include as many tools, but retains syntax highlighting and the ability to use FTP within the editor.

HTML-Kit[33]

This editor is intended for use by web developers, and comes with support for writing HTML, XML and scripts. Among its features are internal preview of your web, integration with HTML Tidy, auto-completion of keywords, etc. Look for the "Previous" version for their free copy.

Application Programming Interfaces

Commonly referred to as APIs, pronounced as the letters of the acronym, application programming interfaces allow us to interact with features and data of a system other than its primary means, whether it is an application or website. Created to address needs of data exchange and integration between systems, APIs provide a controlled method of allowing others to use a system without having direct, unfettered access to the code or database it runs on. Examples of APIs in action are maps on non-google website that are fed from Google Maps with markers, that highlight paths and routes, automate directions, or outline places of interest. All of this is done from within their site or system without you leaving to interact with Google. Another example is the growing popularity of sites for clans or groups of friends in multi-player games that provide results, show game statistics, screen shots, and rankings from a site they create by using the game developer's API to access their data.

Web-based APIs are, essentially, limited websites. They allow the pages and scripts end users create to communicate with the data source by using a predetermined vocabulary and fixed amount of options. When the user's message reaches the API, the API completes the requested task such as getting a certain piece of data, or validating credentials, and returns the results, hiding anything the developers do not want revealed, and only provides the features they are comfortable with others using.

The result is that end users are free (within the limits of the API) to create their own systems exactly as they want, interfacing with their own systems, or creating all new systems the developers of the API had not thought of or decided not to pursue. APIs can cut down on the development time of your own system as you can use them to support your project, like our example of embedding Google Maps instead of creating or installing a map system.

31 http://bluefish.openoffice.nl/
32 http://www.barebones.com/products/textwrangler
33 http://www.chami.com/html-kit/

By combining several disparate systems through their APIs, a mashup is created, which is a new feature, application, or service created by combing several others. APIs are often included as part of a software development kit (SDK) that includes the API, programming tools, and documentation to assist developers in creating applications.

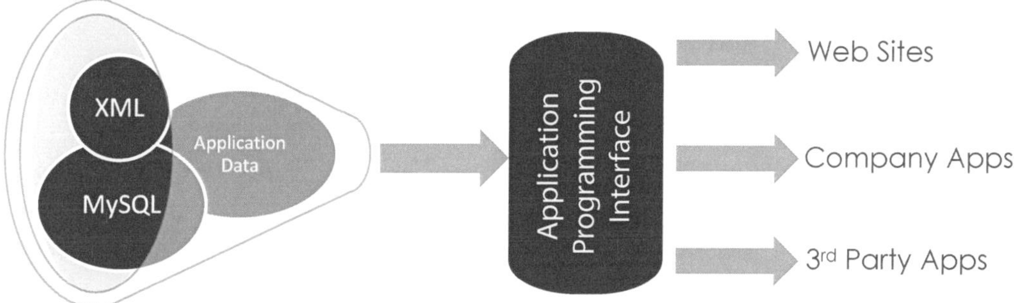

Figure 19 API Data Flow

LEARN MORE

Keywords, search terms: Development methods, coding practices, team development

Cisco Networking Example: http://docwiki.cisco.com/wiki/Internetworking_Basics

List and description of all top level domains: http://www.icann.org/en/resources/registries/tlds

Ongoing comparison of hosting providers: http://www.findmyhosting.com/

Software Development Philosophies: http://en.wikipedia.org/wiki/List_of_software_development_philosophies

Section 1 Assessments

Create Your Own Server

1. Download and install Wamp 2[1] or find a current Mac or Linux equivalent for your operating system.
2. Follow the installation instructions for your system to complete the installation.
3. Select the option, if available, to use an alternate port like :8080 if required by your campus network policy.
4. Test your installation by navigating to http://127.0.0.1:8080 (remove :8080 if you skipped step 3). You should see an image like the one below.
5. Click on the phpinfo and phpmyadmin links to ensure PHP and MySQL are operational.
6. Save this page using your browser's File->Save As option and create an office document.
7. Check the document to ensure it is readable and submit it as proof of your working server.
8. Extra credit: Download, install, and configure Apache, MySQL and PHP separately then configure them to work together. You will need instructions for the versions you download that are appropriate for your operating system, and you will need to create a php configuration page (see Chapter 26) as the page you save to demonstrate everything works.

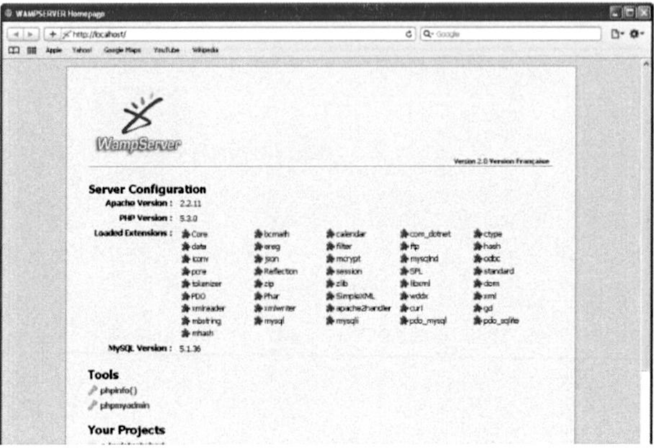

[1] http://www.wampserver.com/en/

Site Map

Draft a site map that meets the description provided below. Show the hierarchy and relationships between pages starting with the index page at the top. Create a digital copy of your site map using a word editor or visual editing program like a mind mapping application or Visio. Be sure to save your document in a format that is widely supported and has a high enough resolution to be legible, like jpg, html, or pdf. Unless you are sure the parties who will receive these types of documents are using the same program you are, you should avoid proprietary file types.

> "I would like my site to be fairly simple. We are opening a new and used store specializing in sports and exercise equipment, so I imagine our visitors will want to know where we are, what our hours are, and what we have on hand. They might also have questions on our trade-in policy and warranty, and I would like them to easily see how much money they could save by buying equipment from us."

Note to the Professor: For a group-based approach to assignments, use this as a starting point to select which site that team of two or more will begin to create, or hold a vote/select a number of projects and create larger project groups to address this site throughout the semester. To build upon the material, these assignments can continue to focus and build on previous work. In teams of two, both students would experience the entire process from the view of the client as well as all aspects of development, by continuing to build their counterpart's site.

Site Wireframe

Design two or three basic layouts for your site, or the alternative example described in the Site Map assignment, including a front page and typical content page for each. Include depictions of where certain pieces of content are expected to be located with their approximate size. Keep in mind a wireframe is about content elements and location, not specific style, color, or actual content.

Include a brief description of which layout you would recommend of the three and why. Create your wireframe digitally using a word processor or visual editor as described under Site Proposal.

Storyboarding

Create a storyboard of a possible user experience your site. You might follow the process of signing in, creating an account, searching for a product, or navigating to a particular piece of content. Find an example that involves at least 4 steps. Create a mockup for each step that includes color and fake content, describing on each panel what action the user will follow to move to the next step.

Create your storyboard frames in a visual editor, saving them as images, and including them in a document editor so you can add your notes under each image.

Discussion / Written Response

1. Compare three web hosting packages. Highlight the differences between their offerings in terms of cost, features, and resiliency. Declare which one you would select and why.
2. Find a current article on net neutrality that discusses a proposed law, regulation, or agreement between governing entities. Defend the proposal or discuss why it is not in the best interest of consumers.
3. Describe three different approaches to developing sites in teams. Include pros and cons of each method and detail when they are best suited for use.
4. Describe the difference between APIs, frameworks, and templates.
5. Find and describe an example of the Internet of Things in use today.
6. Compare and contrast Windows, Mac, and Linux based operating systems.

Questions

TAKE THIS QUIZ ONLINE!

1. Which IP address convention uses both numbers and letters?
   a. IPV4
   b. IPV6
2. Which of the following is not in the OSI 7 layer framework?
   a. Application
   b. Network
   c. Migration
   d. Data Link
3. What name has the acronym PHP not represented over time?
   a. Hypertext Pre-Processer
   b. Personal Home Page
   c. Pre-HTML Processing
4. Which of the following is true?
   a. Open source software is always free in cost
   b. Users can edit the source code at their pleasure
   c. Users can change and sell their version of the product
5. Is open source software always free?
   a. Yes

    b. No

6. Which of these is not a benefit of virtualization?
    a. Reduced hardware footprint
    b. Reduced operating costs
    c. Increased speeds when using systems
7. Which of these best describes cloud computing?
    a. Using servers that are in orbit
    b. Hosting services on virtualized, internet connected hardware
    c. Sharing a file online
8. The predecessor of the internet was
    a. CompuServe
    b. Arpanet
    c. DARPA
    d. Al Gore
9. Cloud computing is
    a. Shared services available online
    b. Portable jump drives
    c. Outsourcing
    d. Portable servers
10. Which of these is not available as a service?
    a. Software
    b. Operating systems
    c. Hardware
    d. None of the above
11. Web warfare has already emerged as a tactic in conflicts between nations.
    a. True
    b. False
12. Botnets are
    a. Local networks
    b. Groups of compromised computers
    c. Viruses
    d. All of the above
13. Which of the following is not part of a standard WAMP server?
    a. HTTP server
    b. Scripting engine
    c. Database

  d. FTP

14. Linux is a(n)
    a. Operating system
    b. HTTP server
    c. Server
    d. All of the above
15. MySQL is a(n)
    a. HTTP server
    b. Database
    c. Server
    d. None of the above
16. PHP is a(n)
    a. Web server
    b. Scripting language
    c. Operating system
    d. Database
17. Open source is always
    a. Free to be modified
    b. Free in cost
    c. Shareable
    d. All of the above
18. Apache is a:
    a. Web server
    b. Scripting language
    c. Database
    d. None of the above
19. FTP stands for ____________.
    a. File Transfer Protocol
    b. Files To Push
    c. File Transmission Pipe
20. HTTP stands for ___________.
    a. Hyper Text Translation Program
    b. Hyper Text Transfer Protocol
    c. Hyper Transfer Text Program
21. The SQL part of MySQL stands for __________.
    a. Super Question Language

   b. Structured Question Language
   c. Structured Query Language

22. An IPV4 address is made up of __ blocks of numbers.
   a. 3
   b. 4
   c. 5
   d. 6

23. An IPV6 address uses both letters and numbers.
   a. True
   b. False

24. URL stands for _______.
   a. Universal Resource Locator
   b. Unordered Resource Location
   c. Unsorted Relational Language

CHECK YOUR ANSWERS ON PAGE 276

Section 2:

Document Markup

Section Contents

Learning Objectives

By the end of this section, you should be able to demonstrate:

- the ability to create an HTML document structured to support CSS styling
- the ability to create a CSS file that adapts styling based on device capabilities
- the ability to create basic images using canvas
- the ability to integrate audio and video to a page
- the ability to utilize special device features
- the ability to integrate external font styles

Chapter 7

Markup Languages

Document markup is a notation method that defines how particular pieces of information are meant to be formatted. The term comes from the practice of marking up manuscripts to notate changes that need to be made. Markup in terms of programming languages is used to identify a language that specifies how a document is to appear.

If you have ever used multiple colors of ink or highlighter when making notes and ascribed meaning to those colors for yourself (e.g., yellow highlighter is important, red ink is a definition) then you have already practiced document markup. You are providing additional layers of information along with the written text, in this case visual cues as to the purpose of the written information.

Some popular markup languages are hypertext markup language (HTML), extensible markup language (XML) and extensible hypertext markup language (XHTML). These were each created to fulfill particular needs in defining the layout and structure of the material.

HTML5

Hypertext markup language is used to aid in the publication of web pages by providing a structure that defines elements like tables, forms, lists and headings, and identifies where different portions of our content begin and end. It can be used to embed other file formats like videos, audio files, documents like PDFs and spreadsheets, among others. HTML is the most relied upon language in the creation of web sites. In this text we will focus on HTML5. While it is technically still in draft form, many proposed elements are already supported by the newer versions of most of the popular browsers.

History

In the beginning, back to the first days of the Internet and ARPA, the primary purpose of creating a page was to share research and information. HTML tags were only meant to provide layout and formatting of a page. As such, early implementations of HTML were somewhat limited as there was little demand for features beyond the basics. Headings, bullets, tables, and color were about all developers had to utilize. As sites were created for other more commercial uses, developers found creative ways of using these tools to get their pages looking more like magazines, advertisements, and what they had drawn on paper. Having been one of those developers, I recall the days of just-get-it-looking-right techniques, splicing page-sized images into tables so graphics were (usually) where we wanted them, nesting tables within tables to create complex layouts, and other methods that violate today's best practices.

Current State

While not formally finalized, many browsers are already supporting a number of features proposed in drafts of HTML5, including things like canvas and media support that greatly improve the browser's ability to process and display complex materials without requiring extensive coding and extensions. In the past, sites that used video and audio players had to integrate support for many players, and would have to include the libraries and formatted files for those systems in their sites. By providing a solution to using these media forms within HTML5, we can improve on the user experience and reduce the efforts necessary to provide them.

While these new features do reduce the amount of programming required to implement higher level elements, and include interactive elements that exceed document markup activities, HTML5 is still considered a markup language.

In these languages, we use tags to ascribe additional meaning to our text, which provide instruction to the browser as to how to display the text on the screen, but are not necessarily displayed to the user. In HTML and XHTML these tags are fixed, or predefined, meaning the names that can be used in the tags are limited to what browsers are able to recognize. In XML, tags are defined by the person creating the content as they are typically used in conjunction with data sources and provide information.

W3C Standards

The World Wide Web Consortium,[1] or W3C, is an international community that supports web development through the creation of open standards that provide the best user experience possible for the widest audience of users. This group of professionals and experts come together to determine how CSS and HTML should operate, what tags should be included as features, and more. The W3C is also your best reference point in determining the accessibility of your site through the use of tools that analyze your code for W3C compliance. These tools confirm if you have fully implemented elements in your code, like providing alternate text descriptions of images in the event that the image cannot load, or the user is visually impaired.

---

1 http://www.w3c.org

In addition to the creation of accessibility standards, among many others, the W3C also provides tutorials and examples and is likely the most exhaustive reference you will find.

CSS

CSS stands for cascading style sheet, and is used to create rules about the color, font, and layout of our pages. It also determines when those rules are to be used, based on information like the device connecting to the page, or in response to a user's action. CSS can be used by not only HTML but any XML-based language. By separating as much of the look and feel of a page from HTML as possible, we actually separate content from appearance. This makes it possible to quickly create several different versions of the appearance of our site, without recreating the content in each version. Our best approach is to use HTML to define the structure (and only structure) of our pages whenever possible, laying the groundwork for CSS to know where to apply the actual style.

History

As HTML grew in popularity, demands on its feature set also grew. Combined with the variety of browser implementations and their varied approaches to rendering and support, creating robust, visually appealing sites involved a significant amount of time and effort. To reduce these, and separate the duties of presentation from those of content, proposals were sought to define a new system of managing these features. CSS was born out of CHSS, or Cascading Hypertext Style Script, and extends our capabilities by allowing us to go far beyond the styling limits of HTML by giving us more power over images, making pages appear more newspaper or magazine-like with layout and typography affects, and reducing load time.

Introduced for public use in 1996, CSS1 contained the ability to apply rules by identifying elements (selectors), and most of the properties still in use today. CSS2 added the ability to adapt for different displays and devices, as well as positioning elements by specific values on the page. CSS2.1 followed with the introduction of additional features, but these were not considered substantial enough to warrant a full version number change.

Current State

While commonly referred to as CSS3, the numbering no longer applies to the language as a whole. The developers have decided to break the language into modules, allowing different aspects of the language to be revised and released independent of one another. This allows for stable modules to stay numbered as they are (since they are not actually changing), while those under more active development can be pushed out as needed. At the moment, most of the "current" modules are at version number 3. Some have not really changed from 2.1, while work on version 4 of selected modules is already underway.

Document Object Model

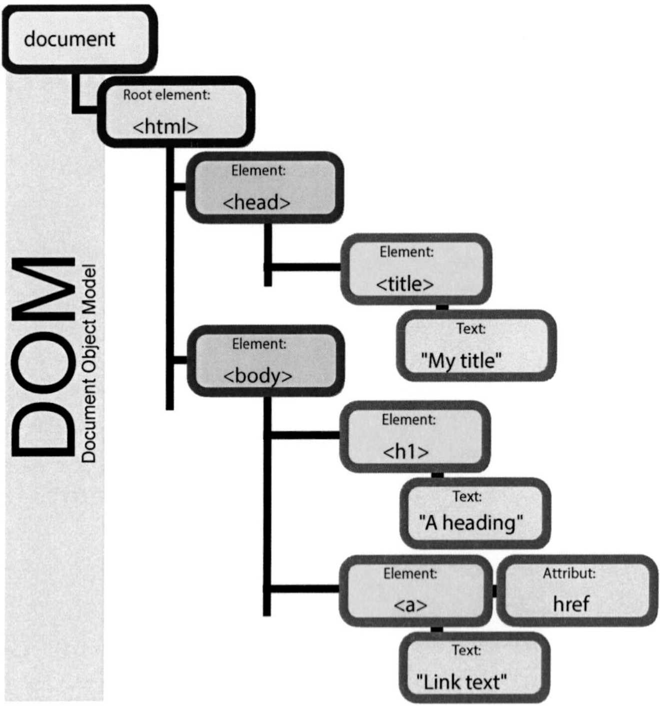

By Birger Eriksson CC-BY-SA-3.0

Figure 20 Document Object Model

Our ability to manipulate and create webpages consistently across formats comes from the document object model API, typically referred to as DOM. This API defines the order and structure of document files as well as how the file is manipulated to create, edit, or remove contents.

The DOM is built to be language and platform independent so any software or programming language can use it to interface with documents. It defines the interface methods and object types that represent elements of documents, the semantics and behavior of attributes of those objects, and also defines how they relate to one another. The DOM, effectively, is what gives rise to the tags we are about to study below. Languages that use the DOM, however, are not required to include all of its features, and may generate additional features of their own.

Figure 20 depicts an example of a document's model in tree format, with nested elements appearing to the right and below their parents. In this example, we are shown an HTML page with a section for the head and the body, which includes a page title and a link as its contents. This structure provides the ability for us to traverse, or move around the document, by referring to an object's name or attribute.

Chapter 8

Creating HTML Files

HTML

File Format

Before we can create our first web page, we need to create a file that our service will recognize as a web page. To do this, we can open our chosen text editor (see a short list of potentials in the section on Integrated Development Environments), and create a new document if one was not created automatically. We will immediately select "Save As" from your editor's File menu, and give your new page its name. If this is going to be the front page, or first page you want a user to see for your site, you should name it index. Index is the default file name most web servers look for in any folder of your website; it saves your users from having to know and type the page name as part of the URL.

In many text editors, underneath or near where you enter the file name is another drop down selector that allows you to pick a file type. This is the extension (what comes after the period in the file name), or file type, that identifies what kind of data the file represents. This tells our operating system, applications, and browsers what conventions were used to create the content so it can be reassembled into usable form. Since we are creating a basic web page, we will use the .htm extension (.html is also acceptable, just be consistent to make your life easier). If your editor does not have .htm or .html in its list, then select "All" and make index.htm your file name.

ADDITIONAL NOTES

If you ever come across an unfamiliar extension and want to know more about it, sites like filext.com can help you determine what programs can open it and what it is for.

Once we have saved our file as index.htm, we are ready to begin. Saving as soon as we create a file is useful as the text editor will then know what syntax is expected. This will enable features like color coding and highlighting that your editor supports.

Document Type

Every HTML page we create should declare its document type (doctype) in the first line. This will identify which spec of HTML is included so the browser knows how to interpret the tags within. Earlier version of the HTML specifications used two definitions for HTML: HTML 4.01 and XHTML. Both of these contained two additional properties of strict and transitional.

With HTML5, much of this has been eliminated, leaving one general doctype declaration of <!DOCTYPE html>. This should be the first line of code in any HTML page you create. We will not cover the older doctype formats as all of our examples will focus on HTML5. Keep in mind, though, that code examples you find online with anything other than the tag above may be outdated approaches to what is shown.

LEARN MORE

Keywords, search terms: xml, html, css, dom, document markup,

W3C Documentation for XML: http://www.w3.org/TR/2004/REC-xml11-20040204/

W3C Documentation for CSS: http://www.w3.org/Style/CSS/

W3C Specifications for HTML:http://www.w3.org/community/webed/wiki/HTML/Specifications

Chapter 9

Page Layout

Tags, Attributes

In order to add content to our page, we will set up our file with some basic structure. First, we will use tags to identify information about where parts of our page start and end. We will do this by using our first set of tags, <html> and </html>. We refer to these as a set because both use the same predefined word (HTML), and the latter uses the backslash (/) to indicate that it marks the close of that tag set. The act of placing a set of tags around content and other code is often referred to as "wrapping" what is between the tags. This is a good way to create a mental picture of what you are doing.

Next, we will put in a few more tags and then save our file and see some results. In between (typically referred to this as "inside") your HTML tags, add an empty set of tags labeled head, and another labeled body. Then create two more sets labeled header and footer inside your body tags. Your resulting file should look like this:

```
<html>
<head>
</head>
<body>
<header>
</header>
<footer>
</footer>
</body>
</html>
```

Now we will add some spacing (see Spacing from our Good Practices section), and the ubiquitous Hello World in between the close of our header and start of our footer tags:

```
<html>
    <head>
    </head>
    <body>
        <header>
        </header>
        Hello World
        <footer>
```

```
        </footer>
    </body>
</html>
```

Now we can better see how elements can be placed within one another, called nesting. If we save our file again, and double click the icon for our file in our documents folder to open it, it should open in your computer's default browser as a white page with Hello World in the upper left corner. Congratulations! You have just made your first web page. Before you ask, though, unless you have created your own server, you will not be able to show your page to someone unless they are at your computer or you send them the file(s) you created. Since only the browser is needed to view the output of HTML, JavaScript, and CSS files, we will be able to view our pages without a server until the PHP examples later on.

As we continue to make changes, you can keep your editor and browser open at the same time. After you save your file in your text editor, you can simply refresh the page in your browser to see your changes.

ADDITIONAL NOTES

As we look at HTML elements, keep in mind that browsers will do their best to adjust for mistakes like missing tags. Different browsers will react to these problems in their own way, so just because it shows up correct in one browser does not mean it will in others.

Some tags, like those for including images, do not need a closing tag in order to work as no content is necessary inside the tags. In this case, we simply use the tag itself where we want it. In older versions of HTML one of the differences between document types was how we closed single tag elements. HTML, for example, wanted a break written as <br> while an XHTML document wanted <br/>. HMTL5 will recognize either of these.

Head

Getting back into our document, we see that the first set of tags is called head. This is where we will put information about the page itself (called metadata) and where we will connect to any other resources like scripts and files that are not part of the page we are using. It is important that your <head> tags are always the first set of tags after <html>, as this is the order in which browsers expect the information.

To provide some basic information about our page or site, we will add some meta tags inside our head to give it a title, keywords, a description, and other details. These pieces of information help the user and bots understand what the page is about.

Each of these items are all parts of the meta tag (<meta/>). Some tags have special features that can be added to their definitions; these are called attributes. Meta tags support attributes like name and content. How we define these attributes will help the browser understand our page better. We will set our title as Our First Page, add the keywords beginning html, learning, and CSIT-107, and for a description we will put in a couple lines about what we are doing, and finally, add our name:

```
<head>
   <title>Our First Page</title>
   <meta name="keywords" content="beginning html, learning,
   CSIT-107" />
   <meta name="description" content="A beginning web page for
   CSIT-107 SUNY Fredonia" />
   <meta name="author" content="Your Name Here" />
</head>
```

There are a few things in this example for us to look at. First, you will note that title has its own tag. What you put in this tag is what will appear as the title in your browser window, and on the tab in your browser for this page (You can only have one set of these tags in a document). Keep in mind, this title will not appear on the page itself. If we want to include it as part of our page content, we would do that from within the body tags.

Next, we see that the values assigned to name and content are placed in quotes. The quotes identify what belongs to that attribute. While it is standard practice to use double-quoted strings, we can also use single quotes. These can be useful when creating HTML statements like those above as output from other languages (we will see examples of this in PHP).

You might also note that our keywords are comma separated, meaning we break them up by placing commas between different values; we do not need to add separate quotes around each word or phrase.

In the HTML5 specs, the meta tag can also have attributes named charset and http-equiv. Charset allows us to specify a particular set of characters we want to use for the page, an http-equiv supports content-type, default-style, and refresh as options. This lets us tell the browser what type of page we have (in our case, text/html), name a default style sheet (we will get to this later) and specify in terms of seconds how often we want to refresh the page, if at all.

Since our content will not be changing unless we change the page ourselves, and we do not have a style sheet yet, we will just add our content type declaration for now:

```
<meta http-equiv="content-type" content="text/html" />
```

Meta is also where we will define cache items like how long our page can be cached before it expires, or if we even want content to expire, as in these examples:

```
<META HTTP-EQUIV="EXPIRES" CONTENT="Mon, 22 Jul 2002 11:12:01
GMT">
<META HTTP-EQUIV="CACHE-CONTROL" CONTENT="NO-CACHE">
```

Body

All of the content that we wish to have on the screen should be encompassed by a set of body tags. The header, content, footer, and div (an all-purpose tag derived from "division") sections are examples of what we can put in our body tags, which we will see in the next example. Keep in mind that using these tags does not prevent us from seeing content that is not within the body. Tags are used to guide the interpreter in how to display the document.

Unless it is specifically within the <head> tags, browsers may elect to display any content that is not properly nested in different ways.

Header, Footer

The header and footer tags are new in HTML5. They were added due to the volume of sites that define a top and bottom section to their pages. Allowing these tags makes it easier to define and find those parts of the layout. The header and footer should be nested within your body tags, but are not a requirement. For our example, we will put a screen title in our header and a copyright in our footer:

```
<body>
    <header>
        <h1>This is our first page!</h1>
    </header>
        Hello World
    <footer>
        &copy; 2013 Your Name Here
    </footer>
</body>
```

After saving your file and refreshing your browser, you should see our sentence in the top left, followed by Hello World, and then © 2013 Your Name Here. We made our title text extra-large by wrapping it in <h1> tags. H1 stands for heading one, the largest heading by default. We can also use h2 through h6 to access additional styles. Just as in a written document, we use these headings to distinguish different portions of our text. Your browser is applying a default style to make h1 look as it does on your screen. Later, we will see how to override this default style to make our headings look how we want them to. Using these headings allows us to quickly identify different portions of content not only for the reader, but also for search engines, which typically consider content in these tags as indicators of what your site is about, reducing our SEO efforts later.

Div/Span

While <p> helps us split up our text, we also need a mechanism to separate different pieces of content like we did when we used header and footer. This will allow us to define more than just a top, middle and bottom to our page. To do this, we can wrap those sections in <div> tags. Div stands for divide—it defines a section of content that should be treated as separate from other content. Span is very similar to div, except that it should identify inline content, meaning material that is within a block of text. Ultimately, a div will place a line break before and after its tags, while a span will not. Aside from this, these tags are functionally equivalent. While these tags seem very plain now, they are very useful when creating complex layouts, and are the tags we will use most often.

While div and span are effective for styling, we should strive to use the best set of tags available so browsers, users, and bots are able to understand our site and its layout, like the <header> and <footer> that we have already used in our code. Just keep in mind, not all of these are supported in all browsers. If you are wondering which browsers will work with what tags, you can refer to caniuse.com to see what is available.

To create organization for our site, we will add some more conceptual sections to our file. You will notice the layout does not actually go left or right as we are labeling our divs (everything will organize top-to-bottom). This is because we need to add CSS for the full effect. We will pick this example up again later to add the CSS needed to create the layout we want:

```
<body>
   <header>
      <h1>This is our first page! </h1>
   </header>
   <div id="left">
      some menu items
   </div>
   <div id="content">
      Hello World
   </div>
   <div id="right">
      and some content on the right
   </div>
   <footer>
      &copy; 2013 Your Name Here
   </footer>
</body>
```

Chapter 10

Text Layout

While all of the following tags are supported in HTML5, some of them are exclusive to the new specification, and will require a browser that is HTML5 compatible to work correctly.

Paragraphs

To build upon our basic structure a bit, we can break a long section of text into paragraphs. We can do this by adding breaks (<br/>) in our code. If we are going to do this a number of times, and if we want to style our paragraphs down the line, we should instead wrap each one in a set of paragraph tags, <p></p>. Using the paragraph tags allows us to automatically add spacing around our content to separate it from the rest of the page.

Before:

```
<body>
    This is some text. It is really long. We want to break this
    into paragraphs so it looks more like a document. This is
    some text. It is really long. We want to break this into
    paragraphs so it looks more like a document. This is some
    text. It is really long. We want to break this into para-
    graphs so it looks more like a document. This is some text.
    It is really long. We want to break this into paragraphs
    so it looks more like a document. This is some text. It
    is really long. We want to break this into paragraphs so
    it looks more like a document. This is some text. It is
    really long. We want to break this into paragraphs so it
    looks more like a document. This is some text. It is really
    long. We want to break this into paragraphs so it looks
    more like a document. This is some text. It is really long.
    We want to break this into paragraphs so it looks more
    like a document. This is some text. It is really long.
    We want to break this into paragraphs so it looks more
    like a document. This is some text. It is really long.
    We want to break this into paragraphs so it looks more
    like a document. This is some text. It is really long.
    We want to break this into paragraphs so it looks more
    like a document. This is some text. It is really long.
```

```
    We want to break this into paragraphs so it looks more
    like a document. This is some text. It is really long. We
    want to break this into paragraphs so it looks more like
    a document. This is some text. It is really long. We want
    to break this into paragraphs so it looks more like a
    document.
</body>
```

After:

```
<body>
    <p>
    This is some text. It is really long. We want to break this
    into paragraphs so it looks more like a document. This is
    some text. It is really long. We want to break this into
    paragraphs so it looks more like a document. This is some
    text. It is really long. We want to break this into para-
    graphs so it looks more like a document. This is some text.
    It is really long. We want to break this into paragraphs
    so it looks more like a document. This is some text. It is
    really long. We want to break this into paragraphs so it
    looks more like a document. This is some text. It is really
    long. We want to break this into paragraphs so it looks
    more like a document.
    </p>
    <p>
    This is some text. It is really long. We want to break this
    into paragraphs so it looks more like a document. This is
    some text. It is really long. We want to break this into
    paragraphs so it looks more like a document. This is some
    text. It is really long. We want to break this into para-
    graphs so it looks more like a document. This is some text.
    It is really long. We want to break this into paragraphs so
    it looks more like a document.
    </p>
    <p>
    This is some text. It is really long. We want to break this
    into paragraphs so it looks more like a document. This is
    some text. It is really long. We want to break this into
    paragraphs so it looks more like a document. This is some
    text. It is really long. We want to break this into para-
    graphs so it looks more like a document. This is some text.
    It is really long. We want to break this into paragraphs so
    it looks more like a document.
    </p>
</body>
```

Ordered, Unordered Lists

If you are not familiar with the protocol for lists, unordered lists are intended for items that relate, but do not need to be in a particular order. Ordered lists, on the other hand, are for items that need to be ordered for a reason, like instructions that need to be followed in correct sequence.

Ordered and unordered lists are alphanumeric and unordered lists of items, respectively. Using these we can create lists to have them display on the screen as we are used to seeing a list of items, or we can take a list we have defined and use it as a group of common objects or ideas to build things like menus and navigation when we add additional CSS.

When we use the tags <ol> (ordered lists) or <ul> (unordered lists), we placed nested <li> tags in each to represent each item in the list.

```
<ol>
   <li>First</li>
   <li>Second</li>
   <li>Third</li>
</ol>
<ul>
   <li>An item</li>
   <li>Another item</li>
   <li>Yet another item</li>
</ul>
```

1. First
2. Second
3. Third

- An item
- Another item
- Yet another item

Definition Lists

A related set of tags can be used when you want to list definitions. These are <dl> for the list itself, with <dt> nested inside for terms and <dd> also nested, for definition, following its corresponding <dt>.

```
<dl>
   <dt>Coffee</dt>
      <dd>Bean-based caffeinated
         beverage </dd>
   <dt>Tea</dt>
      <dd>Leaf-based caffeinated
         beverage</dd>
   <dt>Water</dt>
      <dd>Standard H20</dd>
</dl>
```

Coffee

  Bean-based caffeinated beverage

Tea

  Leaf-based caffeinated beverage

Water

  Standard H20

Address

The address tag allows us to specify text that belongs to an address or contact information for the content creator, making it easier for applications to find the information needed for tools like mapping and generating references.

```
<address>
   Article by <a href="mailto:professor@school.
   edu">Prof. Essor</a>.<br>
   Fredonia, NY<br>
   USA
</address>
```

Article by Prof. Essor.
Fredonia, NY
USA

Article

Article tags are meant to be used on content that can be re-used outside of its original site. It is meant for news articles, blog posts, and other types of content that would be republished in multiple locations.

```
<article>
   <h1>Our Blog Post</h1>
      <p>This is our great content that is now identified as
         something that can exist on its own as a piece of
         work.</p>
</article>
```

Aside

The aside is intended for use when you want to mark a piece of content that is related to the material it is nested within. It created primarily to define related information, like part of an article or blog.

```
<p>
This is some text. It is really long. We want to break this
into paragraphs so it looks more like a document. This is some
text. It is really long. We want to break this into paragraphs
so it looks more like a document. This is some text. It is
really long. We want to break this into paragraphs so it looks
more like a document. This is some text. It is really long.
We want to break this into paragraphs so it looks more like a
document.
</p>
<aside>
   <h4>Side Bar</h4>
      <p>This is something related to our content that is not
         actually a part of it</p>
```

```
</aside>
```

Button

A button is similar to the submit button, but unlike other input styles, it can include text or an image. Its default formatting gives it a beveled button appearance.

```
<button type="button">Click Here!</button>
<button type="button"><img src="ourimage.jpg"/>
</button>
```

Caption

The caption tag is for tables, and allows you to define a label to be printed near the table for reference. You can only have one caption per table, and it must be after the opening table tag.

```
<table>
   <caption>This is our table</caption>
   <tr>
      <td>First Col</td><td>Second Col</
         td><td>Third Col</td>
   </tr>
   <tr>
      <td>1</td><td>2</td><td>3</td>
   </tr>
   <tr>
      <td>4</td><td>5</td><td>6</td>
   </tr>
</table>
```

This is our table

First Col	Second Col	Third Col
1	2	3
4	5	6

Cite

While cite has been included in previous versions of HTML, the current HTML5 specification intends for it to be used to define the title of a work that is included in the document. Previous versions limited this tag to proper citations of written publications.

```
<img src="scream.jpg"
<p><cite>The Scream</cite> E. MunChapter
1893.</p>
```

The Scream E. Munch. 1893.

Entities

In the examples in the Header, Footer section, we placed a copyright symbol on the screen using “©” which told the browser what symbol we wanted to use. This is a reserved symbol, or entity, in HTML. We can call entities by using &[entity name here]; or &[entity number here];. For example,   means non-breaking space, or just a standard space. This is one way to insert extra spaces in our output. Since the browser would skip all the extra spaces in our code, we can add non-breaking space entities to tell the browser we do want it displayed on the screen.

The table below includes examples of other popular symbols (there are plenty more). Keep in mind, when you use entity names, they are case sensitive.

Table 1 HTML Entities

Result	Description	Name	Number
	non-breaking space		
<	less than	<	<
>	greater than	>	>
&	ampersand	&	&
©	copyright	©	©
®	registered trademark	®	®
™	trademark	™	™

Figure

The figure tag allows us to label an image, portrait, or other visual art included in an image tag to identify the content as such.

```
<figure><img src="ourimage.jpg"/></figure>
```

Figcaption

Figcaption, like caption, allows us to add a caption to our image like we would for a table.

```
<figure>
   <img src="ourimage.jpg"/>
   <figcaption>Figure 1</figcaption>
</figure>
```

Mark

Most text altering tags have been skipped in this text as they can be easily achieved through CSS (and to maintain separation of duties). However, the mark tag is worth a look as an easy way to achieve a highlighting effect. It can be useful to insert this tag when generating output for things like search results.

```
<p>Here is a sentence with some
<mark>highlighted</mark> text.</p>
```

Here is a sentence with some highlighted text.

Meter

The meter tag allows us to generate a visual image based on provided values. This is intended for values that are already known or loaded to the screen like a chart or graph. There is also a Progress tag for monitoring file actions in progress like a download.

```
<meter value="3" min="0" max="15">One
Fifth</meter><br>
<meter value="0.65">65%</meter>
```

Nav

If we have a group of links we want in one place (i.e. a menu or list of references), we can include them inside nav tags so browsers recognize them as a group of links. This is especially useful for screen reader software, as the tags provide an indicator as to what the links are for.

```
<nav>
```

```
    <a href="//">Home</a> |
    <a href="/css/">CSS</a> |
    <a href="/js/">JavaScript</a> |
    <a href="/js/jquery/">jQuery</a>
</nav>
```

Progress

The progress tag was created to help display the status of an upload or download. It takes two attributes including the current amount (which we would change using JavaScript) and the total or highest value of what we are monitoring. If we are showing the percentage of an upload we might use:

```
<progress value="46" max="100"></progress>
```

Or, if we want to show the actual amount moved, or are moving a number of items, we can use the number completed and the total number instead of a percent, and the image will calculate it for us:

```
<progress value="345" max="850"></progress>
```

Time

Another new-to-HTML5 element is time. The time tag is flexible in that it can specify a 24 hour formatted value, a full Gregorian calendar date, or both a date and time. The use of this tag by itself will not change any visual styling on the page, but allows applications on our devices to find the information in order to support features like creating calendar entries or reminders based on the information.

```
<p>The daily meeting will be at <time>10:00</time> every
morning.</p>
<p>The next monthly meeting will be on <time datetime="2013-
08-01">August first</time>.</p>
```

Chapter 11

Navigation

A feature found on almost every websites is a navigation system for moving between pages. These are typically menus, where groups of common pages are created to give the site a hierarchical organization. While the approach to visual styling and interaction with menus comes in great variety, most follow a basic principle of using unordered lists of links, and the application of CSS to those lists in order to turn them into the colorful, interactive elements we are accustomed to. While there are drawbacks that we will discuss in Visually Impaired Considerations, alternative approaches can still utilize linked lists to some extent.

Since we created our menu earlier, we already know the contents and structure of our navigation. Our group label, or top-level labels, and the nested <ul>s represent the contents of the list for that menu item.

Some popular approaches to providing a means of navigation are menu bars with drop downs, bread crumbs, and event driven responses. Menu bars are the most frequently utilized element, where hovering or clicking over an item in the menu brings up additional choices related to the main item. Typically referred to as drop down menus, they can be styled to move in any direction. Nesting lists within lists can give us a multi-tier menu that allows us the ability to select from a large number of pages with little effort.

Breadcrumbs are typically depicted as a horizontal delimited list of pages, similar to:

```
Home >> Sports >> Football >> Buffalo Bills >> Patriots >>
Golf
```

The breadcrumb does not follow a hierarchical notation, but acts more like a brief history of where you have been on the site, allowing you to skip back several steps at once without using your browser's back button. These can be helpful in sites with large amounts of content where the user's experience may not be particularly linear, as they move between topics or sections, like news or reference sites.

Event-driven navigation is useful in narrowing the user experience to a fixed set of paths. This method will only make certain links available under certain conditions, restricting the options a user has on a particular page to what they are allowed to do, which may be based on a variety of rules such as if they are logged in, previous links or decisions they have made, or if something in the system needs their attention.

These approaches can be used by themselves, or in combination to provide your user experience.

Linking

Links in HTML can take two forms, both of which are created with the anchor tag (<a>). They can either point to a resource in another location, or to a location within the document. The former are used far more frequently than the latter, however internal links are coming back into popularity with the rise of infinite scrolling.

Absolute, Base, and Relative Path

The href attribute of an anchor tag defines the actual location the link will represent. Absolute and relative paths are two reference methods for connecting sites and pages. While both methods can be used when creating links that point to content in our own site, only absolute can be used when pointing to content that is outside of your domain.

Absolute paths are the entire length of the link required to identify one resource, whether it is a page, image, script, or media file. The URL http://www.msn.com/news/index.htm tells us we want to go to the index page in the news folder of the msn.com website. If this was our site, and we wanted to go to the index.htm file in the sports folder, we could write it as http://www.msn.com/sports/index.htm (absolute) or ../sports/index.htm (relative). The initial .. instructs the browser that our intention is to go back one layer of depth (i.e. "up" one level in folders) and then into the sports folder, which in this example sits in the same parent folder as our news page.

Using just an initial / without .. tells the server that we want to start at the root folder of the server and navigate from there, meaning we start with the base path.

A base path is everything needed to get us to the index page of the root folder of the site. This is typically http://www.yoursitename.com, and is the part you find missing in the relative path above. The combination of the base path, and relative path, equals your absolute path.

Target

While the anchor tag supports several attributes, one of the most important of these is "target." This attribute describes where links will be loaded, like a new tab or the same tab/ browser window we are already using. The attribute can take any of the following values to define that location.

Table 2 Anchor Targets

Value	Description
_blank	Opens the linked document in a new window or tab
_self	Opens the linked document in the same frame as it was clicked (this is default)
_parent	Opens the linked document in the parent frame
_top	Opens the linked document in the full body of the window
framename	Opens the linked document in a named frame

From php.net manual, creative commons 3.0 Attribution

Within the Page

We can add links to a page that move the user around the page itself, which is useful on pages with long content. To do this, we use an anchor tag to define where we want our destination to be. When we create our link, we simply reference the name of our anchor, preceded by a pound sign in place of a traditional URL.

```
Some text here.
<a href="#ourDestination">Click here to go
further down.</a>
Some more text.
Even more text!
<a name="ourDestination">
This is where we want to "jump" to.
```

Some text here.
Click here to go further down.
Some more text.
Even more text!
This is where we want to "jump" to.

Chapter 12

Graphics

Images are the greatest contributors to the visual appeal of your site, and typically account for the majority of bandwidth used in loading your pages. By using a combination of image types, and newer techniques found in HTML5 like canvas, and reproducing images using CSS, we can balance quality against size to reduce our bandwidth needs and allow our site to be more flexible.

Formats

Images are files, just like any other document in your computer, but they can be coded and formatted differently to reproduce the image you want to see. We find these referred to as raster and vector graphics. These formats represent two very different methods of creating an image.

Raster

The image files most of us are already familiar with using are typically raster format. Examples of these are JPEG, GIF and BMP. When we interact with pictures we took on digital cameras for example, we are dealing with JPEG or JPG files. Raster files recreate an image by recording the color value of pixels, which represent the smallest single point on a screen that can be assigned a color by the display. The higher the number of pixels (or density, measured as pixels per inch) translates to how sharp the image is, and how large it can be rendered without losing quality.

The number of colors available in the image file is based on the length of the value available to each point. If we only allowed a single binary character for each pixel point, we would be able to keep our file size as small as possible. This however would mean we could only represent our image in black and white (binary only allows us two options, 0 or 1, so we can only represent two colors.). When we allow longer values to represent a single point, we can assign values a larger range of colors. Once we scale these up, however, we trade away our smaller image sizes in order to have more colorful pictures. Large images can slow down the user experience, and if loading takes too long, users will leave.

Traditionally, we have faced this trade off by using different image formats in different areas of our site. While reserving JPG for our larger images or photos, we can use GIF for smaller icons and indicators. GIFs limit us to 256 colors, but since most icons use few colors, we are able to capitalize on the benefits of this format here. It is important to note that raster images will quickly lose quality when rendered at sizes larger than the original image's width or height.

Vector

Vector images store information about colors and locations as definitions of angles, lines, and curves in mathematical format. The benefit of a vector formatted image is that it can be scaled both up and down in size without distortion or degradation in quality. This is due to the fact that the image is "drawn" by the browser each time it is loaded, and the processor performs the steps necessary to recreate the image. Since the image can be scaled, the same image file can be drawn very large, or very small, without changing the file size. We will get some hands-on experience in how vector images are drawn when we look at the new Canvas features in HTML.

Table 3 Image Formats

Format	Compression	Platforms	Colors	Notes
JPEG (Joint Photographic Experts Group)	Lossy	Unix, Win, Mac	24-bit per pixel; 16.7 million colors.	JPEG is a compression algorithm; the format is actually JFIF (JPEG File Interchange Format)
GIF (Graphic Interchange Format)	Lossless	Unix, Win, Mac	8-bit; 256 colors (216 web palette). Allows transparency.	LZW compression algorithm developed by CompuServe; patent now held by Unisys, which charges for use of the code in graphics programs. Once Unisys began enforcing its patent (in 1995), programs began moving to PNG.
BMP (Bitmap graphics)	Uncompressed	Win	24-bit; 16.7 million colors.	Like all uncompressed formats, these files are very large.
PICT	Lossless	Mac		Very little compres-sion; large files.
TIFF (Tag Interchange File Format)	Lossless or uncompressed	Unix, Mac, Win		TIFF-LZW uses the proprietary LZW compressions (see GIF).
PNG (Portable Network Graphics)	Lossless	Unix, Mac, Win	48-bit; "true color" plus transparency	Will likely replace GIF. Supported in IE, NN 4 and above. A WC3specification.

http://mason.gmu.edu/~dtaciuch

You may notice the compression column. This is the act of removing or modifying the data that represents a file in a manner that makes its overall file size smaller. By doing this, we can transmit files faster, and they will take up less space in memory. When we discuss compression in terms of graphics we need to consider whether it will result in a lossy or lossless result. A lossless result means the compression techniques used do not remove data from the original copy, so we can restore the image to its exact original size and appearance. A lossy compressions structure can result in greater compression, but achieves the extra advantage by removing information from the file.

As an example, imagine a picture of you and your friends on the beach with a clear blue sky behind you. The data in the image file will measure the "blueness" of the sky in varying colors of blue, at a level greater than the eye can distinguish. By averaging the blueness and making more of the sky pixels the same color, we have eliminated information. Certain levels of lossy compression will still be indistinguishable from the original, but at any level, the lossy-compressed version of the file will not be restorable to the original because the extra values were eliminated.

Which is better? As usual, it depends on your intent. If the image can be lossy compressed and is still acceptable to you and your users, and having the smallest possible file sizes (good, of course, for mobile devices) is a priority, then go for it. Quality optimized scenarios will likely call for a lossless compression, like in sites that use large images as their background.

Slicing

For some time, there has been a practice of breaking larger images up into many smaller ones (a process called slicing), in an effort to allow pages to load more quickly. While this gave a visual experience of faster speed (each small image blinking into place as it was loaded) the load time was about the same, if not longer, as the overall file size had not changed, but we instead asked for it over multiple requests instead of waiting for the entire image in one request.

The need for this approach has been largely eliminated by modern versions of CSS (and other techniques we will discuss). This allows us to reproduce many things we used images for (i.e. buttons, hover effects, etc.) without using images at all, and allows us to have the control over layout and formatting that slicing an image used to fulfill. Now a common goal for site developers is to be as "imageless" as possible, using images only where CSS cannot stand in. This reduces load times and gives greater flexibility in site design. As an example of what can be done using CSS3, take a look at this simulated iPhone: http://tjrus.com/iphone#71d465!

Some additional techniques to reduce image weight on a site are right-sizing images, compression (which we just discussed above), caching, and sprites, among others. Right-sizing is editing and creating a copy of an image to the exact size needed where it is shown. For example, small images for items on a product page could simply be the original image rendered at a smaller size. If the user does not look at those products, loading the larger images first only degrades their experience, since every product's large image file needs to be downloaded. Right-sizing and compression both require image editing software with at least some advanced editing features, or use of an online service that covers the basics (with less control on your part) like http://www.imageoptimizer.net.

The process of caching can also help. When your site is completed and your images (and other files) will persist, the use of caching can reduce load times for repeat visitors. Caching means the files the user downloads are marked in the server with an expiration. The next time the user visits the site, their device will check expiration times on the content. If the device's local copy is not expired, it simply uses the one it has, without having to download it again.

The last option we will consider here (there are more, advanced methods) is creating a sprite. Almost the reverse of compression and right sizing, a sprite is one large image that contains all of the icons used throughout the site. Since these smaller images are often repeated, we will download one main image a single time. By using CSS rules to reveal only small piece of the image (i.e. the portion containing one icon) at a time, all of our icons can live in one image file but appear as individual elements on the page.

Favicon

A favicon is a special type of image. It is the small icon that accompanies the page title in the browser's title and tab. This icon is automatically used on each page found in the folder the favicon is stored in. For example, to apply a single icon to your entire site you would place it in the root folder. Any folders below that level can use a different favicon.

These icons are usually 32 by 32 pixel images that represents the site or site's parent company. They are converted to a special format and saved with the extension .ico to identify themselves as site icons. While they are small and provide little to the overall visual experience of a website, sites lacking a favicon tend to appear less legitimate as the icon space will be replaced by the browser's default icon.

Creating favicons can be done in paint or photo editing software that allows you to comply with the size and color density limits of favicons. Additionally, sites like favicon-generator.org or www.favicon.cc among others can help convert existing images into favicons with some basic editing options before saving your new icons.

Chapter 13

Tables

Tables are a method of formatting the content of your page, and are very similar to the concept of a spreadsheet. Tables are composed of rows and columns. Each intersection of the two is referred to as a cell, and is where content is placed. The number of columns and rows you use depends on your need and design.

You will probably find a great number of sites that rely heavily on tables to create the look and feel of their pages. Recognizing I have already admitted to doing this in the past when necessary, I will repeat my earlier statement: Please, do not.

While this was a common method in the past, we now have elements in HTML that are defined for such purposes. Tables should be reserved for creating collections of data or information on your page and nothing else. If you are using them to store information other than how you would in a spreadsheet, you should be using a div or span. Using a table for content organization will create several complications in your code that can be reduced or eliminated by following today's conventions.

First, the formatting of the table is more closely tied to HTML as it is easier to define there than in CSS. Placing these definitions in our HTML breaks our goal of separation of duties to support a responsive design. If we wanted to change the layout, we would have to edit our HTML instead of just our CSS files. Second, it creates extra lines of code to define the layout we are looking for, and the use of column and divs or spans to adjust for different layouts is cumbersome when it comes to code maintenance and readability. Lastly, we lose a great deal of our ability to reorganize our content in multiple ways when using multiple CSS styles. This means that rearranging the content in a table when we want to print or view the content in a different manner is more difficult, or would require a whole different page to accomplish.

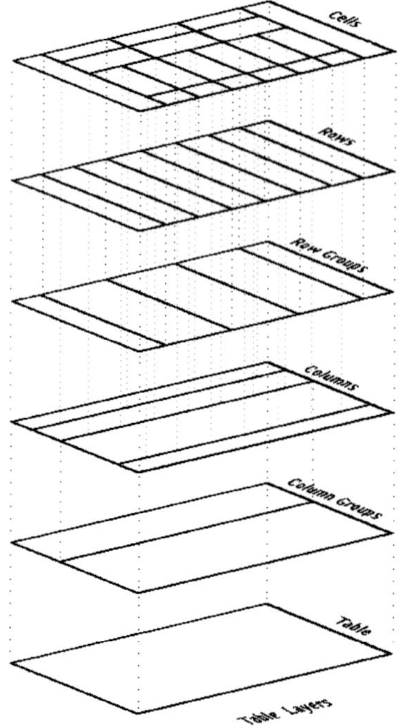

By Tarikash (Own work)CC-BY-SA-3., via Wikimedia Commons

Figure 21 Table Structure

To create a table, we first need to define its beginning and end with tags:

```
<table></table>
```

Next, we can define our heading row by adding our row tags (tr) and nesting dividing tags to represent our columns. Since we want items in this row to be recognized as headings, we use the <th> tag for table heading:

```
<table>
   <tr>
      <th>ID</th><th>First
         Name</th><th>Last
         Name</th>
   </tr>
</table>
```

ID	First Name	Last Name

**Dashed border lines in table examples depict table and cell edges that would not be visible without additional code or CSS.*

To add content to our table, we repeat the process using <td> (for table division) instead of <th> to represent a regular cell of data. Each repetition will add a new row of data to our table.

To build on our example, we will let the first column also be headings, which will represent each row. To do this we use <th> as the first set of tags in each row. We can add a few names as regular content using table division tags as well:

```
<table>
   <tr>
      <th>ID</th><th>First Name</
         th><th>Last Name</th>
   </tr>
   <tr>
      <th>1</th><td>John</td><td>Doe</td>
   </tr>
   <tr>
      <th>2</th><td>Jane</td><td>Doe</td>
   </tr>
</table>
```

ID	First Name	Last Name
1	John	Doe
2	Jane	Doe

Spanning

Using tables to separate several smaller pieces of content horizontally within a layout element is still generally accepted, and is easier than styling divs, but it is still considered a less than ideal approach.

As we create more complicated table layouts, we may want to merge some of these fields together. We can create "extra-large" cells by adding colspan and divspan attributes to the dividing tab (th or td). A colspan value of 2, for example, means the cell will fill two horizontal blocks (left to right) of the table. Likewise, a rowspan of two means the cell will fill two row's worth of space in the column(s) it occupies, as in this example showing staffing for part of a week:

```
<table>
   <tr>
      <th>ID</th><th>First Name</th><th>M</th><th>T</
         th><th>W</th><th>Th</th><th>F</th>
   </tr>
   <tr>
      <th>1</th><td>John</td><td colspan =/2/>work</td><td></
         td><td rowspan=/2/>closed</td><td></td>
   </tr>
   <tr>
      <th>2</th><td>Jane</td><td></td><td></td><td>work</
         td><td>work</td>
   </tr>
</table>
```

<table>
<tr><th>ID</th><th>First Name</th><th>M</th><th>T</th><th>W</th><th>T</th><th>F</th></tr>
<tr><th>1</th><td>John</td><td colspan="2">work</td><td></td><td rowspan="2">closed</td><td></td></tr>
<tr><th>2</th><td>Jane</td><td></td><td></td><td>work</td><td>work</td></tr>
</table>

Keep in mind that spans always move from left to right for columns and top to bottom for rows, starting with the cell you place the attribute in. Your values for the span must always be positive, and larger than zero.

While these examples outline where table cell edges are with dotted lines, we can selectively enable these borders through cell attributes and/or through CSS styling. The best approach is to keep these visual changes in CSS, preserving the structure/style separation of duties between our HTML and CSS, making future visual changes easier to maintain.

Chapter 14

Forms

Forms drive the internet. They are perhaps the most critical element in creating an interactive experience for your end users, and allow you to take in input. Forms define places on a page where the user's interaction can add, change, interact with, or remove the data in your system. The actions and fields you allow in your form determine what the user is allowed to do, and what information he is allowed to see.

Form elements range from username and password style boxes to large text fields, drop down lists, checkboxes and more. All of the elements within a form block are sent from that page to the destination attribute of the form declaration, called an action. When the user hits send this information is then made available in one of several ways to the receiving page or script.

To create a form section, we provide the form with a name, id, action, and method. An example with blank attributes looks like this:

```
<form name="" id="" action="" method=""></form>
```

Our form's name and id are how we will refer to it in our code when interacting with it using CSS, JavaScript, or other languages. The action is where the page should send the information (and where the browser will go when we hit send). Our method is how we will send our information, using either GET or POST.

Get

Sending the data using the get method places all of the form fields by name and value (called a key and value pair) into the address bar, making our URI longer by appending each item to the receiving page's address. An easy way to remember this is that the user "gets" to see the information that was sent, as it will appear in the address bar at the top of the browser. The benefit of using the get method is that the destination can be bookmarked with the data that was sent. So, if your form is used to search a library and filter results, you could save the result as a bookmark, and return to the page in the future, seeing the same results without filling out the form again.

While beneficial, there are two instances in which we DO NOT want to use get: either we do not want the user (or anyone) to see what was sent, such as passwords or confidential information, or we want to send a lot of information. There is a practical limit to how much data can reliably and safely be passed using get, although no formal ceiling. The practical limits are those created by the browser or server's ability to store the information being sent.

When developing large get requests, determine which browsers you want to support, and how old, and figure out which of the oldest has the lowest maximum threshold.

Post

Posted data is sent from the browser to the server in the background, as the client and server first begin to talk. The data is sent in the headers (see) of the communication, and are not visible to the end user. Pages bookmarked with the post method will not have access to the information later on, and that information is lost if the user leaves the page.

How the data is used and values or new content returned bring us to scripting languages. Skip to the server-side language section of this text to learn about that process.

Form Fields

When a webpage with a form is rendered, we can identify a specific field for the user to start with. You may have experienced this in action when you load a website and find the cursor already in a textbox. This is autofocus. To include this function, simply add the attribute autofocus to the field the user will want or need first. We can also apply placeholders to our text fields that tell the user what we want them to enter with the placeholder attribute. To begin, we will add a text input inside our form tags for a name field:

```
<form name="" id="" action="" method="">
    <input type="text" placeholder="Your First Name" autofocus
    name="name" />
</form>
```

Many of the new elements of HTML5 we look at will also assist us with our validation tasks as users fill out forms. These inputs will attempt to validate and/or limit user entry to only valid data. By doing this immediately, we create a better experience for both the user and the programmer. Traditionally, validation had to be done when data was sent to the server, resulting in the page reloading if there were errors. The other popular approach was to perform validation using JavaScript on the client-side (avoiding the reload), but validation would still have to be repeated on the server in the event the end user had JavaScript disabled. Some of the more useful input types are the following:

`<input type="url">` Will attempt to format the user's text into a proper link, or display an error. `<input type="email">` Will make sure an email entered is in proper format, or display an error.

We can also create an input that limits values to a fixed range and increment limitations, which we used to have to display to the user on the page, and then validate after entry:

```
<input type="range" min="10" max="50" step="5" value="30">
```

These limits on a range (shown as a slider) also are valid on a number field as well (shown as arrows):

```
<input type="number" min="10" max="50" step="5" value="30">
```

HTML5 also introduces a wealth of calendar and time controls. We can specify a date, week, or month as well as a time, day and time, and local day and time. Each of these fields will limit the user's entry to valid fields for that type.

Calendar options:

```
<input type="date" name="date"/>
<input type="week" name="week"/>
<input type="month" name="month"/>
```

Time Options:

```
<input type="time" name="time"/>
<input type="datetime" name="dateTime"/>
<input type="datetime-local" name="localDateTime"/>
```

LEARN MORE

Keywords, search terms: Tables, forms

Do not Use Tables For Layout: http://webdesign.about.com/od/layout/a/aa111102a.htm

Mozilla HTML Forms Guide https://developer.mozilla.org/en-US/docs/Web/Guide/HTML/Forms

Chapter 15

Canvas

The canvas element (new as of HTML5) allows us to approach pages with greater control by drawing and creating SVG-style graphics on the page in real time with JavaScript, and giving us the ability to animate and control the motion of our elements. With these new abilities, it is now possible to create browser games and highly interactive pages without the use of flash, additional components, or even pre-existing images (not that this would be a best approach in every situation).

Terminology and integrated functions are focused around the concept of art and media graphics, including functions like stroke() and fill() among others, that expedite your ability to create an image on the screen without a verbose background in graphic arts and mathematical modeling.

Each of the items we create can become an object of its own, and can be grouped with multiple layers or elements as one item. Supporting browsers can understand an object's dimensions and relationship to other elements, bringing native drag-and-drop into play. Page elements that support drag-and-drop can add the draggable attribute to their declaration.

Calling this element a canvas is intentional, and conveys an accurate portrayal of how to treat it. When we create a set of canvas tags and set our width and height, we have effectively "hung" a blank painting on the "wall" of our web page. In our examples below, we will be using a number of values to determine where things we "paint" on the canvas will be.

This is done by using value pairs, or X-Y coordinates. The top-most left-hand corner of the canvas is always (0, 0)—0 pixels to the right, 0 pixels down. This is different from a graph where 0, 0 is in the middle of the page. Our values for X and Y will move our drawing point to the right and down as they grow larger.

In our first example below our canvas size is 300x300, which means the bottom-most right-hand point is (300, 300). Any values large than this, or points with negative values, will move part or all of our drawing off of our canvas.

Rectangles

We will get right into canvas, since it is a visual process, and can be a lot of fun. To begin, we need to create a canvas element on our page:

```
<canvas height="300" width="300"> </canvas>
```

While our canvas is still empty what we have done is allocated a space (just like sizing a div) to declare what part of the page belongs to our div. The width and height tags we provided are required from the start, and since we have not defined an offset or placed the canvas in another container, it will start from the top left corner of our page, again just like a div.

The act of drawing on our canvas is a several-step process. We have to declare how we want our element to appear (for example the fillStyle or strokeStyle attribute), where we want it to start from, and what type of line or shape we intend to create (for example, fillRect or strokeTriangle).

When we declare a shape, we need to convey its size and location. For a rectangle, we do this by setting its starting location (top left corner) as X and Y values, and then by adding its width and height. To add a solid rectangle to our canvas, we will have to add some JavaScript to our page. Since we have not reached JavaScript yet in this text, do not worry if you do not understand every little bit—we will get there. For now, focus on understanding which position of the arguments is used for different settings.

In the header of our page, we need to add the following JavaScript code, identifying what element we want it to affect, and what we want the drawing to be:

```
<!DOCTYPE html>
<html>
   <body>
      <canvas id="canvas" width="300" height="300"
         style="border: 1px solid #c3c3c3;">
      Oh no! This browser does not support HTML5 :(
      </canvas>
      <script>
      var canvas=document.getElementById("canvas");
      var canvas1=canvas.getContext("2d");
      canvas1.fillStyle="#FF0000";
      canvas1.fillRect(50, 50, 50, 50);
      </script>
   </body>
</html>
```

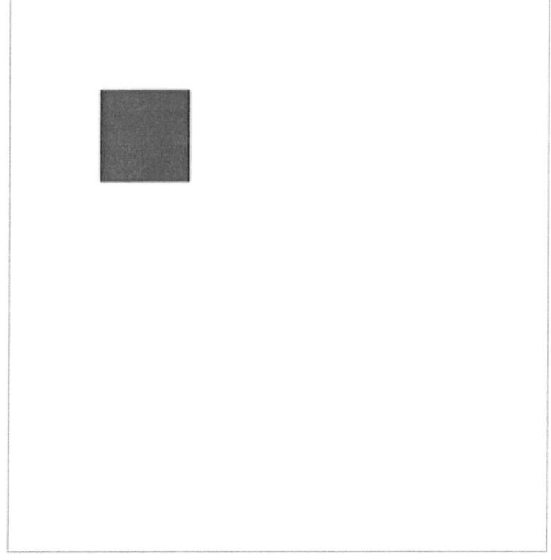

Saving and refreshing our screen should now give you a single lonely rectangle set a little inside the top left corner of your page. You may be wondering about the "Oh no!" line of our example. When our page loads, the "Oh no!" content is placed on our page. When our canvas layers are rendered, this content is then covered up. If HTML5 is not supported (or JavaScript is disabled) our canvas is not drawn, leaving the original text which we can use to tell the user something is wrong. In our fill style declaration we used a color reference as a hex value. We can also use a standard color word like red, or use a function call that takes a red, green, blue, and opacity value set to generate a color. In our fillRect declaration we defined the starting position from the left and top, as well as its width and height, respectively as fillRect(left, top, width, height). In our initial example, all values were 50. Let us add a second rectangle that is wider than it is tall, and move it much further down our page:

```
<!DOCTYPE html>
<html>
   <body>
      <canvas id="canvas" width="300" height="300"
         style="border: 1px solid #c3c3c3;">
      Oh no! This browser does not support HTML5 :(
      </canvas>
      <script>
      var canvas=document.getElementById("canvas");
      var canvas1=canvas.getContext("2d");
      canvas1.fillStyle="#FF0000";
      canvas1.fillRect(50, 50, 50, 50);
      canvas1.fillStyle= "rgba(0, 0, 50, 100)";
      canvas1.fillRect(50, 200, 100, 50);
      </script>
   </body>
</html>
```

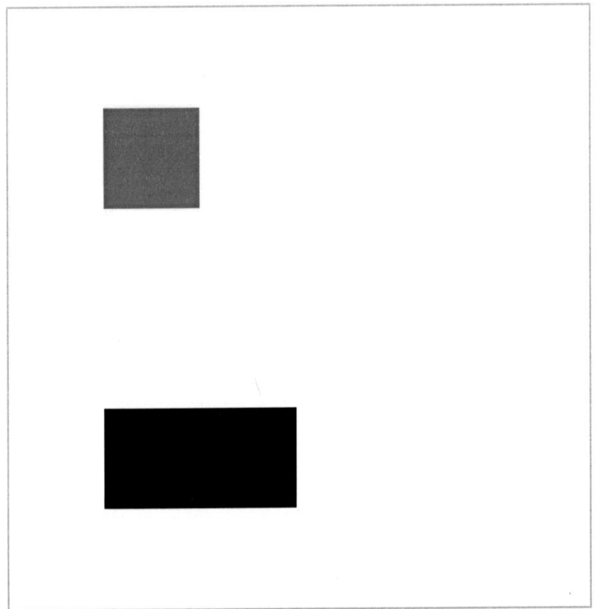

You will notice that even though we now have two blocks, we do not need to change the names we used when declaring our second rectangle from our first. This is because we are setting values, then calling a function to draw the element, and are not storing the values in our script as objects in our JavaScript code.

Keep in mind our drawings can be declared in a manner that draws them outside or extending beyond the confines of our canvas. They will technically be drawn, however the canvas will not expand to meet the needs of your drawing. To see this in action, we can add one more rectangle the same size as our first, but place it so it overdraws our canvas, so we only see a portion of it:

```
<!DOCTYPE html>
<html>
   <body>
      <canvas id="canvas" width="300" height="300"
         style="border: 1px solid #c3c3c3;">
      Oh no! This browser does not support HTML5 :(
      </canvas>
      <script>
      var canvas=document.getElementById("canvas");
      var canvas1=canvas.getContext("2d");
      canvas1.fillStyle="#FF0000";
      canvas1.fillRect(50, 50, 50, 50);
      canvas1.fillStyle= "rgba(0, 0, 50, 100)";
      canvas1.fillRect(50, 200, 100, 50);
      canvas1.fillStyle = "rgba(20, 20, 20, 20)";
      canvas1.fillRect(275, 275, 50, 50);
      </script>
   </body>
</html>
```

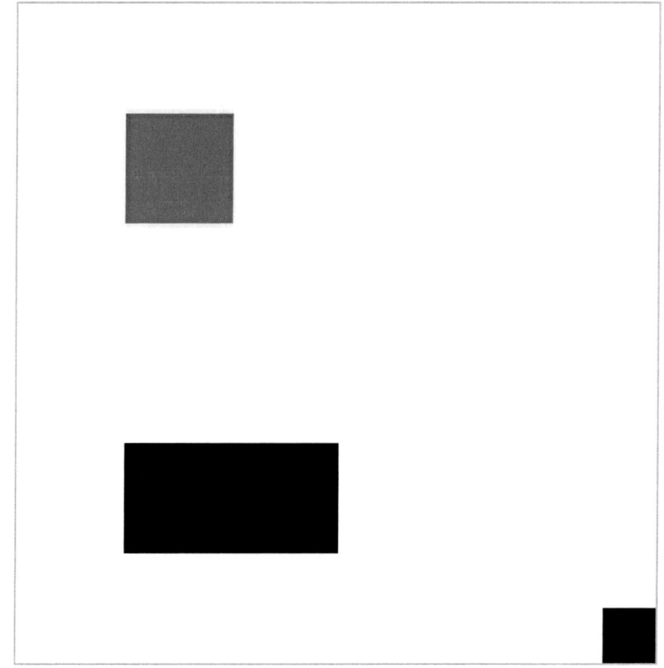

ADDITIONAL NOTES

Keep in mind that JavaScript, which we are getting a sneak preview of, is case sensitive. This means Canvas1 is considered different than canvas1!

Even though this last rectangle is still 50 by 50, we only see the 25x25 of it that fits inside our canvas dimensions. Now that we have played with rectangles, we will replace them with triangles. We will also just give them borders without a fill color. To do this, we will define the line segments that make up our triangle, and use strokeStyle() instead of fillStroke():

Triangles

```
<!DOCTYPE html>
<html>
   <body>
      <canvas id="canvas" width="300" height="300"
         style="border:1px solid #c3c3c3;"> Oh no! This
         browser does not support HTML5 :(
      </canvas>
      <script>
      var canvas=document.getElementById("canvas");
      var canvas1=canvas.getContext("2d");
      canvas1.beginPath(); //declare the beginning of settings
         for our line
      canvas1.strokeStyle = "rgba(50, 0, 0, 0.5)";
      canvas1.moveTo(150,150); // set the starting point of
         our "pen" to the middle
      canvas1.lineTo(150,200); // move our "pen" down 50
         pixels, drawing a line
      canvas1.lineTo(200,200); // move our "pen" 50 pixels to
         the right
      canvas1.closePath(); // Draw a direct line back to our
         starting point
      canvas1.stroke(); // Visually place the defined line on
         the page
      </script>
   </body>
</html>
```

Saving and refreshing should now remove the rectangles we drew earlier and replace them with a right angle triangle positioned with the right angle in the middle of the canvas. By adjusting our X and Y values in moveTo and lineTo variables, we can move our triangle around the page. We will change just one point (our starting point) and see how different our triangle looks:

```
<!DOCTYPE html>
<html>
   <body>
      <canvas id="canvas" width="300" height="300"
         style="border: 1px solid #c3c3c3;"> Oh no! This
         browser does not support HTML5 :(
      </canvas>
      <script>
      var canvas=document.getElementById("canvas");
      var canvas1=canvas.getContext("2d");
      canvas1.beginPath(); //declare the beginning of settings
         for our line
      canvas1.strokeStyle = "rgba(50, 0, 0, 0.5)";
      canvas1.moveTo(75,150); // set the starting point of our
         "pen" to the middle
      canvas1.lineTo(150,200); // move our "pen" down 50
         pixels, drawing a line
      canvas1.lineTo(200,200); // move our "pen" 50 pixels to
         the right
      canvas1.closePath(); // Draw a direct line back to our
         starting point
      canvas1.stroke(); // Visually place the defined line on
         the page
      </script>
```

```
    </body>
</html>
```

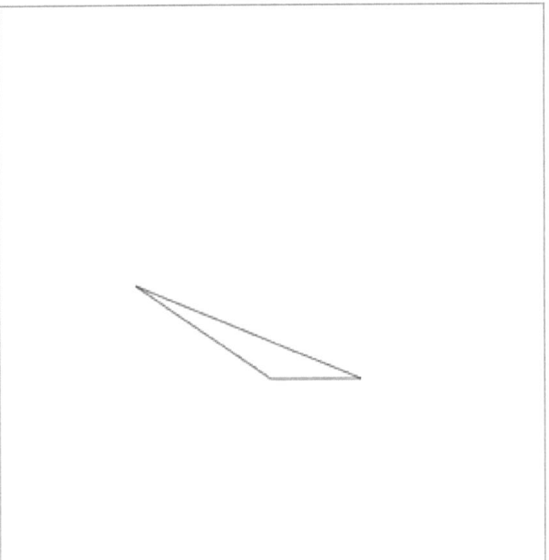

To convert our outlined triangle to a filled, solid object we just need to convert our stroke settings back to fill:

```
<html>
    <body>
        <canvas id="canvas" width="300" height="300"
            style="border: 1px solid #c3c3c3;"> Oh no! This
            browser does not support HTML5 :(
        </canvas>
        <script>
        var canvas=document.getElementById("canvas");
        var canvas1=canvas.getContext("2d");
        canvas1.beginPath(); //declare the beginning of settings
            for our line
        canvas1.fillStyle = "rgba(50, 0, 0, 0.5)";
        canvas1.moveTo(75,150); // set the starting point of our
            "pen" to the middle
        canvas1.lineTo(150,200); // move our "pen" down 50
            pixels, drawing a line
        canvas1.lineTo(200,200); // move our "pen" 50 pixels to
            the right
        canvas1.closePath(); // Draw a direct line back to our
            starting point
        canvas1.fill(); // Visually place the defined line on the
            page
        </script>
    </body>
```

```
</html>
```

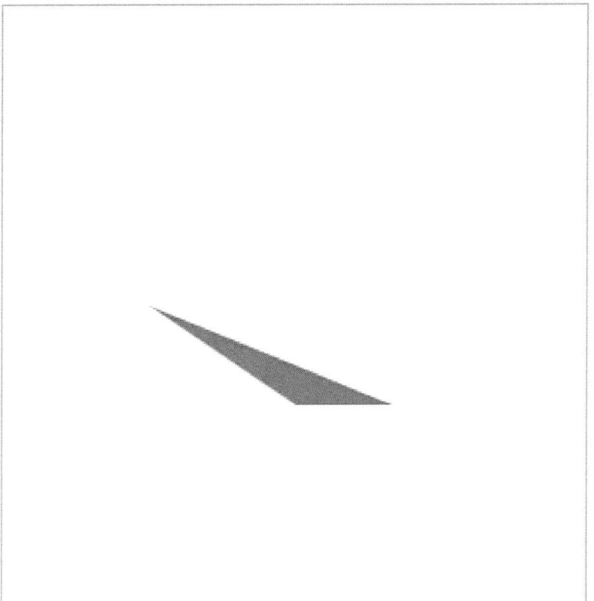

We can move beyond straight lines in order to draw other shapes by using Bezier curves, quadratic curves, and arcs. Each of these allow us to define different points on our lines and to curve our line between those points. For now, we will look at Bezier as an example of how to approach multi-point curves. Bezier lines allow for two control points as opposed to the one allowed in quadratic curve, so the programmatic difference is essentially just one less point defined for a quadratic than a Bezier (limiting the shape your line can take).

Bezier Curve

```
<html>
   <body>
      <canvas id="canvas" width="300" height="300"
         style="border: 1px solid #c3c3c3;"> Oh no! This
         browser does not support HTML5 :(
      </canvas>
      <script>
      context.beginPath();
      context.moveTo(10, 130);
      context.bezierCurveTo(0, 10, 290, 10, 290, 290);
      context.lineWidth = 10;
      context.strokeStyle = /black/;
      context.stroke();
      </script>
   </body>
</html>
```

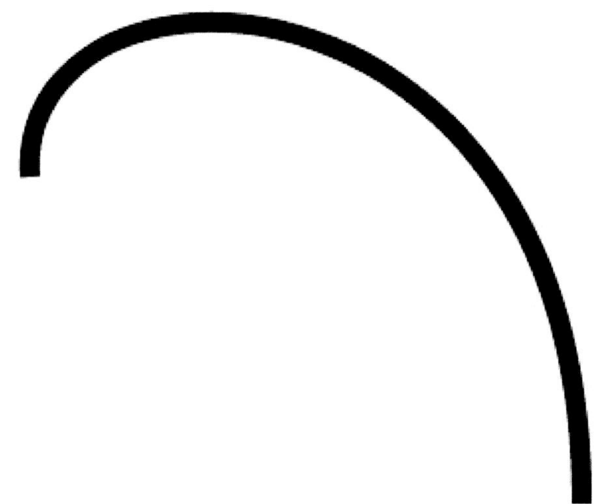

By setting a moveTo point, we are starting our curve from that point just as with a regular line. From here, our Bezier function call takes three sets of points, our two control points, and end point. As a challenge, try adjusting your Bezier points to turn this example into a drop, or marker style, symbol.

Drawn Text

We can even draw text on the screen. While this might seem redundant as we have done that since we began this section, drawing text on a canvas can help us complete logos or draw letters without specifying every line needed to create the letter itself. This means the text becomes part of the canvas and cannot be copy/pasted. To create text, we simply need to define the style, string, and starting location. Replacing our earlier examples, our new canvas1 definition turns into:

```
<script>
   var canvas=document.getElementById("canvas");
   var canvas1=canvas.getContext("2d");
</script>
```

The benefit of creating text as a layer on a canvas instead of styling it with CSS allows us additional mechanisms to manipulate our words.

With this set of techniques, we can now recreate icons and logos without needing actual image files, and can scale them to fit as our page size and layout changes. This also makes it more difficult for your drawn images to be "borrowed." As there is no image file to save, it becomes more difficult (though not impossible) for anyone trying to use your creations. Let us add text to this canvas by setting up a splash of color for our text, then defining our font, text and start location:

```
var gradient=ctx.createLinearGradient(0,0,c.width,0);
gradient.addColorStop("0","red");
gradient.addColorStop("0.5","yellow");
gradient.addColorStop("1.0","blue");
ctx.fillStyle=gradient;
```

```
ctx.fillText("Let's see some color!",10,90);+
```

LEARN MORE

Keywords, search terms: Canvas, css graphics

See what Canvas can do! http://net.tutsplus.com/articles/web-roundups/21-ridiculously-impressive-html5-canvas-experiments/

The full specifications http://www.w3.org/TR/2009/WD-html5-20090825/the-canvas-element.html

Chapter 16

Media Support

Video

The abundance of audio and video material on the internet grew over time as bandwidth improved and storage space became cheaper and ubiquitous. Through this time, many approaches were brought forward to facilitate enjoying the material. Software, file extensions, browser add-ons and more attempted to fill the void. Now, HTML5 has added both audio and video tags to make it easier to integrate media into our pages. These tags make embedding media easier, but (so far) are limited in the number of file formats they support.

ADDITIONAL NOTES

You can convert video files to OGG with any supporting software just as you would convert to any other video format.

Our new video tag supports a number of features through attributes like automatically playing (autoplay), looping the file (looping), on screen controls (controls), preloading the video before it is played (preload), error handling (onerror), and even displaying an image when the file is not in use (poster) and also includes width, height, and source attributes of the file.

The video files we wish to use must be in the OGG format, which is an open source video format. We define our video very similarly to other elements we take into our page. An initial video that simply plays when the page is loaded can be completed by adding the following:

```
<video src="ourfile.ogg" width="200" height="150" autoplay>
```

Take note that this is a pretty rude solution in many cases, as the file will start to play as soon as enough of it is ready, and the user is left with no means of control except closing the page entirely (think about the lovely ads we have all been subject to that use this type of technique). To address this, we will add some more attributes:

```
<video src="ourfile.ogg" width="200" height="150" autoplay
controls preload="auto" poster="videoImage.png">
```

Now we see a splash screen and controls. Our other options for preload (auto lets the browser decide) are none and metadata. None will stop all preloading activity, while metadata loads information about the video like length and dimensions. Audio files are actually identical to this approach (even the use of .ogg files) with exception to the ability to define the width and height. All we need to change is our vocabulary, using the word audio instead of video in our tag.

Audio

```
<audio src="ourAudio.ogg" autoplay
controls preload="auto">
```

The use of audio in a site can add a number of effects, from background music (be kind—allow the user to stop it if they want), to little noises that aid in navigation (these might interfere with screen readers) to embedded players that allow the user to select and play a particular audio file.

Like image formats, audio files can be encoded in a variety of formats that provide different levels of quality. The two formats most commonly found are .mp3 and .wav, standing for motion picture extract group (3rd set of standards) and wave, respectively. The difference lies in their method of compressing and storing the information needed to reproduce the sound. MP3 files are more compressed, meaning they are smaller and require less time and space to transmit, but contain less information and as such have a lower audio quality. Wave files, on the other hand, are typically much larger and sound better. This means they are more taxing on a website as they require more storage space and will take longer to load.

Which format you use will obviously depend on what is more important to you—speed of delivery and space, or quality of sound for the user. Some things to take into consideration are that most users report hearing little difference in quality between the formats, especially when the file is played on a mobile device or computer with basic entry-level speakers attached. If you have ever purchased a digital album or single online, you may have been presented with the option between these or other formats to accommodate the more discerning audiophiles among us.

LEARN MORE

Keywords, search terms: Audio, video, embed(ded) audio video

Example of commercial HTML5-based tools: http://flowplayer.org/Example of flash-based tools: http://www.tubesnack.com/

Chapter 17

Mobile Device Support

When you are creating your HTML pages and following the responsive design patterns that restrict tags to structural as much as possible, you have already laid the groundwork to support mobile devices.

When all of your page content is broken down into logical pieces, and those pieces have ID and/or class attributes, we will be able to show, hide, or reposition those elements using CSS. When we determine the screen dimensions the user has on their device, we can decide what or how to show content from our regular page. The key to this, of course, are the ID and class tags. Anything that you may want or need to control (move, alter, edit, etc.) as a single piece by itself should have an ID tag. Elements that will share the same changes (for example, pictures, links, paragraphs, etc.) should have the same class or classes so they can be changed at the same time.

A single element, say a paragraph in a group of paragraphs, can have both an ID and a class, and can receive style changes from CSS due to both. We will get to this in more depth in CSS, but keep it in mind as you build pages now so they are ready for you later.

If you are reading this chapter looking for examples on HTML5 support of things like Geolocation, these will be found in the JavaScript section as they require the use of a scripting language to function, and are not available through HTML markup.

Important considerations for mobile development go beyond styling changes and begin to include performance measures as well, since mobile devices often lack computing power that can match a desktop or laptop's capacity. Skipping some of your fancier animations or large background images to trim down your loading times is another responsive-style adjustment to your site alongside other CSS changes. See the resources below for some examples of methods that may help your site improve response times.

LEARN MORE

Keywords, search terms: Mobile optimization, mobile performance

Optimization tips and tools http://www.html5rocks.com/en/

mobile/Compatibility Charting: http://mobilehtml5.org/

Test your browser(s): http://html5test.com

Follow new developments: http://www.mobilexweb.com/

Chapter 18

Tags to Avoid

Now that we have focused on the new features of HTML5 and warned about the inefficient methods developers resorted to in the past, let us take a look at a few other tags and methods to avoid using in our code.While some of these are already deprecated, not all are, and they all take away from our goals of separating structure from style and responsive design.

<b>, <i>, <strong>

All of these place emphasis on text, and can be replaced with CSS. Using these within your code means a change to your CSS style will not necessarily determine whether or not the style of text is affected for content wrapped in these tags. It also means you have to edit style in two places, both your CSS and HTML files.

<font>

Again, we can control font (with even more control) using CSS, and hard coding your font into your page can override what you wanted in your CSS.

I know, I have (and will) use breaks in my examples. What I mean to discourage here is using breaks as a quick fix when you should be using <p> or something more appropriate. If another tag better identifies your content, but you do not want some of the automatic styling that comes with the tag, we can override those attributes in our CSS, so use the best tag for your content. We will see how to adjust it to your needs when we look at CSS later.

Styling Attributes

Just like not using tags that style in our HTML, we should avoid using attributes that affect page appearance as well, like aligning content, or applying borders, colors, and other CSS elements.

Chapter 19

Rule Structure

CSS

Selectors

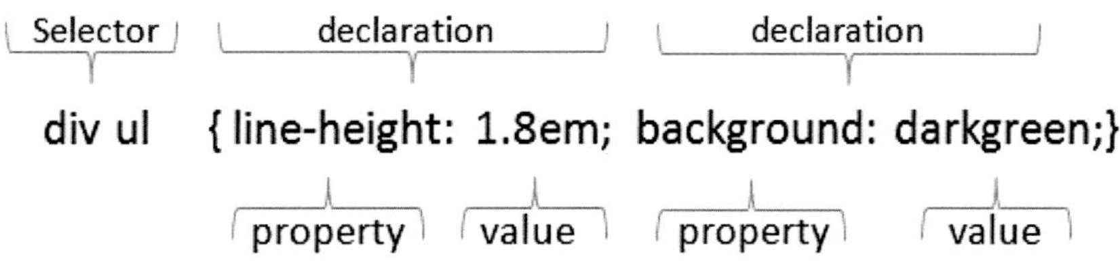

By Armchair [Public domain], via Wikimedia Commons

Figure 22 CSS Rule Structure

The selector is a good place to start with CSS. It is used to identify which item(s) the rule(s) following it will apply to, and is the first element of a rule definition. A selector can refer to an existing tag that is part of the HTML structure like unordered lists, paragraphs, inputs, or it can refer to a custom class, element's name, or ID that we create. Selectors are followed by a set of braces { }, and the rules we enter in between the braces (the property we want to adjust, and the value we want it to have) apply to the selector we specify. We will look at some of these here (there are 40+ as of initial CSS3 components), focusing on those that are more frequently used. Take note that in CSS, we use the colon (:) instead of an equal sign (=) to assign values.

Classes

To take a look at how we can attach a "where" concept to our rules, we will attach some classes to our tags. This allows us to apply different styles to the same selector type, while adding the ability to be more specific about which occurrence we are talking about. We use classes by giving them rules in CSS and referring to them as attributes in elements that support them from our HTML document by using class="nameOfOurClass." When defining classes in our CSS file, we precede their name with a period to specify they are a class.

IDs

The ID attribute is used similar to how a class is used, with two differences:

- The ID is defined with a # instead of a period, e.g., #warning.
- You should use an ID only once on a page, as it should identify something unique to the document.

We already have our ID references in our HTML file anywhere we used id="ourNameHere" attributes in our tags.

Examples

We will begin with a simple example and adjust our unordered list by disabling bullets. For now, we will put the rule in our <head> nested within <style> tags, which will allow the rule to apply anywhere on the page where the selector (in this case, ul) exists:

```
<style>
   ul {
      list-style-type: none;
   }
</style>
```

We could also write this rule in a more condensed form:

```
<style>
   ul {list-style-type: none;}
</style>
```

Since CSS rule sheets ignore white space, the line breaks only serve to make the document more readable when we interact with it. Minifying it (removing all of the extra line breaks by hand or with the use of a script) can reduce the size of larger style sheets, which can help performance (especially in mobile devices where we know this is of more concern).

By adding the rule above, we dictate the appearance of all unordered lists on our page. Rules specify the "What, Where, and When" aspects we want to define for the given selector. The "What" is the actual change we want to see—text in a certain color, an image in a specific location, and so on, just like our example above. In this case, we wanted to hide the default bullet markers. The "Where" is one or more specific locations, defined as a particular named element or when certain conditions are met, i.e. before every paragraph (p.before{}), or every link on the page (a{}). Finally, the "When" aspects allow us to control the site's appearance based on different factors like if the display is mobile sized, or if the user clicked the print button (@media print {}).

By placing these examples in the <head> of our page, we have created an internal style sheet. This denotes that all of the style information we need to reference can be found in the page itself. We could also create external files with our rules. This allows us to have one or more CSS files in our site, and to apply those rules to one or more pages. The external file method is what we will predominantly use as it best fits responsive design, and separates the tasks our files are targeting.

IMPORTANT REMINDER

Using the inline method outside of JavaScript violates our responsive design and separation of duties! Another downside to this method is it would have to be applied to every paragraph we wanted it on within our page.

To connect a CSS file to our webpage, we would move all of our rules (everything inside the <style> tags) into a new document. After saving this new file with the .css extension, the browser will understand that everything contained is to be treated as if it were in our <style> tags. We can connect it to our page much like linking to another page in our server:

```
<link rel="style sheet" type="text/css" href="mystyle.css">
```

In our <link> tag we provide a rel attribute of style sheet to identify the file's purpose. The type attribute tells the browser how to expect the contents to be formatted ("text/css"), and href provides the location of the file. If the file was not in the same folder as the web page we are using, we would adjust the link just as we would in an <a> tag.

Past practice has been to create entirely different sites, complete with customized CSS and HTML pages, to support mobile devices. This kicked off the m.yoursite.com, or mobile.yoursite.com period where heavily modified versions of sites were maintained separate from the primary, desktop version. Now, with the use of responsive design methods and the newer features of CSS3, we can use one master CSS file for all aspects of our site.

You may wish to separate your CSS files while you are working on them, as one master file can become tedious to search through. It may also help to add multi-line or long comments in your file to delineate between organized sections of your CSS. Ultimately, by your release date, you will want to get all of your CSS back into one file. Compressing it with tools like http://www.csscompressor.com/ which remove the whitespace that makes the file readable while developing, and reduces the file size making transmission faster for the user.

Our final method of applying rules is inline. This refers to the practice of inserting the rule inside the attribute tag of the item in question. If we wanted to change the text color of a particular paragraph, we could go right to our HTML file and alter our regular <p> tag to read:

```
<p style="color:red;">Our now RED paragraph!</p>
```

Here we do not need our selector as it is the tag itself, and we also do not need our braces, or quotes within the rules. All we include in our attribute's value are the surrounding quotes and the rules we want to apply, still using : and ; appropriately. This is an effective means of responding to an event, or changing appearance through JavaScript.

There are a number of other things we can do with selectors in order to identify what we want to interact with. The * character can be used to apply to everything within page, or within a selector if one is specified. For example, * { color: blue} would make all text on the page blue (assuming it is the last rule applied… we will get to that) while footer * { color: blue} would make all items in our footer blue. This can be handy for development and testing to quickly adjust a number of items, but should be avoided in production as processing the rule can require examining a large number of elements, potentially increasing page load times.

We can target specific items by referring to them using their ID. To do this, we put a # in front of their ID name. As an example, we will create two divs, one with an ID of todo and another with an ID of complete, to make a quick task list:

```
<div id="todo">
   <ul>
      <li>Check the mail</li>
      <li>Go to the store</li>
      <li>Take the dog to the vet </li>
   </ul>
</div>
<div id="completed">
   <ul>
      <li>Rent a movie</li>
      <li>Make grocery list</li>
      <li>Make vet appointment</li>
   </ul>
</div>
```

- Check the mail
- Go to the store
- Take the dog to the vet

- Rent a movie
- Make grocery list
- Make vet appointment

By adding the following styles to this page, we can turn our To Do list red, and our Completed list green:

```
<style>
   #todo { background-color:red; }
   #completed { background-color: green; }
</style>
```

- Check the mail
- Go to the store
- Take the dog to the vet

- Rent a movie
- Make grocery list
- Make vet appointment

IMPORTANT REMINDER

Keep in mind we can only use an id name once on each page. If you want to apply these rules in more than one place, then you should use a class definition, coming up next!

We can use this technique on any tag that accepts an ID as an attribute (the actual rules we are allowed to use, however, differ depending on the element). To apply rules like this in multiple places, we will need to switch to a class definition. To do this, we simply change our # to a . and instead of relying on an element's ID, we give it a class attribute with a value of the selector name we create in our style definition. We will tweak our last example to split our To Do list into "today" and "tomorrow" lists and rename our completed div to "done."

Then give both to do lists a class of todo, our done list a class of completed, and change our CSS rules to match:

```
<style>
   .todo { background-color:red; }
   .completed { background-color: green; }
</style>
<div id="today" class="todo">
   <ul>
      <li>Check the mail</li>
      <li> Go to the store</li>
   </ul>
</div>
<div id="tomorrow" class="todo">
   <ul>
      <li>Take the dog to the vet </li>
   </ul>
</div>
<div id="done" class="completed">
   <ul>
      <li>Rent a movie</li>
      <li>Make grocery list</li>
      <li>Make vet appointment</li>
   </ul>
</div>
```

- Check the mail
- Go to the store

- Take the dog to the vet

- Rent a movie
- Make grocery list
- Make vet appointment

To add even more emphasis to our completed list we can make the list inside it show text as crossed out. We could do this by applying a style to an ID we assign it, or by giving that ul a class, but we already have enough structure in place to specify what we want by using a descendant selector. This selector type is specified by saying we want elements "a" *inside* elements "b" to have the style applied. In our example, we want <ul>s inside a .completed crossed off, so we will add the following rule to our styles:

```
.completed ul { text-decoration: line-through; }
```

Now, if we add any more sections with a class of completed, they will also be crossed out automatically. You can try splitting your completed <div> into two pieces, like "yesterday" and "last week" to try it out.

ADDITIONAL NOTES

Hover works on more than links! Just about any element has a hover state as long as the cursor position can be associated with it. Note: the z-index and position of layered elements can easily interfere with things like hover.

Hyperlinks are frequently styled so they change in appearance when they are hovered over or have already been clicked. We can assign our styles to these events by creating rules for <a> tags when they are unvisited, visited, or a hover (mouse pointer is over the link) state is attached:

```
a:link {
```

```
        color:blue;
}
a:visited {
        color:grey;
}
a:hover{
        color:red;
        font-weight:bold;
}
```

Try adding a link to your local Veterinarian's office to the task in your todo list, and watch how it changes when you interact with it.

Sometimes you might find it easier to change something for all occurrences of an element that are not members of another rule. Instead of adding additional classes to those elements, we can specify an exception with the not state:

```
div:not(.completed){ font-size:larger; }
```

This rule will make text in any div (whether or not they have the .todo class) text larger. Another handy set of states are :before and :after. These selectors allow us to place and style content as a prepend or append action to our element. If we wanted to prepend a To Do: title to our .todo class elements, we could add the following rule:

```
.todo:before{
        content:"To Do:";
        background-color:yellow;
        color:red;
        font-weight:bold;
}
```

IMPORTANT REMINDER

Note: We cannot use the Content rule to add HTML to an element, only text. To achieve this, we would need to use JavaScript or another language that can manipulate the DOM.

The remainder of the selectors allow us to get even more specific, selecting the elements the appear before or after another given element, matching elements that have a particular attribute, or even matching attributes that contain a certain string as part of their value. For a full reference, I recommend the list at w3schools.com.[2] Our completed example should now look like this:

```
<style>
.todo {
        background-color:red;
}
.completed {
        background-color: green;
}
.completed ul {
```

[2] http://www.w3schools.com/cssref/css_selectors.asp

```
        text-decoration: line-through;
}
div:not(.completed){
        font-size:larger;
}
a:link {
        color:blue;
}
a:visited {
        color:grey;
}
a:hover{
        color:red;
        font-weight:bold;
}
.todo:before{
        content:"To Do:";
        background-color:yellow;
        color:red;
        font-weight:bold;
}
</style>
<div id="today" class="todo">
    <ul>
        <li>Check the mail</li>
        <li> Go to the store</li>
    </ul>
</div>
<div id="tomorrow" class="todo">
    <ul>
        <li>Take the dog to the
            vet </li>
    </ul>
</div>
<div id="yesterday"
class="completed">
    <ul>
        <li>Rent a movie</li>
    </ul>
</div>
<div id="lastWeek"
class="completed">
    <ul>
        <li>Make grocery list</
            li>
```

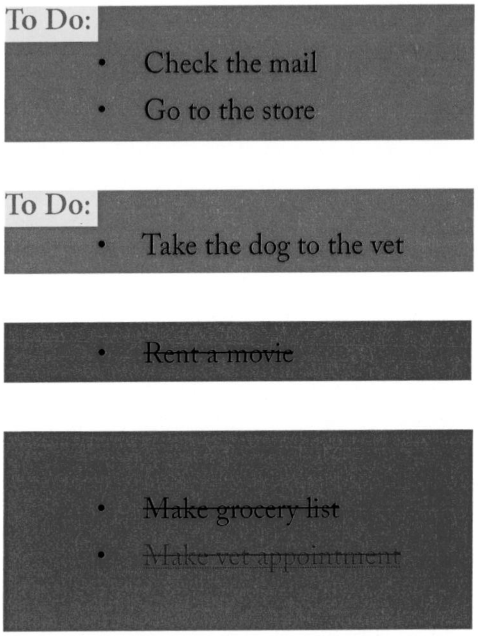

```
        <a href="http://www.dunkirkanimalclinic.com/"><li>Make
           vet appointment</li></a>
    </ul>
</div>
```

Order of Precedence

There are some rules to our rules. There is a hierarchy to how they are applied in order to provide a semblance of order and avoid conflicts. First, we need to consider where the rule is located. In general, the "closer" the CSS file is to the line of code using it, the more likely that particular CSS file will override what is in the others. For example, rules in an external style sheet would be overridden by those in an internal style sheet. Just the same, styles in an internal style sheet would replace the previous style sheet included. Styles that are added to the page, or attributes that are inline with the element they apply to, become the "closest" to what it is targeting.

USEFUL FEATURE

JavaScript code that affects appearance will frequently apply inline modifications to apply style changes to a page, but will not affect the CSS file or other pages.

When we discuss the overriding nature, it is important to remember that this applies to the specific rule. A set of rules for an <a> tag defined in an external sheet will not necessarily be overridden by the <a> tag rules in an internal style sheet. Each rule within the definition is examined, and is still applied if that particular rules does not appear "closer" to the element. For example:

An External Sheet:

```
a {
   color:blue;
   text-decoration:none;
}
```

An Internal Sheet:

```
a { color:red;}
```

Our code:

```
<head>
   <link rel="style sheet" type="text/css" href="mystyle.css">
</head>
<style>
   a { color:red;}
</style>
```

Comparing the above example style sheets, we can see that the external sheet applies two rules: text color is blue, and there should not be an underline. However, our internal style sheet specifies a rule that color should be red. Since this rule is closer, our link will be red. The underline rule, however, is not defined in the internal sheet, so it will carry over and remain.

This also carries into the CSS rules themselves. Definitions can be general, like our example above that would apply to all links on our page, or they can be more specific to target a particular group or single link. The more specific we are, the greater influence our rule will have. For example:

```
<style>
   a{
      color:red;
   }
   div.block a{
      color: blue;
   }
</style>
   <body>
      <a href="">Our RED link</a>
   <div class="block">
      <a href="">Our BLUE link</a><br/>
      <a href="" style="color:green">Our GREEN link</a>
   </div>
```

Above, our "a" style for our links is overridden in our div, as the block style is more particular, or close, to the actual link we want affected. However, our green link overrules our block style as it is inline, and applies to that specific link. From here, only a change in this inline style caused by JavaScript, or an "over-override" from a rule marked !important can trump the inline rule. The easiest way to debug CSS issues is with web developer tools that are an add-on or included in modern browsers like Chrome, that can show you exactly what rules are applied, overridden, and even let you test (temporary) changes before making them in your real file.

Caveat: User-enforced styles (settings the client enters in their browser, or applied by an accessibility program) also fit in to our precedence list, and can override any styles we set.

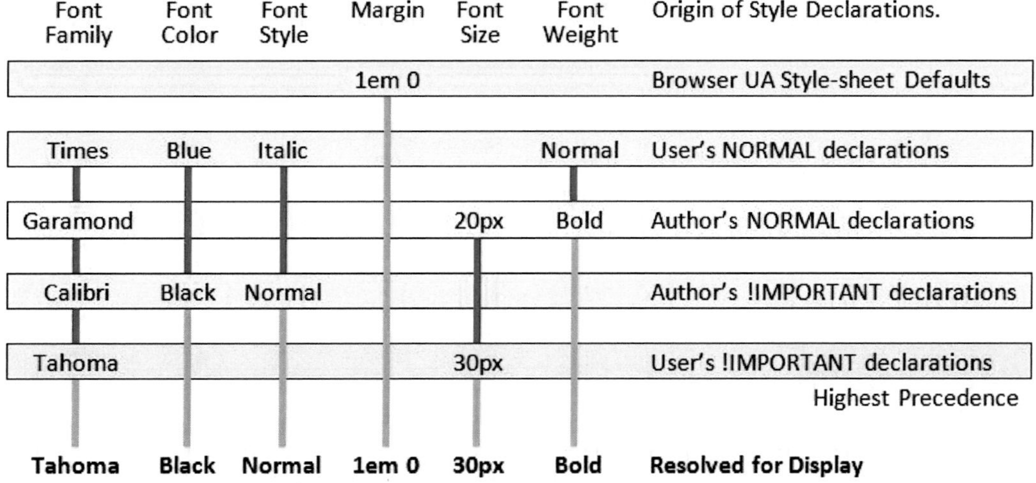

By Armchair [Public domain], via Wikimedia Commons

Figure 23 Document Markup

LEARN MORE

Keywords, search terms: css rules, rule structure, selectors, css classes and ids

A list of all CSS properties: http://www.blooberry.com/indexdot/css/propindex/all.htm

All of the selectors: http://www.w3.org/TR/CSS2/selector.html

Some tips, tricks and more features: http://www.instantshift.com/2010/03/15/47-css-tips-tricks-to-take-your-site-to-the-next-level/

Chapter 20

Layout Formatting

Box Model

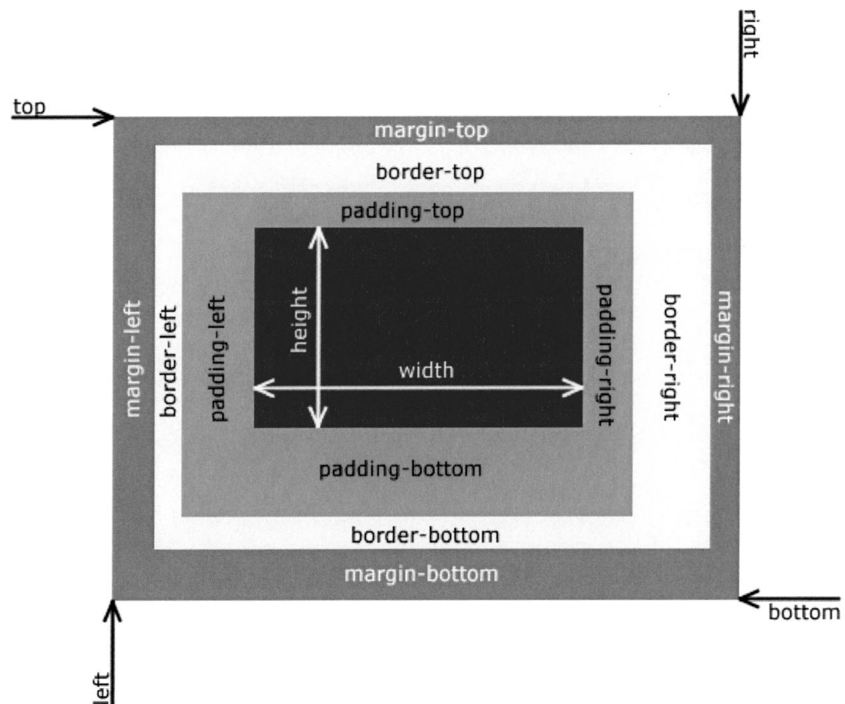

By Matthias Apsel [CC0], via Wikimedia Commons

Figure 24 CSS Box Model

Borders

To better identify where our content falls on a page, and to signify that it is different from the material around it, we can adjust the borders on our elements. Borders can be enabled or disabled by the top, bottom, left and right of the element and can also have different styles like solid, double, grooved, dotted and dashed lines, among others.

To specify a full border, we simply use border, and can apply color, width, and style:

```
<style>
p.one {
	border-style:solid;
	border-width:5px;
}
p.two {
	border-style:groove;
	border-width:medium;
}
p.three {
	border-style:dotted;
	border-width:1px;
	border-color:red;
}
</style>
<p class="one">Some text.</p>
<p class="two">Some more text.</p>
<p class="three">Even more text.</p>
```

Some text.

Some more text.

Even more text.

The full list of possible border styles is as follows:

Table 4 Border Styles

Value	Description
none	No border.
dotted	Dotted border.
dashed	Dashed border.
solid	Solid border.
double	Double (two lines) border.
groove	Grooved, 3d border.
ridge	Ridged, 3d border.
inset	Lowered (sunken) 3d border.
outset	Raised 3d border.
inherit	Inherits the same style as the parent element.

Margin and Padding

These related concepts allow you to control the amount of space between your content and its container, and between the container and objects around it. Padding controls the amount of space inside your container, for instance between text and a set of paragraph tags. You can remember padding as the inside by thinking about a padded room; the padding is only effective if it is on the inside of the walls.

By adding borders to our paragraphs as we did above, we can see the outline of where the paragraph fits into our page. Now, we will see the difference when we apply padding:

```
<style>
   p.one {
      border-style:solid;
      border-width:5px;
   }
   p.two {
      border-style:groove;
      border-width:medium;
   }
   p.three {
      border-style:dotted;
      border-width:1px;
      border-color:red;
   }
   p {padding:10px;}
</style>
<p class="one">Some text.</p>
<p class="two">Some more text.</p>
<p class="three">Even more text.</p>
```

Some text.

Some more text.

Even more text.

You will notice that the paragraphs still have not moved relative to one another, they each simply take up more space. In order to move them further away from each other, we can add a margin:

```
<style>
   p.one {
      border-style:solid;
      border-width:5px;
   }
   p.two {
      border-style:groove;
      border-width:medium;
   }
   p.three {
      border-style:dotted;
      border-width:1px;
      border-color:red;
   }
   p {padding:10px;}
   p {margin:50px;}
</style>
<p class="one">Some text.</p>
<p class="two">Some more text.</p>
<p class="three">Even more text.</p>
```

Some text.

Some more text.

Even more text.

With both examples, we can adjust our values by pixel or percent. We can also control the amount of change by each side of the object, by specifying top, bottom, left or right to our rules. To do this we need to edit our values to only pad the left side of our paragraphs, and only apply a margin to the bottom of each:

```
<style>
   p.one {
      border-style:solid;
      border-width:5px;
   }
   p.two {
      border-style:groove;
      border-width:medium;
   }
   p.three{
      border-style:dotted;
      border-width:1px;
      border-color:red;
   }
   p {padding-left:10px;}
   p {margin-bottom:50px;}
</style>
<p class="one">Some text.</p>
<p class="two">Some more text.</p>
<p class="three">Even more text.</p>
```

Some text.

Some more text.

Even more text.

Instead of writing out multiple rules to adjust sides, we can combine them into one declaration by writing out our values clockwise, starting with top, as padding: top right bottom left or margin: top right bottom left, replacing the words with a fixed or relative value (they can be mixed) and by using zero as a place holder if we do not want the value changed from default:

```
<style>
   p.one {
      border-style:solid;
      border-width:5px;
   }
   p.two {
      border-style:groove;
      border-width:medium;
   }
   p.three {
      border-style:dotted;
      border-width:1px;
      border-color:red;
   }
   p {padding:50px 30px 50px 5px;}
   p {margin:50px;}
</style>
<p class="one">Some text.</p>
<p class="two">Some more text.</p>
<p class="three">Even more text.</p>
```

Some text.

Some more text.

Even more text.

Background

There is a lot we can do with the background of our pages. Colors and images can be applied to all or portions of our content, helping to highlight different elements of our site, and play a large part in the overall look and feel. We can specify colors by their name if they are a basic color like red, white, blue etc. or we can provide its hex value, or the values for its red, green, and blue values.

```
<style>
   p.one {
      border-style:solid;
      border-width:5px;
      Background-color: green;
   }
   p.two {
      border-style:groove;
      border-width:medium;
      Background-color:#ff3355;
   }
   p.three {
      border-style:dotted;
      border-width:1px;
      border-color:red;
      background-color: rgb(33,66,99);
   }
   p {padding:50px 30px 50px 5px;}
   p {margin:50px;}
</style>
<p class="one">Some text.</p>
<p class="two">Some more text.</p>
<p class="three">Even more text.</p>
```

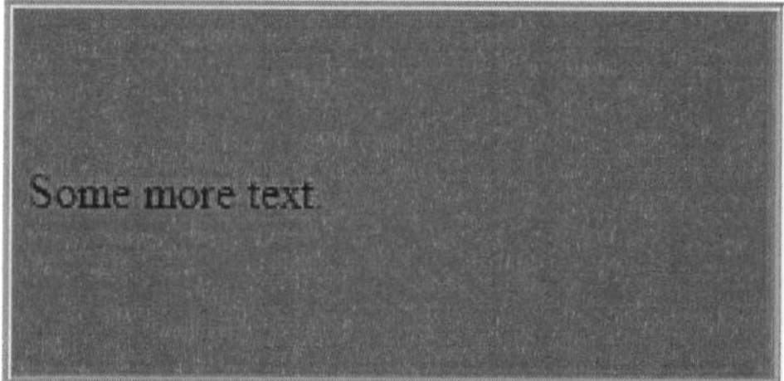

To use images instead of colors, we can specify the image's location in our files, and can also dictate where we want to place it on our page, whether or not it should repeat, and whether it should move or remain in place when the user scrolls the page. By default, images will repeat to fill the space they are placed in. To prevent this, we can add a no-repeat attribute to our definitions. This time, we will use the background attribute as opposed to the background-color attribute. The benefit of this is that you can include both in a set of rules on the same object (image first, color second), allowing you to have an image on top of a background color. Take note that in these examples, you will need to select your own images in place of those used below.

```
<style>
   p.one {
      border-style:solid;
      border-width:5px;
      background:url(clouds.jpg);
      }
   p.two {
      border-style:groove;
      border-width:medium;
      background:url(calendar.jpg) no-repeat;
      background-color:#ff3355;
   }
   p.three {
      border-style:dotted;
      border-width:1px;
      border-color:red;
      background:url(calendar.jpg);
   }
   p {padding:50px 30px 50px 5px;}
   p {margin:50px;}
</style>
<p class="one">Some text.</p>
<p class="two">Some more text.</p>
<p class="three">Even more text.</p>
```

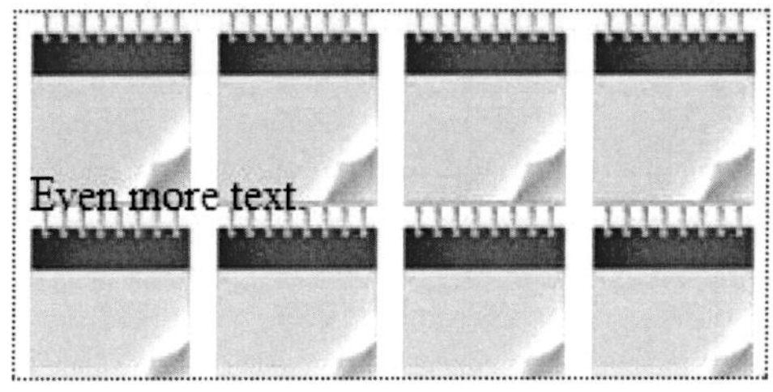

There are two ways of achieving this affect. The first is by using advanced styling through CSS using WebKit features supported by some browsers, and then adding style rules to create the effect as close as possible in other browsers. The second is by creating a repeatable gradient image. The first approach's reliance on WebKit provides support for Apple and Google products. For browsers that do not use WebKit, we have to add extra rules to achieve the same effect. This is a more advanced example as it requires knowledge of each browser's needs to create:

```
<style>
   #ourBackground {
      background-color: #1a82f7;
      background: url(ourFallBackImage.png);
      background-repeat: repeat-x;
      /* Safari 4-5, Chrome 1-9 */
      background: -webkit-gradient(linear, 0% 0%, 0% 100%,
         from(#1a82f7), to(#2F2727));
      /* Safari 5.1, Chrome 10+ */
      background: -webkit-linear-gradient(top, #2F2727,
         #1a82f7);
      /* Firefox 3.6+ */
      background: -moz-linear-gradient(top, #2F2727, #1a82f7);
```

```
        /* IE 10 */
        background: -ms-linear-gradient(top, #2F2727, #1a82f7);
        /* Opera 11.10+ */
        background: -o-linear-gradient(top, #2F2727, #1a82f7);
    }
</style>
<div id="ourBackground" width="300px" height="300px">
    <br/>
    Some <br/>
    Text <br/>
    Here <br/>
    <br/>
</div>
```

This code should produce an almost identical image in every browser, depending on which rule(s) the browser is able to execute:

The first three lines of this style script—

```
background-color: #1a82f7;
background: url(ourFallBackImage.png);
background-repeat: repeat-x;
```

demonstrate how we create the gradient effect through an image. In this example, ourFallBackImage.png would be a very skinny (1 pixel) wide image as tall as we want our gradient to be. By repeating this image across the X axis (moving horizontally) the image will fill the width of the parent object. By specifying the bottom-most pixel color from our image as the background, the gradient will appear to fill the page. The balance of our rules in this example achieve the same result through CSS, but also provides more control over the gradient without needing to create additional images.

Float

Floating an object with CSS allows us to move it around within its parent object, ignoring (to some extent) the other items near it. Note that float is only for left/right values, not top/bottom, even though their movement may feel that way as windows resize.

When multiple objects in the same container have the same float style, they will line up next to each other for as many as the container can fit. While this may sound confusing, we will look at it without the terminology: If you have a big box, and that box has small boxes in it, those boxes will fit as many of themselves left-to-right in a row as they can. Any boxes that do not fit will start a new "row" underneath.

The use of float is a big help to responsive styling. Boxes of content that normally fit side by side on a larger screen will automatically create more "rows," with less items in each, to accommodate screens with less width. Create a page with the following code, and then play around with the size of your browser window to see the resizing in action:

```
<style>
   .thumbnail {
      float:left;
      width:80px;
      height:80px;
      margin:5px;
   }
</style>
<div>
   <img class="thumbnail" src="yourPictureHere.jpg" >
   <img class="thumbnail" src="yourPictureHere.jpg" >
   <img class="thumbnail" src="yourPictureHere.jpg" >
   <img class="thumbnail" src="yourPictureHere.jpg" >
   <img class="thumbnail" src="yourPictureHere.jpg" >
   <img class="thumbnail" src="yourPictureHere.jpg" >
   <img class="thumbnail" src="yourPictureHere.jpg" >
   <img class="thumbnail" src="yourPictureHere.jpg" >
   <img class="thumbnail" src="yourPictureHere.jpg" >
   <img class="thumbnail" src="yourPictureHere.jpg" >
</div>
```

Content before and after a floated element will attempt to wrap around it. When we do not want this to happen, we can add a rule to that element's style to clear the floating effect. To do this, we would add clear: left; clear: right; or clear:both depending which sides we are concerned with.

USEFUL FEATURE

Since relative refers to moving the position from where it would be based on all of the other elements and rules, we can use negative values to "pull" an element in that particular direction.

Positioning

We can specify, with great control, exactly where our elements are ultimately located in our window. CSS allows us to modify location to such an extent that an items position on the page can have no relation to its location in your code. Just as we have seen in many of our other rules, there are two methods to declaring position, fixed and relative. Here fixed elements specify the offset of pixels from a side or corner of the window, and relative declares that our values are moving the content from where it *would* have been if we had not changed it.

Here is how we might take a heading and force it to an offset from the top left corner as an absolute, meaning it will sit there no matter what else is above, underneath, or around it:

```
<style>
   h2 {
      position:absolute;
      left:50px;
      top:100px;
   }
</style>
<h2>This is a heading with an absolute position</h2>
<p>With absolute positioning, an element can be placed any-
where on a page. The heading below is placed 50px from the
left of the page and 100px from the top of the page. As this
text continues, you will see that the heading sits on top of
the text as if it was not even there. As this text continues,
you will see that the heading sits on top of the text as if
it was not even there. As this text continues, you will see
that the heading sits on top of the text as if it was not even
there .As this text continues, you will see that the heading
sits on top of the text as if it was not even there. As this
text continues, you will see that the heading sits on top of
the text as if it was not even there. As this text continues,
you will see that the heading sits on top of the text as if
it was not even there. As this text continues, you will see
that the heading sits on top of the text as if it was not even
there. As this text continues, you will see that the heading
sits on top of the text as if it was not even there.</p>
```

With absolute positioning, an element can be placed anywhere on a page. The heading below is placed 50px from the left of the page and 100px from the top of the page. As this text continues, you will see that the heading sits on top of the text as if it weren't even there.As this text continues, you will see that the heading sits on top of the text as if it weren't even there.As this text continues, you will see that the heading sits on top of the text as if it weren't even there.As this text continues, you will see that the heading sits on top of the text as if it weren't even there.As this text continues, you will see that the heading sits on top of the text as if it weren't even there.As this text continues, you will see that the heading sits on top of the text as if it weren't even there.As this text continues, you will see that the heading sits on top of the text as if it weren't even there.As this text continues, you will see that the heading sits on top of the text as if it weren't even there.

This is a heading with an absolute position

If we wanted to move our heading relative to where it would normally have been positioned (just above our paragraph) we change to relative and provide the offset values that we want. Here, we will move it to the right, move it to the left, and show it as it was:

```
<style>
   h2.pos_left {
      position:relative;
      left:-20px;
   }
```

```
    h2.pos_right {
        position:relative;
        left:20px;
    }
</style>
<h2>This is a heading with no position</h2>
<h2 class="pos_left">This heading is moved left according to
its normal position</h2>
<h2 class="pos_right">This heading is moved right according to
its normal position</h2>
<p>This is our paragraph that has a heading with relative
positioning. Unless we put a negative bottom offset on our
heading large enough to cover it, it will stay above the para-
graph this time. </p>
```

This is a heading with no position

his heading is moved left according to its normal position

This heading is moved right according to its normal position

This is our paragraph that has a heading with relative positioning. Unless we put a negative bottom offset on our heading large enough to cover it, it will stay above the paragraph this time.

Z-index

Just when you thought we had escaped the terrors of precedence and inheritance, we have another factor in our layering to consider. The z-index of an object determines its order in the stack of elements on a page. This is how we can control which items are depicted as on "top" of another when they occupy the same portion of a page. While items are automatically layered according to their location on the page and in our code, these can be modified and overridden by a z-index to set the order we want. A larger value of a z-index forces an object "higher" on the page, or, puts it closer to the "top" of all the elements you are looking at. A page background, for example, is usually the lowest level on your page. As such, other content on your page sits on top of your background layer, and becomes the next layer in the stack. A simple way to ensure important messages are never hidden behind something else is to assign them a z-index of an extremely large like 99999. You should only use such a method for one or two critical items in a site. In our first example, we will see an image with a negative index that ensures it is behind our text. Then we will change our index value to make it higher, putting it on top of the text instead:

```
<style>
    img {
       position:absolute;
       left:0px;
       top:0px;
       z-index:-1;
    }
</style>
<h1>Here is some text</h1>
<img src="http://bglabs.evade.netdna-cdn.
com/files/clouds-seamless-background-824.jpg"
width="100" height="100" />
```

Here is some text

```
<style>
    img {
       position:absolute;
       left:0px;
       top:0px;
       z-index:-1;
    }
</style>
<h1>Here is some text</h1>
<img src="http://bglabs.evade.netdna-cdn.
com/files/clouds-seamless-background-824.jpg"
width="100" height="100" />
```

Mouse Cursor

While this is not a regular feature in most sites, it can be an important player if you intend for your website to act as if it were an application.

We can add cursor rules to our selectors in order to change the appearance of the mouse cursor when that rule is active. Much the same as working in your operating system, we can select the regular icon, wait (also called working, busy, thinking, etc.), text insert, a pointer, a question mark, and a crosshair. While most of these have little use in the average web page, they come in handy when your end product is more application focused.

I would strongly recommend judicious use of cursor changes, and be sure that your changes are reverted back as soon as it is appropriate (i.e. change your waiting/busy back as soon as an event is compete) as forgetting to reset can leave your user thinking your site (or their system) is locked up or endlessly cycling. The full list of the available cursors is as follows:

Table 5 Pointer Styles

Value	Description
auto	(default) let the browser choose
crosshair	Crosshair, or "plus," symbol
default	The default cursor
e-resize	Shows resize to the right (note all resize values are compass combinations)
help	The help (question mark) icon
move	Item can be moved
n-resize	Shows resize up
ne-resize	Shows resize up and right
nw-resize	Shows resize up and left
pointer	A pointer (arrow)
progress	The busy symbol (be careful with this one!)
s-resize	Shows resize down
se-resize	Shows resize down and right
sw-resize	Shows resize down and left
text	Text line (flashing or steady "I")
w-resize	Shows resize left
wait	Shows busy, wait (be careful with this one!)
inherit	Inherits value from parent

Cursor styles can be applied when the element with a CSS attribute that affects the cursor is triggered. This is usually caused by hovering over the object, or when the user initiates an action, in reaction to which we apply the new style using JavaScript. Note that user triggered actions like busy icons normally need to stay "busy" until the script is done. In this case, the body tag should receive the attribute that affects the cursor so it continues to show as busy even if the user moves the mouse off of the button or other trigger that they used.

LEARN MORE

Keywords, search terms: css layout, page formatting, positioning, css layers

LearnLayout: http://learnlayout.com/toc.html

Full layout example without tables: http://www.w3.org/2002/03/csslayout-howto

A set of basic layouts: http://blog.html.it/layoutgala/

Chapter 21

Font and Text Decoration

When we began our testing site, we started using HTML tags wherever we could to provide structure to our content with heading tags. We did this with the understanding that later we would redefine those tags so our headings looked how we wanted them to. That time has come. To start with some basics, we can use what we have already learned above by changing the color of the text and background for our heading tags:

```
<style>
   h1{
      color:red;
      background-color:yellow;
   }
</style>
<h1>This is an H1 heading</h1>
```

This is an H1 heading

We can also adjust our font family and size. You will notice that none of these changes affect anything outside of our headings. While you may see examples using the key terms for size, ranging from "extra extra small" (xx-small) to "extra extra large" (xx-large), it is a good idea to always be as specific as possible, as key terms can be treated differently between browsers. Instead, our examples will use percentage-based and fixed font sizes. To do so, we will make our h1 content italicized and bring the size down to 20px tall:

```
<style>
   h1{
      color:red;
      background-color:yellow;
      font-style:italic;
      font-size:20px;
   }
</style>
<h1>This is an H1 heading</h1>
```

This is an H1 heading

These are just a few examples of the full power of font through CSS. Some "fancier" methods include effects like capitalizing, while simultaneously shrinking, your text (small-caps):

```
<style>
   h1{
      color:red;
      background-color:yellow;
      font-variant:small-caps;
   }
</style>
<h1>This is an H1 heading</h1>
```

THIS IS AN H1 HEADING

Text Styles

While our next example seems like it applies more to font than text, a good way to remember what noun you want to use in your rule is whether the affect changes the way the letters appear or not. If they do, you probably want font. If not, then you probably want text as in these next examples.

First, we might want to add the lead spaces back into our paragraph's definition to make them appear more like a written document. We can also move our text around in our containing element by setting it to left (default), right, center, or stretch to fit with justify:

```
<style>
   p {
      text-indent:15px;
      text-align:justify;
   }
</style>
<p>This is our paragraph for demonstrating some of the things
we can do to text and font through the use of CSS. This is our
paragraph for demonstrating some of the things we can do to
text and font through the use of CSS. This is our paragraph
for demonstrating some of the things we can do to text and
font through the use of CSS. </p>
```

This is our paragraph for demonstrating some of the things we can do to text and font through the use of CSS. This is our paragraph for demonstrating some of the things we can do to text and font through the use of CSS. This is our paragraph for demonstrating some of the things we can do to text and font through the use of CSS.

In addition to adjusting the font itself, we can decorate it with more affects like crossing it out, underlining it, or specifying that it should *not* be decorated, which is especially useful in eliminating the default lines under links:

ADDITIONAL NOTES

Order is Important! Active style rules must come after hover rules, and hover must come after link and visited! Since a link being hovered over can already have been visited, and the active link can be the one with hover on it, this ensures the correct order of application of style.

```
<style>
   .strikeOut{text-
   decoration:line-through;}
   .titles{text-
   decoration:underline;}
   a {text-decoration:none;}
</style>
<span class="strikeOut">Text we
want crossed out</span><br/>
<span class="titles">Hitchiker's
Guide to the Galaxy</span><br/>
<span><a href="">A link with no
underline</span>
```

~~Text we want crossed out~~
Hitchiker's Guide to the Galaxy
A link with no underline

Anchors

Following up on our ability to remove the underline from a link, there are some other special features we can control for our page anchors using CSS. By specifying link, visited, or hover in our link selector, we can control what happens before, during and after a link has been clicked. We can think of these like applying attributes in our HTML tags, except in CSS the special features are called pseudo-classes. Since we can specify any valid CSS rule, we can have our links change colors, alter the backgrounds, change text and font properties, and everything else we will look at. To see some of the basics in action, we will change our text colors for each action, and also our background color when we are hovering. Since you will need to interact with the links to see these in action, we will forgo an image here and you can test the code yourself:

```
<style>
   a:link {color:#FF0000; background-color:yellow;} /* unvis-
   ited link */
   a:visited {color:#00FF00; background-color:orange;} /*
   visited link */
   a:hover {color:#FF00FF; background-color:green;} /* mouse
   over link */
   a:active {color:#0000FF; background-color:white;} /* se-
   lected link */
</style>
<a href="" target="_blank">Here is our fake link!</a>
```

Visually Impaired Considerations

The Internet is obviously a highly visual medium, and it is good practice to keep in mind how your site will be consumed by those with differing visual needs. Here are a few techniques to be better prepared to serve a pleasant user experience.

First is text size. Modern browsers support increasing and decreasing page text on their own (by taking advantage of user style CSS properties). While this reduces the need to provide resizing style sheets for your users to select from, it does mean you should test increasing and decreasing the font size on your site from a browser (usually ctrl and +, ctrl and -). This will allow you to see how far your font size can be pushed before it interferes with your layout. You might need to adjust your style to accommodate these changes. How many levels you wish to account for is up to you, but a general rule of thumb is your page should support +3 with little disruption. You can of course offer special style sheets with links to enable them, giving you better control over the changes while still offering your users an adaptable experience.

Second is the ability to offer your users a text only version of the page. This can be done by applying custom style sheets for actions like printing or different devices that fit under our responsive design, which we will look at in more detail next.

Next is contrast. Color contrast between layered items like a link and a background color can be difficult for many users to distinguish and read. This is not to say that colors should never be layered, but that the contrast between them should be easy to distinguish. A helpful way to test this is to view your site with your brightness and contrast settings turned up and down a bit on your monitor to be sure your site is still legible.

Color combinations can also come into play, for example red and green, and green and blue. When these colors are used together, such as on a submit and cancel button that are next to each other, users with certain forms of color blindness can find them hard to read if not indistinguishable. A better approach is to use a cancel link of regular text next to a large submit button. This makes the options very visually distinct.

For example, the red/green form of colorblindness (Deuterope) makes red and green colors look more alike:

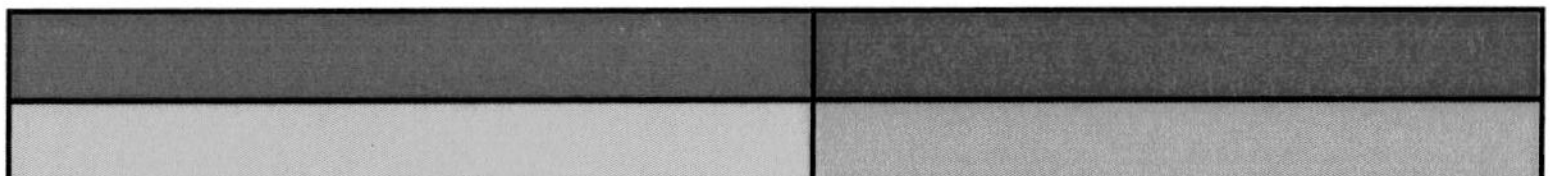

If you are counting on the color of the button to be an important indicator of function, that affect has been lost. Even worse, if you have combined text and background colors that do not lend themselves to readability for the colorblind, they may not be able to interpret the button's function at all!

These considerations are just some examples of a much larger topic, which is accessibility. The W3C maintains a full list of items[3] to be considered to improve your site for the widest variety of users, and there are a number of sites that can scan your pages to provide notes and tips that follow the W3C guide, including one from the W3C itself at http://validator.w3.org/. Sites that pass the W3C validation can add "stamps" to their pages that identify their efforts and support, and to indicate that those considerations have been made.

[3] http://www.w3.org/standards/webdesign/accessibility

Chapter 22

Responsive Styling

Our last rule concept of "When" can be applied to responsive design. It applies to rule conditions being, such as a user has a device with a mobile screen, or is trying to print our page. Since these are not within our default display, we may wish to remove elements or modify our layout to support a small screen, or remove background images and colors to make printed versions easier to read and less taxing on ink supplies.

To do this from within our style sheet, we need to specify the differences between our selectors that apply to these use cases. When we want to make style changes based on the user's device, it is best to test for the existence of the feature in the browser, or for a specific feature or setting of a device, instead of the name and version that it identifies itself as. For example, if we consider the browser's current width, it does not matter what the device is. A user could be on a desktop but have the browser much smaller than full screen. We also do not want to maintain a list in our code of every mobile phone size, especially when most of them fall within a limited range. By just checking the size, we can categorize the device and give it a best-guess-fit appearance.

Another argument for this approach is how the level of support for features changes both as standards change and as browsers are updated. If we only check the browser name, and a newer release than we were aware of supports the feature we want, we would lose out on the feature we want to implement. Instead, we can try and "test load" some of the features we want, or include fall back rules (like we did in our gradient example) to give ourselves the widest amount of support we can.

To test by feature or capability, we use the media queries feature of CSS. We will use screen size as an example. While not a perfect science, there are roughly 4 basic screens to consider, along with their average sizes:

- Smart phones (portrait)—320 pixels
- Tablets (portrait)—768 pixels
- Tablets (landscape), netbooks—1024 pixels
- Laptops, desktops—1024 or higher

This by no means captures every device or possible resolution. For example mini-tablets (or the trend of phablets/oversized cell phones) can fall around the 480 pixel range. Whether you want to support different layouts for these devices will determine if you need to consider more variety than the list above, but once we implement more responsive features you will see how these devices will usually receive an acceptable viewing experience. Next we will create new sections in our CSS that define what changes are necessary for those sizes.

Some browsers and devices, like Apple's Safari browser, will attempt to fit the entire page into their device screen by reporting to be a full size device. To prevent this, we can add the following meta tag to our HTML:

```
<meta name="viewport" content="width=device-width;
initial-scale=1.0">
```

This line tells the browser to report its actual device width so we can provide the proper view.

Next, we need to create a series of selectors that will test for our different scenarios. Using media queries to guide our decision:

```
@media only screen and (max-width: 959px) {}
// Smaller than desktop/laptop (tablets, netbooks)
@media only screen and (min-width: 768px) and (max-width:
959px) {} //Portrait or landscape tablets, netbooks
@media only screen and (max-width: 767px) {}
// devices smaller than portrait tablets (mobile)
@media only screen and (min-width: 480px) and (max-width:
767px) {} // mobile landscape to tablet portrait
@media only screen and (max-width: 479px) {}
// mobile up to landscape mode
```

If you already have some CSS written, you can add these selectors below your existing code. Any rules in your existing code that are not overwritten by one of these selectors will remain in use, and become your "fall back" rules. This is why we did not include a media query for full size devices (although you could, if you wanted a different set of rules to be your fall back, say to assume a smaller device instead of a full size device as your default style).

Within each of these new selectors is where we would override our "normal" style to adjust our user experience. Anywhere we used floating divs will automatically adjust (within their parent container) as the window size changes. With these selectors, we can move other pieces of content around or even turn off some items that are unwieldy on smaller devices. Larger ads may be too large in screen size and file size for easy consumption on a mobile device. To disable it, we add a rule to the media section for smaller devices that hides that content. Imagine we have the following layout:

<table>
<tr><td colspan="3">Logo</td></tr>
<tr><td>Link 1
Link 2
Link 3</td><td>Flash ad
Content</td><td>An ad
Another ad</td></tr>
<tr><td colspan="3">Contact information</td></tr>
</table>

This layout could be represented by the following HTML and CSS:

```
<header><img src="ourlogo.png"></header>
<div id="container">
   <div id="left">
      <ul>
      <li><a href="">Link 1</a></li>
      <li><a href="">Link 2</a></li>
      <li><a href="">Link 3</a></li>
      </ul>
   </div>
   <div id="main">
      <div id="splash">[flash with id
         "video"]</div>
      <div id="content">Our text content
         here</div>
   </div>
   <div id="right">
      <div class="ad">an ad here</div>
      <div class="ad">another ad </div>
   </div>
   <br style="clear: left;" />
</div>
<footer>Contact Information</footer>
```

```
<style>
      div{
         border-style:dashed;
         border-width:1px;
      }
      header{
         background:url(ourlogo.png)
            no-repeat;
         background-size:200px 100px;
         background-position:center;
         height:100px;
      }
      #left{
         min-width:100px;
         max-width:150px;
         float:left;
      }
      #main{
         float:left;
      }
      #right{
         min-width:100px;
         max-width:150px;
         float:left;
      }
</style>
```

Which, in turn, could generate something like this once we add actual content:

Since we are using floated divs, the site will (eventually) conform to a top to bottom format that retains all content when it cannot fit across the display it is on. This is because float will place the elements in a line when the container is wide enough to hold them. When content is wider than the row, it is wrapped down to a new line. The max and min widths will help to ensure that content is not clipped, but while this helps us in some cases, the bulky flash video and large logo reduce the user's ability to browse from a mobile device. To adapt this example for users on smaller screens, we want to preserve all of the pertinent content while also preserving a good user experience. To do this, we will hide the video, put our links at the top, and move our ads to the bottom, all by adding media queries to our CSS. We will also opt for a smaller version of our logo. Since our current design was deemed flexible enough for other devices, we will just add the CSS selector for small screens:

```
<header><img src="ourlogo.png"></header>
<div id="container">
     <div id="left">
        <ul>
        <li><a href="">Link 1</a></li>
        <li><a href="">Link 2</a></li>
        <li><a href="">Link 3</a></li>
        </ul>
     </div>
     <div id="main">
        <div id="splash">[flash width id "video"]</div>
        <div id="content">Our text content here</div>
     </div>
     <div id="right">
        <div class="ad">an ad here</div>
        <div class="ad">another ad </div>
     </div>
     <br style="clear: left;" />
</div>
<footer>Contact Information</footer>
  <style>
     div{
        border-style:dashed;
        border-width: 1px;
     }
     header{
        background:url(ourlogo.png) no-repeat;
        background-size:200px 100px;
        background-position:center;
        height:100px;
     }
     #left{
        min-width:100px;
        max-width:150px;
        float:left;
     }
     #main{
        float:left;
```

```
    }
    #right{
        min-width:100px;
        max-width:150px;
        float:left;
    }
@media only screen and (max-width: 479px){
    video{ display:none; }
    #left{
        width:100%;
        float:none;
    }
    #main{
        width:100%;
        float:none;
    }
    #right{
        width:100%;
        float:none;
    }
    #header{
        background:url(http://www.vectortemplates.com/raster/
            batman-logo-big.gif) no-repeat;
        background-size:100px 60px;
        background-position:center;
        height:100px;
    }
}
</style>
```

Now, our floats and min/max rules will do the best they can until the device screen is less than 480 pixels. At that point our special style will kick in for mobile devices, putting our divs in a vertical row, hiding and resizing content, and making the divs as wide as the screen. Our site, without changing any HTML, will now look like the following:

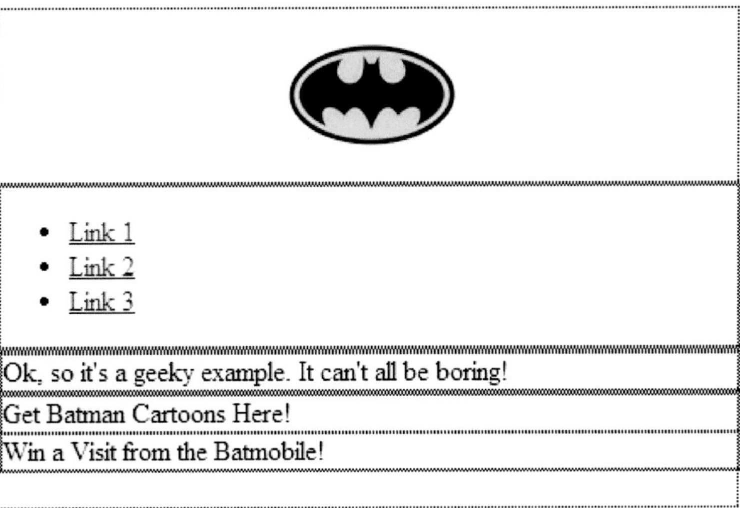

We can also use media queries to set styling for when a user prints our page, without requiring them to click a link to a special version (selecting print from a browser menu would trigger this style) by using @media print{}.

The full list of options for @media are as follows:

Table 6 Media Types

Name	Description
all	All devices.
aural	Text-to-speech readers.
braille	Tactile responsive devices.
embossed	Printing to braille printers.
handheld	Small portable devices.
print	Print view.
projection	Slides and presentations.
screen	Computer screens (regular size and up).
tty	Teletype terminals.
tv	TV displays.

Section 2 Assessments

For each of these assignment, complete each bulleted step and submit all files (HTML, CSS, scripts, images, etc.) necessary by zipping and submitting your assignment folder.

Your First Page:

- Your name, the course, and semester commented at the top of the file
- Create body, header, and footer sections
- Create a div named content between your header and footer
- Set a page title that displays in the browser tab
- Place an address in an address tag in your footer
- Your name at the top of the page as an <h1> heading in your header
- Add a few paragraphs about yourself to your content div
- Add a list of hobbies or interest displayed as an HTML unordered list to content
- Link at least two of your hobbies or interests to websites related to those interests

Fun with Media

- Your name, the course, and semester commented at the top of the file
- One image as part of your page
- A short audio clip (or link to available audio filand player
- A short video clip (or link to available videand player
- Set both audio and video clips to have controls and not play automatically
- Give your video clip a placeholder image

Tables on Chairs

- Recreate the following table in HTML
- Use style attributes to set cell colors as needed
- Use the caption tag to label your table

Production Levels for Chairs This Week:

	Monday	Tuesday	Wednesday	Thursday	Friday	Total
Stools	5	5	5	(quota met)		15
Rolling	(out of materials)			10	15	25
Standard Leg	4	8	12	4		28

Registration Form

- Create a form with an action attribute of post
- Give it the following fields, and a submit button:
  - First Name, Last Name
  - Email Address, Email Address Again
  - Age
  - A "Plan" select box that contains Basic, Premium, Titanium options
- A checkbox asking if the user wishes to be added to a mailing list
- A shirt size radio set that has values of Small, Medium, Large

Adding Some Style

- Using CSS rules, modify your "Your First Page" submission to include:
  - A background image that repeats to fill the screen
  - A background color on your content div
  - Modifying H1 to be 32 point and a different color from default
- Split your About Me and Hobbies sections into separate divs within Content
- Give your new divs a fixed width of 400 each and set them to sit side by side

Responsive Styling

- Add rules to your CSS to achieve the following:
  - Allow divs in your content section to shrink to 200px
  - Vertically align your content divs for screens smaller than the typical tablet
  - Shrink your h1 to fit on one line when on tablets and phones if needed
  - Only show the first paragraph of your About Me section on phones

Discussion / Written Response

1. Explain the W3C's stated reasoning as to why it was decided to stop moving all of CSS through version numbers as one cohesive unit. Do you agree or disagree

with this position, and why?

2. Discuss pros and cons of creating web applications using HTML5, CSS3, and other languages against creating the same application for each device's platform (i.e. Apple' iTunes, Google Play, Windows Store).

3. Discuss how XML differs from HTML, and where it is commonly used today.

4. Why is HTML considered a document markup languages as opposed to a programming language?

Questions

TAKE THIS QUIZ ONLINE!

1. What does HTML stand for?
    a. Hyperlinks and Text Markup Language
    b. Hyper Text Markup Language
    c. Home Tool Markup Language
    d. Hyper Text Manipulation Language
2. Choose the correct HTML tag for the largest heading.
    a. <heading>
    b. <h1>
    c. <header>
    d. <h6>
3. Which of these is a properly formatted link?
    a. <a link="www.google.com">Link</a>
    b. <a href="www.google.com"/>
    c. <link location="www.google.com">Link</a>
    d. <a href="www.google.com">Link</a>
4. How can you open a link in a new tab/browser window?
    a. <a href="url" target="_blank">
    b. <a href="url" target="new">
    c. <a href="url" new>
5. Which doctype is correct for HTML5?
    a. <!DOCTYPE HTML5>
    b. <!DOCTYPE html>

c. <!DOCTYPE HTML PUBLIC "-//W3C//DTD HTML 5.0//EN" "http://www.w3.org/TR/html5/strict.dtd">

6. What is the correct HTML for making a drop-down list?
   a. <select>
   b. <input type="dropdown">
   c. <input type="list">
   d. <list>
7. Which of the following is correct?
   a. HTML is used for exchanging data, XML is not.
   b. XML is used for exchanging data, HTML is not.
   c. HTML can have user defined tags, XML cannot.
   d. Both b and c above.
8. What is the correct HTML5 element for playing video files?
   a. <movie>
   b. <video>
   c. <source>
   d. None of the above
9. What is the correct HTML for inserting an image?
   a. <img src="image.gif" alt="MyImage">
   b. <image src="image.gif" alt="MyImage">
   c. <img href="image.gif" alt="MyImage">
   d. <img alt="MyImage">image.gif</img>
10. The <canvas> element in HTML5 is used to:
    a. Display database records
    b. Manipulate data in MySQL
    c. Create draggable elements
    d. Draw graphics
11. In HTML5, which attribute is used to specify that an input field must be filled out?
    a. Formvalidate
    b. Validate
    c. placeholder
    d. required
12. Which HTML5 element is used to display a measurement within a fixed range?
    a. <gauge>
    b. <range>
    c. <measure>

d. <meter>

13. What does CSS stand for?
    a. Cross-site scripting
    b. Cascading Style Sheets
    c. Creative style sheets
    d. Compiled site styles
14. Given the following, what value does the left margin have?: margin: 10px 5px 20px 15px;
    a. 10px
    b. 5px
    c. 20px
    d. 15px
15. Which style rule overrides the other?
    a. Class
    b. Id
16. What property creates space between HTML elements?
    a. Margin
    b. Padding
    c. Spacing
    d. Float
17. What property creates space within an element?
    a. Margin
    b. Padding
    c. Spacing
    d. Float
18. Which set of tags are used to define CSS within the page?
    a. <style type="css"></style>
    b. <class type="text/css"></class>
    c. <inline css></inline>
    d. None of the above
19. Which of these is the correct way to define a hover state for an anchor tag?
    a. :onHover
    b. :mouseOver
    c. :hover
    d. None of These

20. Which property of a position rule will force content to a position regardless of other elements?
    a. Fixed
    b. Absolute
    c. Relative
    d. Strict
21. Responsive styling allows us to support many devices with one style sheet.
    a. True
    b. False
22. Which of the following is the best fit for defining styles on small mobile devices?
    a. @media only screen and (max-width: 479p)
    b. @media only screen and (max-width: 769p)
    c. @media only screen and (max-width: 120p)

CHECK YOUR ANSWERS ON PAGE 280

Section 3:

Scripting Languages

Section Contents:

Server-Side and Client-Side Scripting
Creating PHP Files
PHP Errors
PHP Output
Data Storage
Data Manipulation
Email
File Interaction
Structures
Functions
Objects and Classes
JavaScript Syntax
JavaScript Examples
jQuery

Learning Objectives:

By the end of this section, you should be able to demonstrate:

1. An ability to create PHP scripts
2. An ability to receive, store, and manipulate user data
3. An ability to interact with files
4. The ability to create and send basic email
5. The ability to use logic and control structures in scripts
6. The ability to create functions and simple classes
7. Altering a page using JavaScript and jQuery

Chapter 23

Server-Side and Client-Side Scripting

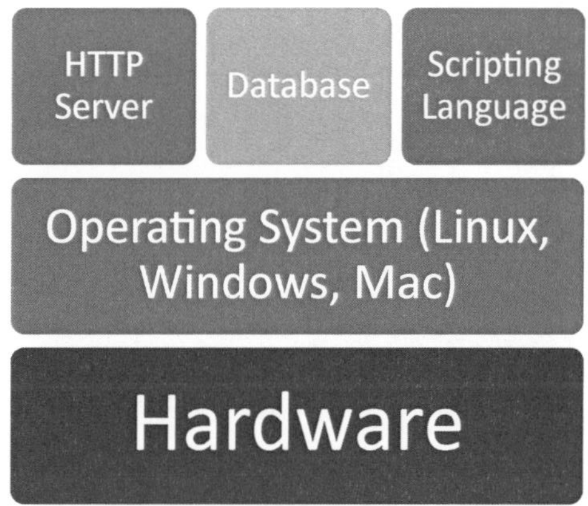

PHP

Created in 1994 at the hands of Rasmus Lerdorf, PHP began as a set of CGI scripts developed to track views of his resume online. Rasmus continued adding scripts to his collection so he could do more with his websites. Over time, some friends began to use it as well. By June of 1995, enough of a framework was in place that Rasmus decided to make PHP public. As others embraced it, and began to submit their own work, PHP grew. By version 3 it was decided that the time had come for a more professional name. In homage to its original name of Personal Home Page, the PHP acronym was kept, but was changed to a recursive representation of "hypertext preprocessor." PHP was now an independent language, with object-oriented capabilities, high extensibility, and had a growing following.

As the community grew, the core team of Rasmus, Andi Gutmans and Zeev Suraski continued their work. Gutmans and Suraski rewrote the core of the engine, and dubbed version 4 Zend, a blend of Gutmans and Suraski's first names. Now with dozens of developers and even more contributors, PHP has grown to version 5, and is installed on tens of millions of servers around the world. It continues to rank as one of the top ten web development languages.

With strong semblance to languages like C++ and Perl, the goal was to create a language that allowed fast development of dynamic pages. It is a server-side language, which means it runs on the server before anything is sent to the user's computer. This is in contrast to client-side languages, where the code is sent to the user's computer to be processed locally with languages like JavaScript.

Some advantages to server-side languages are that the code is hidden from the user, and secures what is taking place in the background. It also reduces the work load that the user's computer is burdened with. This, however, also means the server must be powerful enough to support the number of users requesting pages, as it must bear the brunt of the computation.

PHP is a parsing engine, which means it examines the php file, performs any php related tasks it finds, and passes the result to the web server. This makes it an interpreted language, as the output and script are run on demand, as opposed to a compiled language where the code is transformed and saved into a runnable form.

JavaScript

JavaScript is a client-side script, meaning the browser processes the code instead of the web server. Client-side scripts are commonly used when we want to validate data before sending it to the web server, adjusting the interface in response to user feedback, and for implementing other advanced features. Since JavaScript is part of the browser, it can be run without a web server present. If the computer is slow or busy, the performance of our code may be reduced. If JavaScript is disabled (less of a concern today than just a few years ago) then our script will not run. This being said, this is less of an issue now, and JavaScript can reduce the number of communications to a server, reducing transmission time and improving performance.

JavaScript will be our client-side scripting example. As JavaScript can be handled within the browser, we can capitalize on it to validate user data, react to user actions that affect appearance, and interact with the user's computer, without requiring the involvement of their internet connection or our server. Like CSS, JavaScript is not a fully formed language that can stand on its own. Like PHP and Java, JavaScript is an object-oriented language that is multi-platform. Unlike Java (but still like PHP) it is a loose, typed language.

There is a common misconception that Java and JavaScript are the same thing. Review some of the larger differences between them below if you are already familiar with Java.

Table 7 Java vs JavaScript

JavaScript	Java
Object-oriented. No distinction between types of objects. Inheritance is through the prototype mechanism, and properties and methods can be added to any object dynamically.	Class-based. Objects are divided into classes and instances with all inheritance through the class hierarchy. Classes and instances cannot have properties or methods added dynamically.
Variable data types are not declared (dynamic typing).	Variable data types must be declared (static typing).
Cannot automatically write to hard disk.	Cannot automatically write to hard disk.

Writing JavaScript code is a lot like writing PHP. Both languages use many of the same concepts and can look very similar in terms of code. Since we will have covered many of the foundational concepts JavaScript uses in the PHP section, we will focus on differences between JavaScript and PHP. We will look at examples that highlight how JavaScript can be integrated with other languages, like responding to event driven actions to modify our pages in real time. Bear in mind that the power of the language can be used to perform many of the same tasks we have examined already in PHP.

A best practice for using JavaScript in your site is to create your entire site without it, and then add it where it can improve the user experience (a process called progressive enhancement). This will help ensure that your site will still operate (albeit maybe not as attractively) if JavaScript is not present.

Chapter 24

Creating PHP Files

Like the HTML and CSS files we have already created, PHP also uses a special file format to identify its contents. When you want to use PHP in a file, even if it was already .htm or .html, you will need to set (or create) the file format as .php.

If you do not have access to a server with PHP, you can follow along this section of the text by using http://writecodeonline.com/php/ to try the examples and write your own code.

ADDITIONAL NOTES

Technically, you could insert PHP code into HTML files (or other formats) and have it run, by changing settings on your server for how it serves and interacts with the file extension in question. You could also do the same with HTML in a text file, or other combinations. The drawback is this could also affect other files on your server, and makes your site less portable to other servers.

Long, Short Tags

As you begin to work with PHP, you will undoubtedly see code examples that begin with <?php or <?, while both will end with ?>. These are tags, just like in HTML, and are used to mark the start and end of a section of code that contains PHP (we could even use <script language='php'></script>). PHP can be interspersed, or cohabitate, in a web page among HTML and other languages like JavaScript. The difference between the two opening tags is that <?php is longhand writing, while <? Is considered shorthand. By default, all PHP capable servers will recognize longhand while shorthand is an option that must be enabled. For best support of your code, and to better recognize what language is being used, always use longhand when writing your code.

Chapter 25

PHP Errors

Before starting, an understanding of errors will help you quickly recognize where problems exist (and if they are truly problems) in your code, which will lend to faster debugging and understanding where to look for problems.

To start with, we can tell PHP what kind of errors we want to know about before we even run a script. While the full list of supported reporting levels (see Table 8 PHP Errors) covers a variety of concerns, there are a few (notices, errors, and warnings) that cover what we will run into most often.

Notices

```
Notice: Undefined index: message in /home/example.php on line 9
```

Notices, technically, are not errors. They will notify us of things that we may have intended or wanted, but that PHP can do without. For example, using a variable on a page without declaring it first will generate a notice. PHP will create the variable as soon as it is called, even if we did not declare it, without creating a formal error (other languages would consider this an error worthy of breaking execution). By notifying us but still continuing, if we had already declared or used the variable elsewhere, this notice would indicate a spelling error or mistyped variable name.

Warnings

```
Warning: main(): Failed opening 'noFileHere.php' for inclusion
on line 2
```

Warnings still will not stop our script from running, but indicate that something has gone wrong during execution of a script. Attempting to use include() on a file that does not exist would create a warning.

Errors

```
PHP Fatal error: Undefined class constant 'MYSQL_ATTR_USE_BUFF-
ERED_QUERY' in database.inc on line 43
```

Finally, errors are unrecoverable (execution will stop). Typical causes of errors are parsing errors like missing semi-colons, function, or class definitions, or other problems the engine does not know how to resolve. If we used require() on a file instead of include, an error would be triggered instead.

Most errors that we will receive are parsing errors. They are typically problems caused by *what* we wrote in our code, like missing brackets, semi-colons, or typos. When we receive an error, the compiler will tell us what problem it discovered and where. Keep in mind that we are being told where an error was *found* not necessary where the source of the problem exists. For example, a missing semi colon or bracket may have occurred several lines before it created a problems for the compiler.

The other category of errors we will run into are logical. These are errors caused by *how* we wrote our code, and can be much more frustrating. Logical errors are usually discovered when the script does not behave as expected. The source can be mistakes in what code we run in different parts of an if/then statement or even an error in math used in a function that gives us the wrong solution.

Resolving errors can be something of an art form. With parse errors, the engine can guide you to the area to help you begin looking for the source of the error. Logical errors can usually be resolved by adding extra, temporary outputs to follow the value of a variable or trace execution of logic statements through a script. This technique can help you find where what happens differs from what you expect. Unit testing your functions will go a long way toward preventing many of these issues, as does iterative programming.

To dictate what errors we do and do not wish to see in our script output, we will use the error_reporting() function. By passing one or more of the constants below, we control what is reported. For example, maybe we want information on warnings and errors, but do not care about notices. To do this, we can call error_reporting(E_WARNING | E_ERROR). The pipe symbol (|)works as an or in this case. If we want to see everything except notices we can use E_ALL but leave out notices with the carrot (^) character to indicate an exception with error_reporting(E_ALL ^ E_NOTICE). It is good practice to set your error reporting level close to the top of your script, so you can easily find it and change settings:

```
<?php
   error_reporting(E_WARNING | E_ERROR);
//This next line will trigger a notice that the variable does
not exist, but we will not see it
echo $test;
?>
<?php
   error_reporting(E_ALL);
//This time we will see the notice
echo $test;
?>
Notice: Undefined variable: test on line 3
```

You may be wondering why we would selectively show or hide errors; when we are developing our code, the system errors we will need to see in order to debug are different from what we would want end users to see for a system in production. Revealing, verbatim, the system generated error message is not only confusing to non-programmers but can expose sensitive information to those with malicious intent. Instead, we would provide a message we chose in the error's place. Take a look at the full list of error reporting levels:

Table 8 PHP Errors

Constant	Description
E_ERROR	Fatal run-time errors. These indicate errors that cannot be recovered from, such as a memory allocation problem. Execution of the script is halted.
E_WARNING	Run-time warnings (non-fatal errors). Execution of the script is not halted.
E_PARSE	Compile-time parse errors. Parse errors should only be generated by the parser.
E_NOTICE	Run-time notices. Indicate that the script encountered something that could indicate an error, but could also happen in the normal course of running a script.
E_CORE_ERROR	Fatal errors that occur during PHP's initial startup. This is like an E_ERROR, except it is generated by the core of PHP.
E_CORE_WARNING	Warnings (non-fatal errors) that occur during PHP's initial startup. This is like an E_WARNING, except it is generated by the core of PHP.
E_COMPILE_ERROR	Fatal compile-time errors. This is like an E_ERROR, except it is generated by the Zend Scripting Engine.
E_COMPILE_WARNING	Compile-time warnings (non-fatal errors). This is like an E_WARNING, except it is generated by the Zend Scripting Engine.
E_USER_ERROR	User-generated error message. This is like an E_ERROR, except it is generated in PHP code by using the PHP function trigger_error().
E_USER_WARNING	User-generated warning message. This is like an E_WARNING, except it is generated in PHP code by using the PHP function trigger_error().
E_USER_NOTICE	User-generated notice message. This is like an E_NOTICE, except it is generated in PHP code by using the PHP function trigger_error().
E_STRICT	Enable to have PHP suggest changes to your code which will ensure the best interoperability and forward compatibility of your code.
E_RECOVERABLE_ERROR	Catchable fatal error. It indicates that a probably dangerous error occurred, but did not leave the Engine in an unstable state. If the error is not caught by a user defined handle (see also set_error_handler()), the application aborts as it was an E_ERROR.
E_DEPRECATED	Run-time notices. Enable this to receive warnings about code that will not work in future versions.
E_USER_DEPRECATED	User-generated warning message. This is like an E_DEPRECATED, except it is generated in PHP code by using the PHP function trigger_error().
E_ALL	All errors and warnings, as supported, except of level E_STRICT prior to PHP 5.4.0.

Adapted from php.net, Creative Commons 3.0 Attribution Unported

Chapter 26

PHP Output

Print, Echo

PHP allows for two methods of sending output to the screen. One is called print, the other echo. While they provide the same functionality, echo is a construct (it will be treated as a command), where print is an expression (it will be evaluated and will return a value). When we use print or echo in PHP, both can be used as constructs (called without parenthesis after them, as if they are a command) or as a function (called with parenthesis like a function call). Print will return a 1 as a result when it is used, while echo will not return anything.

Ultimately, the differences between print and echo are negligible. Debates over which to use range from consistency of verbiage, speed of processing (print technically takes four operating commands to echo's three as it has one more step of returning the 1), and obscure examples of where one might win out over the other.

For our examination here, use what you like. In extreme examples, a high volume of echos will be faster than a high volume of print statements, but there are far more important places to consider refining code for speed than any gains you might find here.

To send output to the screen, we can start with the famous example of Hello, World!

```
<?php echo "Hello, World!"; ?>
```

We can also wrap the string in parenthesis as we discussed above if you feel it makes things more clear:

```
<?php echo ("Hello, World!"); ?>
```

Congratulations, you have just created your first PHP web page!

We can get a little more in depth before moving on with another example. When functions return something to us, we usually save that value and then take action on it. We can also send the output directly to the screen if we know it is formatted how we want to view it. The phpinfo() function for example gives us access to all the details about our server. If we use it without requesting a specific piece of information, it defaults to returning a full web page with all the details about our server. We can see this by using the following:

```
<?php echo phpinfo(); ?>
```

This screen shot is just a portion of the entire response, which is usually several pages long. Keep this function in mind, as it is a convenient way of finding the settings of your server without digging into your config files.

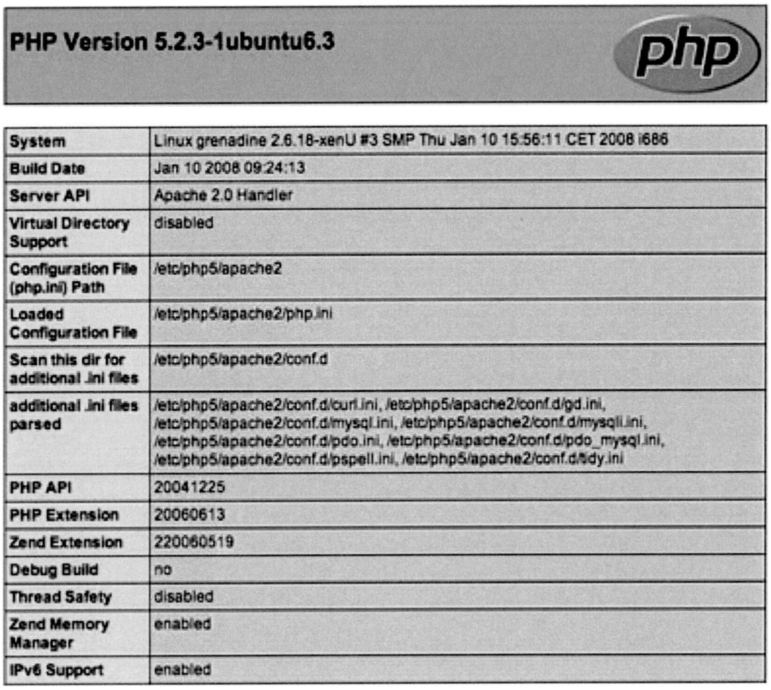

PHP Version 5.2.3-1ubuntu6.3 php

System	Linux grenadine 2.6.18-xenU #3 SMP Thu Jan 10 15:56:11 CET 2008 i686
Build Date	Jan 10 2008 09:24:13
Server API	Apache 2.0 Handler
Virtual Directory Support	disabled
Configuration File (php.ini) Path	/etc/php5/apache2
Loaded Configuration File	/etc/php5/apache2/php.ini
Scan this dir for additional .ini files	/etc/php5/apache2/conf.d
additional .ini files parsed	/etc/php5/apache2/conf.d/curl.ini, /etc/php5/apache2/conf.d/gd.ini, /etc/php5/apache2/conf.d/mysql.ini, /etc/php5/apache2/conf.d/mysqli.ini, /etc/php5/apache2/conf.d/pdo.ini, /etc/php5/apache2/conf.d/pdo_mysql.ini, /etc/php5/apache2/conf.d/pspell.ini, /etc/php5/apache2/conf.d/tidy.ini
PHP API	20041225
PHP Extension	20060613
Zend Extension	220060519
Debug Build	no
Thread Safety	disabled
Zend Memory Manager	enabled
IPv6 Support	enabled

LEARN MORE

Keywords, search terms: Troubleshooting php, common programming errors

Common Programming Mistakes: http://www.dummies.com/how-to/content/troubleshooting-a-php-script.html

Debugging with Print and Eclipse: http://www.ibm.com/developerworks/library/os-debug/

Chapter 27

Data Storage

Variables

Variables are created and used when our script runs in order to create references to (store copies of) pieces of information that are needed for a short span of time, or are expected to change value as the script runs. They contain a reference to a place in the server's memory where the value is stored, not the actual content. This tells the parser where to look to find the information we want. PHP is a loosely typed language, which means we do not have to tell the computer what type of information we are going to keep in a variable. In strictly typed languages, we would have to specify if the variable was going to be an integer, string, float, or other option supported by the language in use. Trying to store a different type of information than declared in a variable would result in an error. PHP will not give us an error or check this by default. This eliminates the need to declare variables, but this can result in some confusing bugs in your code. Those of you with experience in a strictly typed language like C++ will be happy to note that although not required, PHP will allow declarations, and will then give errors upon their misuse.

Variables in PHP must start with a dollar sign ($), and can be followed by an underscore (_) or letter (a through z, both upper and lower case). Variables cannot start with a number, but may contain numbers after an underscore or at least one letter; they also cannot contain a space, as spaces are used to determine where commands, variables, and other elements start and end. See the table below for examples:

Table 9 PHP Variable Naming

GOOD	BAD
$_first	$1st
$LastName	$(first)name
$standard_tax_rate	$first name
$last4SSN	$final$

- Booleans Can have a value of 0 or 1
- Integers Whole numbers (1, 3, 20, etc.)
- Floating point numbers Decimal values (1.33, 34.2325)
- Strings Contain any number of characters
- Arrays Structured lists of information
- Objects Collections of related variables and functions
- Resources Special variables that hold reference points to things like files
- NULL An empty (unused or unset) variable
- Callbacks A mechanism to reference a function declared elsewhere

In the scope of this text we will cover most of these items with exception to callbacks, and with only a cursory examination of objects. If you plan to focus on application development, this would be a good area to continue studying. For most web development, there is little call for robust object-oriented programming.

To create a variable in PHP, we first give the name we wish to use, followed by what we want to assign to the variable. In PHP, the equal sign (=) is used to assign what is on the right hand side to what is on the left hand side (we will see how to check login statements later on). To create a variable called ourString with the value of Hello World, we would enter the following:

```
$ourString = 'Hello World';
```

We can now refer to $ourString in one or more places of our code in order to access the string Hello World and use it or modify it.

You might notice the semi-colon (;) at the end of the line. Semi-colons are used to tell the interpreter where a statement ends, and where the next one begins. They are easy to forget! If you see a syntax error, you will want to look at the line before the error to see if a semi-colon is missing.

PHP also maintains some variables of its own, called predefined variables. These start with underscores, and will hold certain types of values for us (avoiding the use of underscores at the start of your variables will help avoid colliding with these reserved variables). Several of these variables ($_GET, $_POST and $_FILES) will hold items a user has typed or submitted using forms. $_COOKIE and $_SESSION are used to hold information throughout a user's visit, and $_ENV holds information about the server.

Incrementing Methods

Until now, we have been using the equal sign strictly for assigning strings to variables. We can also use some short hand methods of modifying numerical variables within our code. For example, adding 1 to the variable $counter can be done with:

```
$counter = $counter + 1;
```

But we can shorten that by using the "plus equal":

```
$counter +=1;
```

Or if we only need to add 1, the "plus plus":

```
$counter++;
```

In these example, each one would add 1 to the counter. In the first two examples, we could add more than one, or perform a calculation to be added. We can also perform the opposite calculation, in that we can subtract and assign a given number as well by using -= or --. Where and how you choose to embrace these is up to you, but you should be familiar with each form in order to fully understand any code you are examining.

Strings

In our first echo examples, we printed a string to the screen. Strings are a type of variable that hold, as seems obvious, strings of words. Full sentences can be stored in one variable name, or can be built by combining other variables. Manipulating strings in PHP can be done through a number of functions, which can complete tasks like finding and replacing words, breaking strings apart, capitalizing one or all words, and a number of other useful tasks.

Strings can be used to create output that the user reads, generate part or all of the HTML code for a page to display, and even commands that can be passed to other languages to direct their operation.

Single, Double Quotes

Until now, when we have used strings, they have been double quoted. PHP actually lets us use both single and double quotes when defining our strings to support different functions. There is an important difference between the two that we need to keep in mind. Single quoted strings are treated by the interpreter as plain text, meaning the output to the screen will be exactly what is in quotes. Double quoted strings will be examined by the interpreter for anything that can be processed by PHP, which means items like special characters and variables will be replaced with what they represent before the output is sent to the screen. For example, if we set a variable named string to Hello and use it in our output, single quotes will ignore it while double quotes will process it:

```
$string = "Hello"; // The quotes we use here do not matter for
this example
echo "$string there";
echo '$string there';
Hello there
$string there
```

Escaping

Escape characters are symbols with special, secondary meaning when coupled with the language's escaping method. We can indicate that we want a new line in a text file by using \n. In this example, n is not "just an n," it represents that we want a newline because it is preceded by a backslash, PHP's escaping character. In PHP, escape characters are commonly used in double-quoted strings, so we can include special characters (single quoted string will ignore this, just like other PHP commands, variables, and the like).

A helpful way to think about the escape character is that it "reverses" the character or symbol that comes after it. If it precedes a letter, then it is supposed to do something, not display the letter. If it precedes a symbol, the symbol has a special value in PHP, but we actually want to see the character.

Table 10 Character Escaping

\"	Print the double quote, not use it as a string opening or closing marker
\'	Print the single quote, not use it as a string opening or closing marker
\n	Print a new line character (for text or output files, not on the screen)
\t	Print a tab character
\r	Print a carriage return (for text or output files, not on the screen)
\$	Print the next character as a dollar sign, not as part of a variable
\\	Print the next character as a backslash, not an escape character

Writing $string = "I want to spend $5.00"; would result in a name error. Instead, we can use $string= "I want to spend \$5.00"; to achieve the output we are looking for. If we wanted to use the backslash, we could write a folder location as $address = "c:\\www\\ourfolder\\sometext.txt";. While we could more easily do this with single quotes as $address = 'c:\www\ourfolder\sometext.txt'; we would need to append any variables we wanted to reference into the string that is single quoted.

Constants

Sometimes we need to store a piece of information, but we do not want it to change while our script is running. To do this, we can create a constant—essentially, a variable that we are not allowed to change. Creating a constant is done by calling the define function, and passing a string of our constant's name and its contents:

```
define("OURCONSTANT", "Our constant value");
```

You will notice we do not have a dollar sign in front of our constant name. In fact, to use it, we can just echo the name:

```
echo OURCONSTANT;
```

Our example here has the constant name all uppercase. This is a practice many people use to help distinguish between variables and constants. There are also some predefined constants in PHP that can be useful to us, such as PHP_VERSION and PHP_OS. The former will give us the version number for PHP, and the latter will give us details on the operating system the server is running on. Since constants do not have a leading dollar sign, we cannot embed them in a string, but instead need to concatenate them if we want to use them with other output:

```
echo " This server runs on " . PHP_OS;
```

Concatenation is the act of connecting several items into one variable or output. A period is used as we did above to denote where those pieces start and end. If we wanted to add more to our statement, we can keep adding periods like this:

```
echo "This server runs on ". PHP_OS . " and use PHP version ".
PHP_VERSION;
```

Arrays

Arrays are a much dreaded topic to many programmers, and almost as frustrating as a missing terminating character. For the uninitiated, an array is a method of storing multiple values under one variable name as a linked list of information. This allows us to keep related values together, and to establish relationships between data. Typically, array information is stored in one of two different formats, either numeric or associative. In numerical format, each element in the list (or, each piece of information) is found by referring to its place in line. Depending on your programming language, counting may start at 1 or 0. In our case, by default, PHP starts with 0. In order to take a look at an array, we should follow best practices and declare our variable as an empty one to begin with. We can do this with:

```
$ourFirstArray = array();
```

Now the system will know that we intend to use this variable as an array. If we try to echo or print our array, we would see the following output:

```
Array
```

In order to see the contents of an array, we need to refer to an actual position or view the entire contents. Since we have not added anything yet, we will move along for now.

Here we will create a new array, but one in which we already know what we want the first few values to be. We will set up the cast of Family Guy as an array called theGriffins.

```
$theGriffins = array("Peter","Lois","Stewie","Chris","Brian");
```

Now we can take a look at some output. If we wanted to see what the first element of the array held, we could:

```
echo $theGriffins[0];
```

which would give us:

```
Peter
```

Or, to take a quick look at the entire array, we can use the built in function print_r, which means print recursively, and will output each value for us in a preformatted manner:

```
print_r($theGriffins);
Array(
0: Peter
1: Lois
2: Stewie
3: Chris
4: Brian
)
```

Now, something seems amiss. Is someone missing? Oh yes, Meg. Let's add her to our array. To add a new element to the end of an array, we do not need to worry about knowing how long it is, or what number to assign to the new element. With PHP we can simply append [] to our variable name, adding Meg as a new element at the end of our array:

```
$theGriffins[]='Meg';
```

Now if we run print_r, we would see:

```
Array(
0: Peter
1: Lois
```

```
2: Stewie
3: Chris
4: Brian
5: Meg
)
```

Perhaps we want to make things a little more formal, and use full first names. In this case, we need to update a few things. First, we should change Stewie to Stewart. Since we have the reference right above this text we can see that Stewie is at position 2 (item 3) in the array. So let us set that position to his full name:

```
$theGriffins[2]='Stewart';
```

Your print $theGriffins[2]; should now give you Stewart instead of Stewie! By placing the item's position number in the brackets of our array variable, we are specifying that we want to see the information that is stored in that spot. Perhaps you have forgotten where in the array you stored a particular value. Most languages supporting arrays will already have built in functions for common tasks such as this. In PHP, we can use the array_search function. In this case, we pass the values as a "needle in a haystack" pair, giving the function first what we are looking for, and then the array in which we hope to find it:

```
echo array_search("Meg", $theGriffins);
```

will give us:

```
4
```

Note that close matches would be ignored. The interpreter does not know that Pete and Peter, or Meg and Megan represent the same common name. For these types of searches, we would need much more complex algorithms.

In order to update the Meg value to Megan, we will combine our techniques:

```
$location = array_search("Meg", $theGriffins);
$theGriffins[$location] = 'Megan';
```

We could, for the sake of brevity, take advantage of the inner first nature of the PHP interpreter and combine our statements:

```
$theGriffins[array_search("Meg", $theGriffins)]='Megan';
```

Now that we are a bit more comfortable with numbered arrays, we will take a look at associative. In this approach, we provide the reference in which we want a position in the array to be named. For instance, perhaps we want to give short descriptions of each character so someone unfamiliar with the show is better able to recognize them. To distinguish details by character, we will use their names in place of numbers. Our initial array from before with names and descriptions could look as follows:

```
$theGriffins = array("Peter"=>"The fat guy", "Lois=>"The red
head", "Stewie"=>"The baby", "Chris"=>"The awkward boy",
"Brian"=>"The Dog");
```

Now that our array is associative, we pass the identifying piece of information we are looking for. This is done as a key and value pair, where the key is the associative word you can reference and the values is still what is stored. You will notice we used => in our declaration this time, which identifies what comes before the => as the key, and what follows as the value. So to find out what we know about Lois:

```
print $theGriffins['lois'];
```

gives us:

```
The red head
```

Note that we need to put the associative key in quotes (single or double) when using print or echo.

Reading Get, Post

Earlier we discussed how to set a form to use Get or Post to transmit data to be processed. To access these pieces of information, PHP has two built in arrays that store what is transmitted under $_POST and $_GET. These are reserved variables that are always available in your code whether or not any information was sent in that manner (in which case, the variable will simply be an empty array). When we want to see the value of a form element sent using Get with a field name of firstName, we would use:

```
print $_GET['firstName'];
```

If it was sent using post, all we would change is the variable name:

```
print $_POST['firstName'];
```

To save changes to the variable, we can place the results of the desired change to a local variable we create, or assign them back to the array position in our GET or POST array. The only way of keeping the changed material for use on another page, though, is to resubmit the data to the page. I recommend using local variables so this is easier to keep in mind.

Note that when you use GET or POST variables inside of a double quoted string, the single quote characters are not needed in the array element request and will create an error. For example:

```
print "My first name is $_POST[firstName]";
```

We can also easily see everything that was sent by using the print_r function or var_dump like this:

```
print_r($_GET);
```

Now that we are interacting with data that is not under our control (given to us by the user, or another outside source) we have to keep in mind that what they send us cannot be trusted. If the user gave us a value we did not expect, or if someone is attempting to be malicious, we would be interacting with data that could cause errors or introduce security problems in our site. We address this through validation and sanitization (see Integration Examples), which are techniques that help us address potential problems with data we did not create.

Cookies and Sessions

Cookies and sessions are mechanisms we can use to store and use information from any page on our site. These approaches allow us to do this without having to pass information between pages using forms or special links as we have up to this point. Cookies achieve this by storing very small files on the user's computer. They are typically used to hold onto information that identifies the user, whether or not they are logged in, or other information the user needs to achieve their full experience with the site. Cookies can be set to expire after a fixed amount of time, or "forever," by setting an expiration date far after the computer or user is likely to still be around.

Sessions allow the same storing of information, but achieve it by storing the information on the server (instead of your computer) for a fixed amount of time (usually up to 15 minutes unless the user stays active). This means sessions will still work even when the user's security settings block cookies. The use of cookies can be disabled a number of ways such as the use of security software, browser settings, and ad blockers. For this reason it can be useful to use both in your site, allowing as much functional use as possible even when cookies are denied, but still capitalizing on their longer persistence when they are available.

To create a cookie, we need to call the setcookie() function and pass it some variables. At a minimum, we need to give our cookie a name and a value for it to store. The name is how we will refer to it, and the value is what we want stored, just like any other variable we would create. Additionally, we can provide setcookie() with an expiration time, a path, a domain, and a secure flag.

The time, if passed, must be the number of seconds after creation that the cookie is considered valid for. We can achieve this by passing the time() function, which defaults to the current time, and adding seconds to it. For example, passing time()+60 means the current time plus 60 seconds. If we want to make it 15 minutes, we can pass the math along instead of doing it ourselves by passing time()+60*15. 60 seconds, 15 times, is 15 minutes. One whole day (60 seconds, 60 times = 1 hour. 24 hours in a day) would be time()+60*60*24.

By default, our cookie will be considered valid on all pages within the folder we are in when we create it. We can specify another folder (and its subfolders) by placing it in the path option. The same holds true for domain, where we can specify that a cookie is only good in certain parts of our site like an admin subdomain.

Finally, we can pass a true or false (false is the default) for secure. When set to true, the cookie can only be used on an https connection to our site.

We can pass the values we want in the following order:

```
setcookie(name, value, expire, path, domain, secure);
```

A simple example setting user=12345 for a day in our admin section of our site could look like the following:

```
<?php setcookie("user","12345",time()+60*60*24,,admin.oursite.
com); ?>
```

From any page in the admin.oursite.com portion of our domain, we can now use $_COOKIE["user"] to get the value 12345. If we want to store other values, we can pass an array to our cookie, or create other cookies for other values. To change a value in our cookie, we simply use setcookie and give the same name with our new value:

```
<?php setcookie("user","23456"); ?>
```

Finally, if we want to get rid of our cookie early (i.e. our user logs out) then we simply set the cookie to a time in the past, and the user's computer will immediately get rid of it as it is expired:

```
<?php setcookie("users","",time()-60*60); ?>
```

In this example we set our cookie to an hour ago.

A session works much the same way, and can be created by calling session_start(); at the top of our page. We can then set, update, and delete variables from the session like any other array by using the reserved array $_SESSION[]. To add our user again, we would type:

```
<?php session_start(); $_SESSION["user"]="12345"; ?> <html>
rest of page here...
```

It is important to remember that session_start() must be before the opening of any content, thus above the <html> tag. Once on a different page, we would call session_start() at the top again to declare that session values are allowed to be used on that page. Once we have done that, we can continue to use $_SESSION[] values anywhere on that page. If the user is inactive (does not leave the page or, click any links, or otherwise trigger an action to the server) for 15 minutes (the default value) the session is automatically destroyed.

We can manually remove items from our session by calling unset(), for example:

```
<?php session_start(); unset($_SESSION['User']; ?>
```

Or we can jump right to ending the entire session by using the session_destroy function:

```
<?php session_destroy(); ?>
```

This will remove the entire $_SESSION[] array from memory. Create or modify another PHP page in your collection (in the same folder and site as the current example). In this second page, you will be able to call the same values out of your cookie or session (as long as you include session_start() in this file as well) without passing any information directly between the pages.

LEARN MORE

Keywords, search terms: Variables, strings, arrays, cookies, session, data persistence

Sorting Arrays: http://php.net/manual/en/array.sorting.php

All string functions: http://php.net/manual/en/ref.strings.php

PHP Sessions: http://www.sitepoint.com/php-sessions/

Evolving Toward a Persistence Layer: http://net.tutsplus.com/tutorials/php/evolving-toward-a-persistence-layer/

Chapter 28

Data Manipulation

Comparison Operators

PHP supports many of the mathematical comparisons common to programming languages, such as equivalence and relative value comparison. The symbols used however may be different than what you are used to. In the chart below we will look at how to represent each comparison test, and under what condition we can expect the test to come back as true.

Table 11 Comparison Operators

Example	Name	Result
\$a == \$b	Equal	TRUE if *\$a* is equal to *\$b*.
\$a === \$b	Identical	TRUE if *\$a* is equal to *\$b*, and they are of the same type. (introduced in PHP 4)
\$a != \$b	Not equal	TRUE if *\$a* is not equal to *\$b*.
\$a <> \$b	Not equal	TRUE if *\$a* is not equal to *\$b*.
\$a !== \$b	Not identical	TRUE if *\$a* is not equal to *\$b*, or they are not of the same type. (introduced in PHP 4)
\$a < \$b	Less than	TRUE if *\$a* is strictly less than *\$b*.
\$a > \$b	Greater than	TRUE if *\$a* is strictly greater than *\$b*.
\$a <= \$b	Less than or equal to	TRUE if *\$a* is less than or equal to *\$b*.
\$a >= \$b	Greater than or equal to	TRUE if *\$a* is greater than or equal to *\$b*.

These tests will come in handy as we move into logic structures. The results of these comparisons can help us determine a course of action like what is displayed to the user, how we modify or create data, or respond to user input. Pay close attention to the difference between the equal (==) and identical (===) tests. Equal means the comparison of each side is considered the same. For example, 1 and True are considered equal, because PHP will treat a 1 as both an integer and a binary representation of true. If we want to ensure elements are the same in both value and type, we would use strictly equal. This test returns a false in our example, as 1 and true are not both integers of the value 1. Also, do not forget at least the second =, as just one will be treated as assignment, not a logical test!

Order of Operations

PHP follows the traditional order of operations used in mathematics, as found below. An associativity of "left" means the parser will read left to right across the equation. "Right" means it will move right to left (i.e.: assign the equation to the element on the left of the = sign). Precedence takes place from the top down, meaning the operators higher in this list will be evaluated before those beneath them. Just as in mathematics, parenthesis will interrupt this list by treating the contents of each set of parenthesis (from the inner most out) as a statement by itself. The portion of the table in yellow highlights the operators most used for development below application level.

ADDITIONAL NOTES

Take Note! While using the words "and" and "or" in your logic statements, PHP will not give you an error, as they are in the order of precedence below. Take note that they are below the = sign—this will affect your logic equations. The vast majority of the time you will want to use "&&" and "||", as they will be evaluated before assignment.

Table 12 Operator Precedence

Associativity	Operators
non-associative	clone new
left	[
non-associative	++ —
right	~—(int) (float) (string) (array) (object) (bool) @
non-associative	instance of
right	!
left	* / %
left	+—.
left	<< >>
non-associative	< <= > >= <>
non-associative	== != === !==
left	&
left	^
left	|
left	&&
left	||
left	? :

right	= += -= *= /= .= %= &= |= ^= <<= >>= =>
left	and
left	xor
left	or
left	,

Let us look at a few examples to demonstrate precedence in PHP:

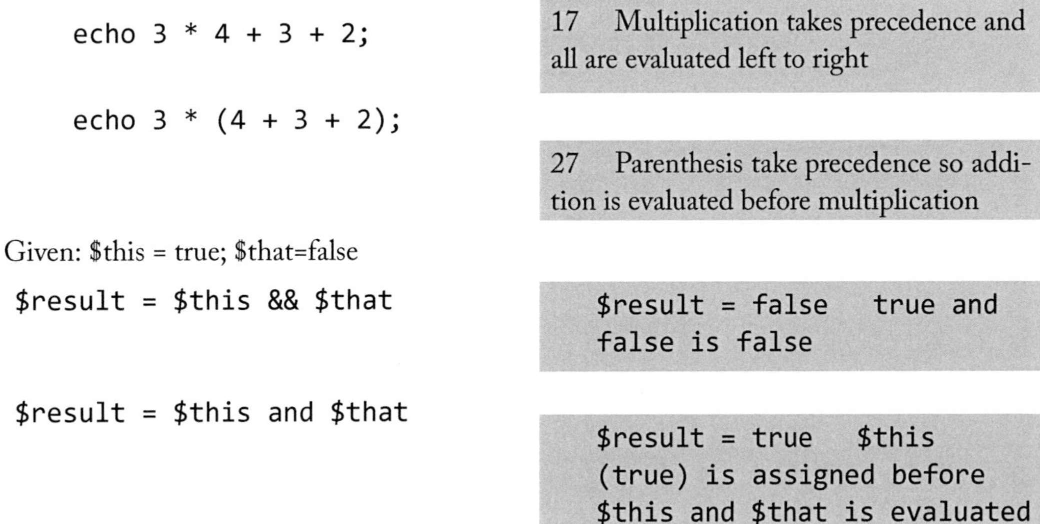

Manipulating Data Streams

Data streams are long strings of characters specially formatted to convey information between systems. They typically focus on the ability to quickly convey all the information in as readable a format as possible, resulting in a compressed syntax to identify the information and its meaning. Two of the most popular methods of streaming data today are JSON and XML.

Data streams do not have to be raw, or complete, records of an entire system. They are frequently used to transmit responses between the back-end system (server or database) and the system that generates content the viewer sees (browser and/or scripting language).

JSON

An acronym for JavaScript Object Notation, JSON delimits objects with nested brackets and quoted values, denoting key and value pairs with colons. This is a very short, concise method of delivering data, but the recipient will need to get the meaning of the information elsewhere like documentation, and the string is not easily human readable. It is useful when the volume of data is high, and speed is important.

If we asked our system to give us the family members from Family Guy, we might get the following:

```
{"Griffins":{"Peter":"Father", "Lois":"Mother", "Stewie":"Son",
"Chris":"Son", "Meg":"Daughter", "Brian":"Dog"} }
```

If we asked for the Griffins *and* Quagmire, we might get:

```
{"Griffins":
{"Peter":"Father", "Lois":"Mother", "Stewie":"Son",
"Chris":"Son", "Meg":"Daughter", "Brian":"Dog"},
{"Quagmire":"Neighbor"}
}
```

XML

An abbreviation of eXtensible Markup Language, XML wraps pieces of information in tags, similar to HTML, but the names of the tags are user-defined. Grouping of information is done by nesting the tags within each other. Using our Family Guy example above, our XML response would be as follows:

```
<Response>
<Griffin>
<Peter >father</Peter>
<Lois>mother</Lois>
<Stewie>son</Stewie>
<Chris>son</Chris>
<Meg>daughter</Meg>
<Brian>dog</Brian>
</Griffin>
<Quagmire>
<Glen>neighbor</Glen >
</Quagmire>
</Response>
```

USEFUL FEATURE

You can test validate JSON and XML strings that you create or receive by copying and pasting them into validation sites like jsonlint.com and xmlvalidation.com. They can help you identify problem areas in your strings to make sure your data is stored correctly.

Take note that I specify that this is how your code *might* look in these examples. The actual output's format would vary based on how the developers decides to create the response string, and also based on any options available to the user as to how they want the information organized. For example, we might want character ages instead of relationships like father or daughter, or the developer might group the results by gender and put first and last names as the value pairs.

It is important to note that when you actually interact with data streams they will not look as they do above, but will be long strings without the spacing and line breaks, as this reduces the size of the string. The formatting you see above is often referred to as the "pretty print" format, which adds extra spacing and formatting to make it more human readable.

We can create both XML and JSON in PHP. You can do this by creating the exact string necessary to format it, or we can use functions in PHP to help us along. The SimpleXML package allows us to create, navigate, and edit XML content, while the json_encode and json_decode functions allow us an easy means to convert JSON to and from arrays.

For brevity, we will consider examples of receiving data in these two formats. While converting JSON into, an out of, arrays is easily done with json_encode() and json_decode(), creating data by hand in these formats would necessitate a much deeper look at both XML and JSON. Your journey there can begin with the Learn More section. I would recommend you explore at least one format in depth, as you will come into contact with these formats when you interact with APIs. Current trending has JSON getting more attention in new development, but there are plenty of already built XML systems in place, and plenty more that offer both.

An easy way to interact with XML or JSON data in PHP is to convert it into arrays that we can more easily traverse. When we are working with XML we can use the SimpleXML package integrated in PHP to read our string or file using $data = simplexml_load_string($ourXML); or $data = simplexml_load_file("ourXmlFile.xml");. We can open JSON files to string or receive them from another source, and decode them using $data = json_decode($ourJson). Just like we did with arrays we created earlier, we can see our data by using print_r($data);.

```
$ourJson =
'{"Griffins":{"Peter":"Father",
"Lois":"Mother", "Stewie":"Son",
"Chris":"Son", "Meg":"Daughter",
"Brian":"Dog"}, }';
$familyGuy =
json_decode($ourJson,1);
print_r($familyGuy);
```

```
Array ( [Griffins] => Array (
[Peter] => Father [Lois] =>
Mother [Stewie] => Son [Chris]
=> Son [Meg] => Daughter
[Brian] => Dog ) )
```

Be sure to place the 1 as our second option in our json_decode() call, as it instructs the function to return the data as an array instead of objects. The same transfer to array for

XML becomes a little more complicated, as PHP does not natively support this type of conversion, so we need to do more to get our full list displayed as arrays:

```
$ourXML= '<Response>
<Griffin>
<Peter >Father</Peter>
<Lois>Mother</Lois>
<Stewie>Son</Stewie>
<Chris>Son</Chris>
<Meg>Daughter</Meg>
<Brian>Dog</Brian>
</Griffin>
<Quagmire>
<Glen>Neighbor</Glen>
</Quagmire>
</Response>';
$familyGuy =
simplexml_load_string($ourXML);
$familyGuy = (array) $familyGuy;
foreach ($familyGuy as &$group)
{$group = (array) $group;}
print_r($familyGuy);
```

```
Array ( [Griffin] => Array ( [Peter] => Father [Lois] => Mother [Stewie] => Son [Chris] => Son [Meg] => Daughter [Brian] => Dog ) [Quagmire] => Array ( [Glen] => Neighbor ) )
```

While we were able to make the outermost layer of the data an array just by re-declaring its type, the type casting conversion in PHP is not recursive. However, simplexml_load_string turns our XML into objects not arrays, so by looping through our array again and recasting each element to an array, we can correct the data in the second layer. This process would need to be repeated for each nested layer of data.

LEARN MORE

Keywords, search terms: json, xml, data formatting, data structures

Essential XML Quick Reference: http://bookos.org/book/491155/a86a21

Json.org: http://www.json.org/

Data Structures Succinctly (Pt 1): http://www.syncfusion.com/resources/techportal/ebooks/datastructurespart1

Chapter 29

Email

Disclaimer: Unless you are working on a server that already has email capability, this chapter may not work for you. WAMP 2.0 (or just Apache, MySQL, and PHP by themselves) do not contain the ability to act as an email server in and of themselves. If you have an email account that uses an exchange email server or another hosted solution, you can research how to configure that account into your server to use your address to send email. Since this process will differ depending on the service you use, comprehensive directions on how to do so are not possible here.

In short, you will need account credentials such as a username and password, some connection settings that can be found in your account settings that may be stored in your email software, web settings, or phone settings, and you will need to edit your php.ini file's sendmail settings. Once you have made the necessary changes, do not forget to stop and start your server for them to take effect.

Text-Based

Regardless of what service you use to facilitate sending email, you will always use the same function in PHP to trigger it. The mail() function allows us to specify the "Who, What, and Where" settings. Through this function we can support multimedia (HTML-based) emails and attachments as well.

The minimum information necessary to send an email is the recipient and message, assuming you have placed an email address in the "From" portion of the php.ini settings file:

```
mail("ourRecipient@nowhere.com", "That is a nice inbox you got
there!");
```

The full list of options at our disposal includes the following:

```
mail([to], [subject], [message], [headers]);
```

The headers section allows us to pass further information like a different "from" address than our default, a reply email, CCs, BCCs, and information on other features like HTML content or attachments. Since this last section and our actual message can be quite long, it is helpful to declare all of these elements as variables first to keep our actual mail function call readable:

```
$to = "ourRecipient@nowhere.com";
$subject= "You Win a million dollars!";
$message = "Not really. We just wanted you to read this.";
$headers .= 'From: Us <us@somewhereOutThere.com>' . "\r\n";
```

```
$headers .= 'Cc: someoneelse@nowhere.com . "\r\n";
$headers .= 'Bcc: hiddenPerson@definatelyNotHere.com' . "\r\n";
mail($to, $subject, $message, $headers);
```

You will notice that our headers string actually contains the labels of the email, and that line breaks are included at the end of each piece. This helps translate the string into separate pieces of information when we submit the variable to the mail function in order to create our actual email.

HTML

To make our messages look better and incorporate things like color and images, we can add HTML to our message. We can do this by inserting two more lines to our header that specify this:

```
$headers .= "MIME-Version: 1.0\r\n";
$headers .= "Content-Type: text/html; charset=ISO-8859-1\r\n";
```

Declaring our MIME Type version and content type of text/html allows us to include HTML in our message. At this point, we can edit our message string to include HTML tags. Since it is still a PHP string, we can include variables and concatenate results from functions just as we can in other strings, allowing us to create messages that include content specific to the user or recipient:

```
$message = "<table width=*20%'><tr><td>First:</td><td>Jose</
td></tr>
<tr><td>Last:</td><td>Jalapeno</td></tr></table>";
```

Now we have sent our user some information formatted into a table. While we can include a lot of HTML in a message, keep in mind your users will be viewing them on a number of different devices and through different programs. The more complex the content, the more likely your user will not see it as you intend.

In fact, best practices for HTML email are to include the content formatted for email clients that only support text, or as a fall back when something else goes awry. To do this, we need to add a few more lines of code to specify which parts of our message belong to the HTML version, and which parts belong to the text version. Part of this involves creating an indicator that specifies where sections start and end. To do this, we need a unique string—unique enough that it would never be an intended part of our message. An easy way to do this is to use the md5 and time functions to generate our string. **This does not mean we have encrypted our email.** The use of md5 simply helps us generate a long, random string:

```
$divider = md5((date('r', time()));
```

We also need to edit our header line to announce that our message is multipart and not just HTML:

```
$headers .= "MIME-Version: 1.0\r\n";
$headers .= " Content-Type: multipart/alternative;
boundary=\"PHP-alt-".$random_hash; charset=ISO-8859-1\r\n";
```

Now we will add our $divider where our message starts, where we fall back from HTML to text, and then at the end of our text section. Whenever we start a new section, we need to specify which MIME format we are using. This allows us to mix and match multiple things, even text, HTML, and attachments, all in one message. Since things are getting a bit more complex, we will introduce a new concept, output buffering, to keep things cleaner.

Output buffering allows us to "stop" outputting anything to the screen or browser. By using the buffer, we can create larger sections of text to use elsewhere. When we are done, we will store the buffer contents into our message variable.

```
<?php ob_start(); ?>
—PHP-alt-<?php echo $divider; ?>
Content-Type: text/html; charset="iso-8859-1"
Content-Transfer-Encoding: 7bit

<table width=*20%'><tr><td>First:</td><td>Jose</td></tr>
<tr><td>Last:</td><td>Jalapeno</td></tr></table>

—PHP-alt-<?php echo $divider; ?>
Content-Type: text/plain; charset="iso-8859-1"
Content-Transfer-Encoding: 7bit

First: Jose
Last: Jalapeno

—PHP-alt-<?php echo $divider; –
$message = ob_get_clean(); ?>
```

You will note that we closed our PHP tags after starting our output buffer. This means everything that follows would be treated as HTML to be rendered, so we still need to open and close PHP tags when we want to insert dynamic content into our message. Once we are done with our message(s), we use the ob_get_clean() function to dump the buffer's content into our message variable. This action also closes, or clears, the buffer we were using. Now we have an email that supports an HTML and plain text version of our message. To add an attachment, we would add one more MIME type section that names the file format we want to attach, then include in our buffer content the file's content. Since we cannot drop the actual file into our code, we need to encode it. We can take care of all of this by adding a couple extra lines at the start of our section for our attachment.

```
—PHP-mixed-<?php echo $division; ?>
Content-Type: application/zip; name="ourFile.pdf"
Content-Transfer-Encoding: base64
Content-Disposition: attachment

<?php echo $attachment; ?>
—PHP-mixed-<?php echo $division; ?>—
```

When you send attachments, you will want to keep in mind the size of the file(s) that you are attaching. Just because your server is able to process and send the file does not mean your recipient's server will be able to accept it. Emails with attachments should be accompanied by a body as well. If there is no text in the body of the email, the recipient's email client may elect to treat the attachment as the body of the message.

Chapter 30

File Interaction

We can use PHP to create and read files in a variety of formats, allowing us to create whole new pages, store information in document form, copy files, and plenty more. The first step in this process is creating a new file, or opening an existing file, that we want to work with. To do this, we use the function fopen() to declare the file's location and how we intend to interact with its contents.

File Permissions

PHP follows the Unix/Linux approach to file permissions, which is more granular to what Microsoft and Apple users are typically used to. In this approach, a particular file can have different permission levels depending on if the person editing the file is the owner, belongs to the same system group as the owner, or falls into the "anyone else" category. Within these three categories we can also specify whether or not the person is allowed to read, write, or execute the file, in any combination.

One of the methods used to depict permissions is with a string of letters and dashes, using R, W, and X to represent read write and execute. In this approach, three groupings of these letters are strung together in the order of owner, group, other, by read, write and execute. A file that everyone has full permissions would be represented by rwxrwxrwx, while a file where the owner can do anything, others in his group can read and execute, and anyone else can execute would be shown as rwxr-xr—. The dashes here indicate that the permission is lacking. Group membership refers to the group your account is associated with on the server, which can be anything the server is told to recognize like administrators, users, guests, professor, student, and so on. If the owner of our imaginary file was in the administrator group, other administrators could read and execute the file, where anyone in any other group would only be able to execute it without seeing its contents.

Understanding this structure is important to understanding why file open methods are necessary, and can also help us understand problems opening files when appropriate permissions are not used. Any time we open a file in PHP we need to use one of the following methods, which will determine what PHP lets us do with the file.

Table 13 PHP File Methods

mode	Description
'r'	Open for reading only; place the file pointer at the beginning of the file.
'r+'	Open for reading and writing; place the file pointer at the beginning of the file.
'w'	Open for writing only; place the file pointer at the beginning of the file and truncate the file to zero length. If the file does not exist, attempt to create it.
'w+'	Open for reading and writing; place the file pointer at the beginning of the file and truncate the file to zero length. If the file does not exist, attempt to create it.
'a'	Open for writing only; place the file pointer at the end of the file. If the file does not exist, attempt to create it.
'a+'	Open for reading and writing; place the file pointer at the end of the file. If the file does not exist, attempt to create it.
'x'	Create and open for writing only; place the file pointer at the beginning of the file. If the file already exists, the **fopen()** call will fail by returning **FALSE** and generating an error of level **E_WARNING**. If the file does not exist, attempt to create it. This is equivalent to specifying **O_EXCL|O_CREAT** flags for the underlying**open(2)** system call.
'x+'	Create and open for reading and writing; otherwise it has the same behavior as 'x'.
'c'	Open the file for writing only. If the file does not exist, it is created. If it exists, it is neither truncated (as opposed to 'w'), nor the call to this function fails (as is the case with 'x'). The file pointer is positioned on the beginning of the file. This may be useful if it is desired to get an advisory lock (see flock()) before attempting to modify the file, as using 'w' could truncate the file before the lock was obtained (if truncation is desired, ftruncate() can be used after the lock is requested).
'c+'	Open the file for reading and writing; otherwise it has the same behavior as 'c'.

PHP.net [CC-A 3.0]

File Actions

Assuming we want our file in the same folder as our page and that the web server has permission to create files in that location, we can start a new file with the following:

```
$handler = fopen("ourFile.txt", 'x+');
```

If all was successful in creating our new file, the $handler variable would now represent the system's position in our open file as a reference. If the file already existed, we would have received an error (this keeps us from accidently overwriting a file we wanted). If no permissions errors cropped up, you can now add content to your file. If you do have permission errors, you will need to change folders to one your web server can write to, or give your server permissions on that folder. Since this is an operating system task, you will need to find instructions on how to achieve this based on your OS type, version, and web server settings.

We can now add whatever we want to our file, so long as it results in valid content for the file type we are creating. For example, any HTML placed in a text file will appear as plain text, not a web page. We would need to create our file as ourFIle.html for that type of content to render correctly. If we had a large block of text already stored in a variable called content, we can add it to our file by using fwrite(). Each time we call fwrite, the variable passed to it will be appended to what we have already sent. If we had opened an existing file, the content might be appended ('a') or overwrite what exists ('w+') depending on how we opened it. When we are done, we need to close the file, which actually writes the content using the $handler variable and saves it in our folder:

```
fwrite($content);
fwrite($moreContent);
fclose($handler);
```

If we browse to our file from our operating system, you should be able to open it in a text editor and see the text you stored in your $content variable.

Uploading Files

In order to allow users to upload files to our server, we have to create a folder that allows the web server to write to it, and make the following changes in our php.ini file:

```
File_uploads = on
Upload_tmp_dir = [location of our upload folder]
Upload_max_filesize = [size in megs, i.e. 5M = 5 megs]
```

After making these changes and restarting our web server, our users will be able to use upload form elements, which we create using an input with a type attribute of file:

```
<input type="file" name="userUpload" id="userUpload">
```

On the page that processes our form we can access the file (and information describing it) by using the reserved PHP array $_FILES:

```
echo "File name:" . $_FILES["userUpload"]["name"] . "<br>";
echo "Type:" . $_FILES["userUpload"]["type"] . "<br>";
echo "Size:" . ($_FILES["userUpload"]["size"] / 1024) .
"kB<br>";
echo "Stored in:" . $_FILES["userUpload"]["tmp_name"];
```

Chapter 31

Structures

Referred to as selection, control, or loop structures, this set of elements dictate conditions under which certain sections code are executed. They allow our program to be flexible, instead of restricting it to the same actions every iteration. Here, we will consider all of them together, as structures in general.

If

"If" is perhaps the simplest test we can apply in logic. In programming, the "then" side is implied in the code contained in the definition of our statement—If [some condition] is true, then do something. We can use this to put exceptions into our code, or to redirect to a different action. Within the If statement we can perform simple comparisons or have the interpreter perform calculations and get returns from functions as part of its comparison task.

To run some examples, we will check if a variable called coffee is equal to hot. If it is, we want to run the drink function.

```
if("hot" == $coffee){
      drink($coffee);
}
```

ADDITIONAL NOTES

Remember that = is an assignment operation! == or === must be used when testing if both sides of the operand are equivalent.

Else

Next we will assume our drink() function tells us if we want more or feel full, prompting us to take new actions, like cleaning up after ourselves. This means we need to take one of two actions, which can do by extending our If/Then by adding Else:

```
if(drink($coffee)=='full'){
   cleanUp();
```

```
}
else{ //We want more!
      drink($coffee);
}
```

elseIf

We can use elseIf when we want to follow up a failed If statement with another check. While the same affect can be created by placing an If inside of our Else, we can eliminate a layer of nesting. We can still follow up an elseIf with its own Else as well:

```
if ($a > $b) {
      echo "a is bigger than b";
} elseif ($a == $b) {
      echo "a is equal to b";
} else {
      echo "a is smaller than b";
}
```

While

While statements will repeatedly execute until the condition we provide is no longer true. The code will start over, in a loop, as long as the requirement is met.

Be careful with While statements! You can easily create infinite loops using While, in which your code will continue to run until forced to stop by closing the page or resetting your web service. The first method of prevention is to ensure that you have at least one place in your While loop that can affect the value (or values) in your while condition. The second method of prevention is to make sure that at least one result of those changes satisfies your While condition.

While loops are very similar to If in terms of structure. Here we will pretend $ourValue is a 4:

```
$ourValue=4;
while($ourValue!=6){
      echo "Wait for it...<br/>";
      $ourValue++;
}
echo "6!";
```

```
Wait for it...
Wait for it...
6!
```

Let us try one that counts for us:

```
$ourValue=4;
while($ourValue!=10){
      echo "$ourValue," ;
      $ourValue++;
}
```

```
4, 5, 6, 7, 8, 9,
```

To see a broken While statement in action, change $ourValue to 11 and refresh your page!

Do While

Do While loops are very similar to While loops with the difference that every Do While loop will run at least one time. This is because a Do While loop evaluates the equation after each loop, not before. Since it does not check if conditions are met until the end, the first loop will never be checked. For example, compare the following loops and their output:

```
do {
   echo $i;
} while ($i > 0);
echo "<br/> done";
```

```
0
done
```

```
while ($i>0){
   echo $i;
}
echo "<br/> done";
```

```
done
```

LEARN MORE

Keywords, search terms: Control structures, logic

Alternative syntax: http://www.brian2000.com/php/understanding-alternative-syntax-for-control-structures-in-php/

More examples: http://www.informit.com/articles/article.aspx?p=30092&seqNum=2

For

For loops are very similar to While loops, but they execute code only while the condition is within the given range. When using a For loop, we need to provide it with the value we want to monitor, the condition we want to stop on, and how we want to change it, right in the declaration. As a result, the body of the loop is strictly what we want to happen while the For's conditions are true. Let us say we want to watch $x (we will pretend it is 5 right now). We want to keep running until it is greater than 10, and we want to add 2 each time we finish the loop:

```
$x=5;
for($x;$x<10;$x+=2){
      echo "$x is less than 10
         <br/>";
}
echo "$x is greater than 10!";
```

```
5 is less than 10
7 is less than 10
9 is less than 10
11 is greater than
10!
```

Unlike the While loop, you will notice we did not have to change the value of $x inside our loop, it was done automatically each time the end of the loop was reached. If the termination condition (in our example x would be greater or equal to 10) is not met, the loop starts again. Let us look at another example. This time, if a secondary condition that we test for occurs, we will force the For to stop by changing $x ourselves to something that satisfies the termination condition:

```
$x=5;
for($x;$x<10;$x+=2){
      echo "$x is less than 10 <br/>";
      if($x==7)$x=11;
}
echo "$x is greater than 10!";
```

```
5 is less than 10
7 is less than 10
11 is greater than
10!
```

Foreach

Although we took a brief look at Foreach when we reviewed pseudo-code, we will take a look at an actual implementation now. This loop format is used to iterate over arrays, allowing us an opportunity to manipulate each element inside. Since it is designed specifically for interacting with arrays, these are the only objects you can pass to it. The function takes the array we want to look at as well as what we want to call each element as we look at it. Alternatively, we can ask that the function take each element as a key and value pair, which can be very useful when position value is needed or associative arrays are in play.

When we use a Foreach, the engine makes a copy of the array, leaving the original intact, eliminating the need to track and reset the original array's pointer or reset the array when we are done. This also means that while we are interacting with the elements inside our array, we need to keep in mind that we are dealing with a copy. No changes that are applied to our copy will persist unless we call the function while applying an ampersand (&) before the variable name, which instructs the function to apply changes directly to our original array.

In order to apply changes to our array, the original that is passed must be a variable already stored in memory, and not an array declared in the function call. Let us look at some examples to clear some of this up by mimicking print_r().

```
$array = array(1, 2, 3, 4, 5);
foreach($array as $number){
      echo "Our value is $number <br
         />";
}
```

```
Our value is 1
Our value is 2
Our value is 3
Our value is 4
Our value is 5
```

To play with an associative array and see the key and the value, we will adjust both our starting array and what we pass in the function call:

```
$array = array("Mike"=>42,
"Frank"=>38, "Anne"=>28);
foreach($array as $key=>$value){
      echo "$key is $value years
         old.<br />";
}
```

```
Mike is 42 years old.
Frank is 38 years old.
Anne is 28 years old.
```

Finally, we will take a look at applying our changes back to the array, multiplying our original array's values by 2:

```
$array = array(1, 2, 3, 4, 5);
foreach($array as &$number){
      $number = $number * 2;
}
print_r($array);
```

```
Array(
    0 => 2
    1 => 4
    2 => 6
    3 => 8
    4 => 10
)
```

Switch

A switch statement lets us run several tests to determine the proper course of action, or to apply one or more changes to our variable or elsewhere in our code, when the condition of our case is met. Some indicators that a switch is appropriate are when you find yourself running several If Then statements on the same variable, or have nested multiple logic statements attempting to control the action of your script.

To create an example, let us write a switch that gives information about a number passed to it. First, we will design it to determine the smallest positive value of 2 through 9 that $value is a multiple of, and then we will tweak it a bit so it can tell us all the values of 2 through 9 $value is a multiple of. If we just want the smallest value, we only need to test 2, 3, 5, and 7 since 4, 6, 8 and 9 are multiples of these numbers anyway, so they could not be the smallest. Now, if the number we check is divisible by one of these numbers, it would not have a remainder. To check specifically for a remainder, we can use modular division, which in PHP is represented by a %, and returns a 0 or 1. If we get a zero, there is no remainder. So let us create a switch with empty test cases for 2, 3, 5 and 7:

```
switch($value){
      case ($value % 2 == 0 ):
      case ($value % 3 == 0 ):
      case ($value % 5 == 0 ):
      case ($value % 7 == 0 ):
      default:
}
```

Each case can be followed by a set of parenthesis denoting our logical test or a value, which is followed by a colon that denotes the start of what we want to happen when the case is true. If we wanted a case where the value IS 2, we would use:

```
Case 2:
```

Or, if we wanted to test if the value is the WORD two, we would use:

```
Case "two":
```

By default, each case will be tested until the switch is complete, or we tell it we want it to stop. This ability will be useful in a moment, but for now, we want the switch to stop as soon as we find a value, since we are testing in smallest to largest order, and only need one test to be true. To do this, we put a "break;" wherever we want the execution of our switch to stop. Typically this is the last line before the following case, but if the case we are in has additional logic tests we might have more than one "break;" depending on the extra conditions we are testing.

You will also notice the "default:" that snuck in at the bottom. The default case must be last, but is optional, and gives us a "catch all" action in the event that none of our cases were met. We do not need a "break;" after our default, since it will always be the last case in our switch.

To complete our example, we will want to let the user know what the smallest value we found was, so we need to fill out our code:

```
switch($value){
case ($value % 2 == 0 ):
   echo "$value is divisible by 2 <br/>";
   break;
case ($value % 3 == 0 ):
   echo "$value is divisible by 3 <br/>";
   break;
case ($value % 5 == 0 ):
   echo "$value is divisible by 5 <br/>";
   break;
case ($value % 7 == 0 ):
   echo "$value is divisible by 7 <br/>";
   break;
default:
   echo "$value is not divisible by 2 through 9.";
}
```

With this example, if $value was 4, we would get "4 is divisible by 2." If $value was 12, we would get "12 is divisible by 2" but would not get a response for 3, 4, or 6 since we included breaks after each test, and it stopped after 2. If $value was 11, we would get all the way to "11 is not divisible by 2 through 9." In this scenario, it is because 11 is a prime number, which by definition is only divisible by itself and 1.

Now let us tweak our switch statement so it tells us all of the values between 2 and 9 that can divide our number without a remainder. First, we will have to start testing the values we could skip earlier. For example, 8 is not divisible by 6 even though both are divisible by 2. Second, we no longer want to stop after one expression is true. To do this, we will get rid of all of our breaks except for the one in the case preceding the default, ensuring that if any of the cases were true, we will not still see our default statement. That gives us:

ADDITIONAL NOTES

This does not mean our switch will find all prime numbers! Prime numbers have to be tested against the range 2 to $n^{1/2}$ to ensure there are no dividends.

```
switch($value){
case ($value % 2 == 0 ):
   echo "$value is divisible by 2 <br/>";
case ($value % 3 == 0 ):
   echo "$value is divisible by 3 <br/>";
```

```
case ($value % 4 == 0 ):
   echo "$value is divisible by 4 <br/>";
case ($value % 5 == 0 ):
   echo "$value is divisible by 5 <br/>";
case ($value % 6 == 0 ):
   echo "$value is divisible by 6 <br/>";
case ($value % 7 == 0 ):
   echo "$value is divisible by 7 <br/>";
case ($value % 8 == 0 ):
   echo "$value is divisible by 8 <br/>";
case ($value % 9 == 0 ):
   echo "$value is divisible by 9 <br/>";
   break;
default:
   echo "$value is not divisible by 2 through 9.";
}
```

To repeat our examples using 4, 12, and 11, respectfully we would see the following responses:

```
4 is divisible by 2
4 is divisible by 4
12 is divisible by 2
12 is divisible by 3
12 is divisible by 4
12 is divisible by 6
11 is not divisible by 2 through 9
```

Chapter 32

Functions

Now that we are comfortable creating some code, let us take a look at how to do more with what we have. In any language we use, there are concepts that are not always translatable from one to the next, if the concept is even present in both. In spoken languages, words for a particular concept also may have no direct translation to another language. For example, the German word *Kummerspeck* is a single word to convey the concept of excess weight gained by emotion-related overeating. Not only does the English language lack a word defining this concept, its closest literal translation in English would be "grief bacon." Similarly, in Wagiman (Australia) there is an infinitive murr-ma, which means "to walk along in the water searching for something with your feet,"[1] which is both much more specific and requires a significantly longer English sentence to convey.

The development of words that specify such lengthy or concise ideas arise out of the popularity of, or need to convey that concept often in a society. It is far easier to say "I am going to the gym to get rid of this Kummerspeck" than "I am going to the gym to get rid of the weight I gained from overeating due to my emotions," which allows for the concept to be used more often.

In programming languages, we can find a parallel to this when functions or abilities in one language are not available in another, or require additional code to achieve. For example, in PHP you can retrieve items available to the page using the GET method by referencing the built-in $_GET array:

```
<?php echo $_GET['variable name']; ?>
```

Attempting to implement the same functionality in JavaScript requires much more effort, even with the assistance of its built-in location.search function:

```
var $_GET = {},
variablesList = location.search.substr(1).split(/&/);
for (var x=0; i<variablesList.length; ++i) {
var tmp = variablesList[x].split(/=/);
if (tmp[0] != "") {
   $_GET[decodeURIComponent(tmp[0])] =decodeURIComponent(tmp.
   slice(1).join("").replace("+", " "));}}
```

The programming equivalent of creating a word to describe a concept is the ability to create our own algorithms and functions, to describe new actions. In the example above, we

[1] Jacot, de Boinod, Adam. Global Wording. *Smithsonian Magazine*. March 2006. Web. 15 Dec. 2012

could take our JavaScript code and wrap it in a function definition, and add a return call to send the results back to where you called the function, like this:

```
function findValues(){
    var $_GET = {},
    variablesList = location.search.substr(1).split(/&/);
    for (var x=0; i<variablesList.length; ++i) {
        var tmp = variablesList[x].split(/=/);
        if (tmp[0] != "") {
        $_GET[decodeURIComponent(tmp[0])] =
            decodeURIComponent(tmp.slice(1).join("").replace("+",
            " "));
    }
    }
    return $_GET;
}
```

Now, anytime you wanted to find your values using JavaScript, you could include this function and simply type:

```
var $_GET = findValues(); document.write($_GET['variable
name'];
```

Creating a function also allows us to reference it in more than one place, without having to retype or copy and paste those lines into every place we want to use them. This also means that debugging only requires fixing the original block of code in your function, as it is the only place the line exists, since each function call is a reference to this single definition.

Creating a function in PHP is much like the example we looked at for JavaScript above. To create a function, we use the word function (denoting that we are creating one, not calling one to use it) followed by the name we want to give it and any variables we would like it to use in parenthesis. A set of braces are used to identify the code that belongs to the definition. An empty function called Add that does not accept any variables would look like this:

```
function Add(){ }
```

Note that a terminating semi-colon is not needed after the closing brace. The brace tells PHP that the statement is complete, just as it does when using a logic or control statement. To pass variables into our Add function, the function will need to know what to expect to receive. We do this by adding parameters (names we give to the variables passed to the function) to the definition. Here we will add two parameters:

```
function Add($num1, $num2){ }
```

Now, we will tell the function to add these numbers and give us the result:

```
$var1 = 4; $var2= 5;
function Add($num1, $num2){
        $temp = $num1 + $num2;
        return $temp;
}
$value = Add($var1, $var2);
```

When we use the function and pass it actual values (in this example, $var1 and $var2) those variables are called arguments; they contain the data we actually want to use. Another example of function output you may see are ones that send output right to the screen, like this:

```
$var1=4; $var2=5;
function Add($num1, $num2){
      $temp = $num1 + $num2;
      print $temp;
}
Add($var1, $var2);
```

They might also output more than we expect, not just the result of the equation:

```
function Add($num1, $num2){
   $temp = $num1 + $num2;
   print "$num1 + $num2 = $temp";
   $oddEven = $temp % 2;
   if ($oddEven == 0){ print "<br/>$temp is even"; }
   else{ print "<br/>$temp is odd"; }
}
Add(7,9);
```

While all of these example are effective, the second two examples actually limit our ability to use them again, namely by performing multiple actions, and by mixing action and output. Since the power of a function lies largely in our ability to reuse it, these are attributes we will want to eliminate. To make functions as useful as possible, they should do one thing, and do it well.

In this example the intent of our function is to add numbers. Our expectation is that we will provide it numbers, and it will provide the sum. Any other actions or steps needed to solve a larger problem should reside elsewhere in your code, or in another function. By doing this, we know that when we use add() all it will do is give us a number. If the function shows our output instead of returning it, we would not be able to use if it we did not want it to show on the screen. By returning it and storing it, we can choose where and when it is displayed, or use it somewhere else.

To simplify our function and follow these practices, let us refine it to the following:

```
function Add($num1, $num2){ return $num1 + $num2; }
```

Now we can call the function and store it to a variable:

```
$sum = Add(3,5);
```

Or we would chose to display it on the screen:

```
echo Add(3,5);
```

USEFUL FEATURE

Wait! Where did the $temp variable go?! By skipping the use of declaring $temp to hold our sum, we have eliminated one reserved memory space while the function is running. In terms of the size of this function, the number of variables we needed, and the time for it to execute, we would never know the difference. However, in much larger programs, especially when memory is limited, these steps can improve performance.

Let us take a look at how we can put all of this together:

```
<?php
function Add($num1, $num2){
      return $num1 + $num2;
}
echo "Welcome to the number adding page! <br/>";
echo "The sum of 3 and 5 is " . Add(3,5);echo "<br/>The sum of
9 and 12 is " . Add(9, 12);
?>
```

ADDITIONAL NOTES

Do not forget your SCOPE! Functions cannot see anything outside of their braces that are not given to them when they are called. Once you leave your function, any local variables created in it that were not returned are gone!

Seeing as the ability to add numbers is already built into PHP, let us look at a more advanced example. We will design a function that tells us how much to add to a bill for a tip. To do this, we will need to create a function that takes in the total of our bill, calculates the tip amount, and tells us how much the tip would be.

Remember, a function should do one thing only, so before we worry about final totals or any other issues, let us at least get that far:

```
function tip($billTotal){
      $tip = $billTotal * .15;
      return $tip;
}
```

In the above example, we assumed a 15% tip. What if that is not the standard where you are? Or maybe the service was better or worse than you expected. This is an additional use case we need to consider. To do this, we will allow the user to tell us the percentage they want, and assume that if they do not tell us, it is still 15%:

```
function tip($billTotal, $percent=.15){
      $tip = $billTotal * $percent;
      return $tip;
}
```

Setting $percent equal to a value in the function definition tells the function that if a second value is not passed, assume it to be .15. This allows that variable to be optional, so we can call this function as tip(45.99,.20) or just tip(45.99). We are still only doing one thing, but now we have some flexibility. What about other use cases, like splitting the bill? While we could tell the function how many people to divide the total by, that would violate our "one thing" rule. Instead, we can divide the total outside of the function, and give tip() the result to figure out how much each person's contribution to the tip would be.

If you have been testing out our function as we have progressed, you have probably had some tip values that resulted in half pennies and even smaller fractions of currency to fulfill. This is because our function does not know we are dealing with money—it is just doing the math. Since we only need to calculate to the second decimal point for this type of problem, we can round out our answer to match. PHP already provides us with a rounding function called round, so we will use that to refine our response:

```
function tip($billTotal, $percent=.15){
      $tip = $billTotal * $percent;
      $roundedTip = round($tip, 2);
      return $roundedTip;
}
```

Lastly we will combine our statements, as we did before, to eliminate extra variables and shorten our code:

```
function tip($billTotal, $percent=.15){ return
round(($billTotal * $percent),2) }
```

Now we have a concise function that can perform a single task and perform it well. We can refer to it anywhere in our page as often as we need to without having to copy and paste the code. In fact, this is the perfect time to introduce a set of functions that allow us to import other files into our page.

ADDITIONAL NOTES

Order helps! If all of your optional variables are at the end (right hand side) of the definition, you will not have to pass empty quotes as place holders if you only want to send the required variables.

The functions include(), require(), and require_once() all allow us to pass a file location on our server that we want to use as part of our code. By importing these outside files, we can create libraries of functions or class files and insert them into any page we want to use them on. Each of these functions runs the same way, by passing a file location. If the contents of the file are not critical to your page, you may want to only use include, as it will not generate an error if the file is missing. Errors will be thrown by using require() or require_once(). The former will always insert the contents of the file, while the latter will only load the file if its contents are not already available. Using required_once() will save us from redefinition errors caused by redefining functions or classes we already have. If the contents of the file tip.php was our function, we could reference it in any page like this:

```
<?php
require_once("tip.php");
echo tip(49.99);
?>
```

LEARN MORE

Keywords, search terms: Functions, function scope

Tizag's function review: http://www.tizag.com/phpT/phpfunctions.php

Helper Functions : http://net.tutsplus.com/tutorials/php/increase-productivity-by-creating-php-helper-functions/

Chapter 33

Objects and Classes

We can group related functions together into an item called a class. Classes are collections of functions (when they are in classes, they are called methods) and variables that are related or collectively represent our knowledge or actions that can be performed on a concept. We can create a class by writing:

```
class math(){
}
```

This gives us an empty class called Math. Let us include our adding function:

```
class math(){
   function add($num1, $num2){
      return ($num1 + $num2);
}
}
```

and add a couple more functions:

```
class math(){
   function add($num1, $num2){
      return ($num1 + $num2);
}
   function subtract($num1, $num2){
      return ($num1–$num2);
}
   function divide($num1, $num2){
      if($num2!=0){return ($num1 / $num2);}
      else return "error";
}
}
```

By creating the class, we have declared that add, subtract, and divide all belong to Math. To use our new class, we create a copy of it, called an instance, in our script. In the divide function you can see we check to make sure we will not divide by zero, which would cause an error. This is an example of how we can use classes and functions to expand functionality and protect our program. We can reference the variable that is our object to use the functions and data members (variables that are inside a class) inside it:

```
$ourMath = new math();
echo $ourMath->add(5,9);
```

The arrow tells us to use something inside our class, in this case the add method. We can use these methods over several lines:

```
$temp = $ourMath->add(5,9);
$temp = $ourMath->divide($temp/2);
```

or nest them:

```
$temp = $ourMath->divide($ourMath->add(5,9),2);
```

Classes are commonly used to create libraries of related actions, like the Math example we made, or to create collections of methods and data members that pertain to a concept in our system. For example, if this was an online course system we might have objects to represent concepts like students and courses.

Methods in the student class would revolve around the student, like calculating their GPA or generating a list of courses the student is enrolled in. The courses class might have a similar method that calculates the overall average of all students in a class, but these could only be run from an object of the appropriate type and permission. An object is an instance (or copy) of the class that represents a particular item, like a particular student or course.

While most functions in PHP can be used by any script, we can control what pieces of our class structures can be accessed by programmers when an instance of the class is used. We do this with the keywords public, private, and protected that precede our methods or data members in our class. This gives us a means to protect our information and/or control what can be done when the object is being used.

Public items can be accessed by "anyone" (or anything, such as other classes), meaning we can reference them using -> just like in our example. Protected items can be accessed by other methods in the class, or by methods in parent or child classes that use the class in question—we will cover class inheritance here though. Finally, private items can only be accessed by the class itself. This means that a method or data member marked private in our Math example could only be used by other methods in the class, not by us when we write code to use an object-based on the class. To see this in action, we will look at public and private in action by adjusting our math class. To learn more about inheritance and protected methods, you can refer to this chapter's "Learn more" section.

```
class math(){
    public function add($num1, $num2){
        return ($num1 + $num2);
}
    private function subtract($num1, $num2){
        return ($num1–$num2);
}
    public function divide($num1, $num2){
        return ($num1 / $num2);
}
}
```

Since our add and divide methods are set to public, our previous example still works—we are able to add and divide from our code without any issues. If you try to use subtract though ($ourMath->subtract(5,2);) you will end up with an error:

```
Fatal error: Call to private method math::subtract()
```

The only way for the subtract method to be used is by being called from within another method in the Math class. If we had a more advanced method like calculating a longer formula, that method could call subtract as part of its execution.

LEARN MORE

Keywords, search terms: Functions, classes, objects, inheritance

More examples: http://php.net/manual/en/language.oop5.visibility.php

Constructors and inheritance: http://net.tutsplus.com/tutorials/php/object-oriented-php-for-beginners/

PHP Objects Patterns and Practice 3rd Edition: http://it-ebooks.info/book/411/

Chapter 34

JavaScript Syntax

Tags

Defining your block of JavaScript code in HTML is done with the use of another set of HTML tags we have not used yet, <script>. The script tags allow us to link to a script file or mark off a section of our code for our JavaScript to reside in. We can place script tags in any section of our HTML. Traditionally, JavaScript is placed in the head of the page, especially when the code consists of functions to be called or actions that are to occur on page load. If your JavaScript will be shorter or creates some simple output, you might find it easier to place it in your code where you want the output to be.

As the <script> tags can be used for more than just JavaScript, it is recommended to clarify what type of code the tags contain. To start with an example where we link to an external JavaScript file, we will use a <script> tag and give it attributes to define what our code is and where it lives.

ADDITIONAL NOTES

If your JavaScript's action or output is not critical to visual layout or output of your page, you can move <script> tags to the bottom of your page. This allows the page to render before processing your JavaScript, and gives the user a faster (seeming) experience.

```
<script type="text/javascript " src="http://someplace.com/
scripts/ourscript.js">
```

This example would populate the <script> tag set with the contents of the JavaScript file just like we did with CSS. Also like our CSS examples, we can place our JavaScript entirely in the HTML as well. To use the ubiquitous Hello World example yet again, we would replace our example above with the following:

```
<script type="text/javascript">
   alert("Hello World!");
</script>
```

The alert function in JavaScript will create the pop up box in our browser that must be closed by the user. By placing this block of code into either the head or body of a blank page as follows, we will get an alert box instead of text on the page:

```
<html>
   <head>
      <script type="text/javascript">
      alert("Hello World!");
      </script>
   </head>
<body/>
</html>
```

Not only is this a little more exciting than just printing it onto our page, we can even add some control to when we receive this output by giving it a trigger event. A trigger event is anything that can be monitored in order to cause another action to occur. In this case, our trigger event will be a click of a button. To do this, we need to stop our alert from running as soon as the page loads. We will do that by wrapping it in a function declaration so it only runs when we call it, and then add a button that calls the function:

```
<head>
   <script>
      function howdy(){
      alert("Hello world!");
      }
   </script>
</head>
<body>
   <input type="button"
   onclick="howdy()" value="Our
   Button" />
</body>
```

Our Button

The page at www.w3schools.com says:

Hello world!

OK

Now when we load our page, the alert window will not show up until we click our button. If it does not, you may need to check your JavaScript settings to make sure it is allowed in your browser. If you are unfamiliar with how to do this, search the Internet for your browser type, version number, and the words enable JavaScript for directions. JavaScript is usually enabled by default, so a double check of your code for typos may also be in order.

Variables

Creating variables in JavaScript is very similar to PHP. The variable names still need to begin with a letter, and are case sensitive. They can also start with $ or _ to help us identify them. One difference is that when we declare variables in JavaScript, we do so by putting "var" in front of them. This identifies what follows as a variable, like the $ in PHP. To convert our example into a string variable, we would adjust it as follows:

```
<head>
   <script>
      function howdy(){
      var str="Hello World";
      alert(str);
      }
```

```
    </script>
  </head>
  <body>
    <input type="button" onclick="howdy()" value="Our Button"
    />
  </body>
```

Output

The "echo" or "print" equivalent in JavaScript can be achieved by instructing it to place the text you want into the DOM (Document Object Model). We reference the document object in JavaScript with the word document, and call the write method to produce our output:

```
<script language="javascript">
   document.write ("Some output from <b>JavaScript!</b>");
</script>
```

We can be more specific as to the exact place(s) on the page we wish to put our content. In PHP, we would simply place our print or echo statement where we want the content to appear. With JavaScript we can continue to take advantage of the document object model to specify where we want output to be. This also means the script that makes the content can be stored in a separate location from the output location itself:

```
<script language="javascript">
   document.getElementById("ourText").innerHTML ="Hello
   World";
</script>
<div id="ourText"></div>
```

No matter where the "ourText" div is on our page, or where the script is, the div would contain Hello World as its text. This is the basic approach taken when we use JavaScript to make changes to our page.

Strings

While strings work largely the same as they do in PHP and other languages, concatenation is achieved by the use of the concat() function, or the plus (+) sign instead of PHP's use of period (.). Let us take a look at a couple examples to see the difference:

```
str1 = "Hello World!";
str2 = "How are you?";
output = str1.concat(str2); // Note we use . to access
concat() from the string
output = str1 + " " + str2; // Concating with +, which works
like PHP's .
```

Arrays

Arrays in JavaScript work in much the same way as PHP. All we need to keep in mind is that our output needs to use DOM manipulation:

```
<script>
//Some examples of setting and using array variables
   var x;
   var mycars = new Array();
   mycars[0] = "Saab";
   mycars[1] = "Volvo";
   mycars[2] = "BMW";
   for (x=0; x<stooges.length; x++){
      document.write(mycars[x] + "<br>");
   }
</script>
```

Braces and Semi-colons

When a control structure only has one line, JavaScript will allow us to skip the curly brackets that would normally outline its contents. We also do not need to include semi-colons as long as we include a line break after most statements. However, leaving either of these items out can create bugs by inconsistent coding. Adding a second line to your condition statement when not using brackets might work in some cases, but not all. Instead of a syntax error, though, it would be interpreted as part of the next statement after it. This will create a harder to find logic error.

LEARN MORE

Keywords, search terms: JavaScript syntax

Mozilla Developer Network: https://developer.mozilla.org/en-US/docs/Web/JavaScript?redirectlocale=en-US&redirectslug=JavaScript

Chapter 35

JavaScript Examples

DOM Navigation

Now we will look at some other techniques we can use to interact with the DOM using JavaScript. We specified we wanted to use a particular element by referencing its ID (getElementById()) but we can also interact with groups of elements that share a special type or class. To reference by type we would call the getElementsByTagName method, giving us a list of elements that we can review, or modify:

```
<div id="output"></div>
<input type="text" size="20"><br>
<input type="text" size="20"><br>
<input type="text" size="20"><br><br>
<input type="button" value="Submit Form">
<script>
   var x=document.getElementsByTagName("input");
   document.getElementById("output").innerHTML = ("Number of
   elements: "+x.length);
</script>
```

Perhaps we only want elements inside of another specific element. We can grab inputs from a particular form. To do this, we change our reference from the document as a whole to the element we want to inspect:

```
<div id="output"></div>
<form id="form1">
   <input type="text" size="20"><br>
   <input type="text" size="20"><br>
   <input type="text" size="20"><br><br>
   <input type="button" value="Submit Form">
</form>
<form id="form2">
   <input type="text" size="20"><br>
   <input type="text" size="20"><br>
   <input type="text" size="20"><br><br>
   <input type="button" value="Submit Form">
</form>
```

```
<script>
   var x=document.getElementsByTagName("input");
   document.getElementById("output").innerHTML = ("Number
   of elements: "+x.length+"</br>Number in form2: "+form2.
   getElementsByTagName("input").length;
</script>
```

In this example all we changed was doubling our inputs and putting them into forms. We also used form2 as our reference instead of document to create our second output, although this time we just tacked it onto the end without creating a second variable. You can see in this example that not only can we concat function results easily in JavaScript, we were still able to refer to the length() method, even though it was added to the end of the getElementsByTagName method. This chain is perfectly valid in JavaScript, and will always be evaluated from the inside out just like sets of parenthesis. In this case, counting the inputs in form2 occurred first, creating a temporary object that ".length" was instructed to access.

Events

It is important to keep in mind that JavaScript is not living within the confines of an object or function and will be processed as soon as it is loaded. Depending on its placement in the document this means our script may attempt to utilize something in the DOM that has not been created yet as the page is still loading. If we want our code to wait until the full page is complete, we need to wrap our code into one of these two items and then use a trigger, or event, to signify when the page is ready. One approach to this is adding an onload attribute to our body tag:

```
<body onload="ourFunction()">
```

We can even monitor events that do not involve the document itself like the location of the mouse. Monitoring the location of the mouse may have little practical application in the average website, but it can be useful in web-based games and analytics applications, where knowing the position of the mouse can influence how the page acts:

```
<script>
   function getCoords(event){
      var x=event.clientX;
      var y=event.clientY;
      alert("X: " + x + ", Y: " + y);
   }
</script>
<p onmousedown="getCoords(event)">Click anywhere on this sen-
tence to see the x and y coordinates of the mouse. Clear the
alert and try again to see the numbers change.</p>
```

While we are waiting for an event to occur, we can execute other steps before it is processed, or even replace it. We can see an example of this by saying goodbye before a visitor leaves our page:

```
<script>
   function sayGoodbye(){
```

```
        alert("Thanks for visiting!");
    }
</script>
<body onunload="sayGoodbye()">
```

To stop an event, we can use the preventDefault() method, which allows us to supersede what would have taken place. For instance, we may want to use a link to trigger a JavaScript function, but do not want to the page to reload, or follow the URL that was clicked on. In this example, we could have the following:

```
<script type="text/javascript">
    addEventListener("load",function(){
    var link= document.getElementById("google");
    links.addEventListener("click",function(e){
        e.preventDefault(); //prevent event action
    }
});
</script>
<body>
    <a href=http://www.google.com id="google">Google</a>
</body>
```

Geolocation

Devices and browsers that have access to GPS, cellular, or wireless router location data may provide that information to web pages (usually also in conjunction with user permission). When this data is available, our webpage can receive the information from the device. We can use it to improve the user experience, or provide features that are location dependent, like finding the nearest restaurant, or offering local deals. This example demonstrates how to access the information if it is available. Once we have the coordinates, we can write additional scripts on our backend (PHP and/or MySQL) that use them in order to tailor the user experience.

Keep in mind most browsers/devices allow the user to turn these features on and off, and not all devices will have access to or share this type of information. Because of this, it should not be a required or relied upon features unless you are sure your target users will be on such a device, and are aware that this type of feature is a requirement.

```
<p id="text">Where am I?</p>
<button onclick="getLocation()">Find Me</button>
<script>
    var response=document.getElementById("text");
    function getLocation(){
        if(navigator.geolocation){
        navigator.geolocation.getCurrentPosition(position);
    }
    else{response.innerHTML="Geolocation is not available from
    this device or browser.";}
    }
```

```
    function position(loc){
        response.innerHTML="Latitude: " + loc.coords.latitude +
        "<br>Longitude: " + loc.coords.longitude;
    }
</script>
```

Chapter 36

jQuery

jQuery is a freely available library add-on to JavaScript. It reduces the amount of code and complexity required to produce features and effects commonly used in creating today's sites. This library rapidly extends how much, and how fast, you can improve upon your site. In addition to jQuery, additional library extensions have been created that extend the jQuery library to automate even more tasks.

Before we begin to look at jQuery, we should consider implementation. The jQuery library is hosted for free on Google's servers at ajax.googleapis.com/ajax/libs/jquery/1.10.2/jquery.js (you may need to adjust the version number for future releases). While you are free to save any number of versions to your own site, there are benefits to using Google's copy. Among them are decreased latency (Google's copies are distributed on servers around the world), decreased communication load on your server, and a caching benefit—the more sites using Google as their source increases the chance your user will already have a recent copy on their device.

Once you have connected to Google, you may want a fall back—Google or not, things can happen. To do this, we need a mechanism to detect whether or not our Google hosted copy loaded correctly. To achieve this, we can test for a feature that is only present in jQuery after we have attempted to load it. If this feature fails, we can assume something went wrong, and then load our fallback copy. All of this can be done by adding two lines in our code:

```
<script src="//ajax.googleapis.com/ajax/libs/
jquery/1.10.2/jquery.min.js"></script>
<script>window.jQuery || document.write('<script
src="link/to/our/jquery-1.10.2.js"><\/script>')</script>
```

Once we have connected to the jQuery library, we can begin to use it in our JavaScript code. jQuery statements begin with a $ and then expect information on the selector we wish to use or the method we wish to access in order to take action. Using the document object method (DOM) to select a page element in JavaScript bears resemblance to the chain selector approach of Java:

```
document.getElementByID('ourAttributeName');
```

Meanwhile, jQuery allows us to identify the same element simply by referencing the same attribute:

```
$('#ourAttributeName');
```

While neither of these examples actually interact with the attribute, both identify the same unique place in our document. With jQuery, the use of the pound sign (#) in our selector specifies that we are looking for an ID. The #, in this case, takes the place of typing out document.getElementByID.

Alternatively, if we wanted to select all elements on our page with a particular class, we would exchange our pound sign for a period. This specifies that we want to select all items of the identified class:

```
$('.ourClassName');
```

Once we have declared our selector, it takes on aspects of an object, something that we can interact with whether it represent one or many elements on our page. For example, we can hide all paragraphs on a page by setting a button to do so:

```
<script>
$(document).ready(function(){
   $("button").click(function(){
      $("p").hide();
   });
});
</script>
<h2>Hide those paragraphs!</h2>
<p>This is a paragraph.</p>
<p>This is also a paragraph.</p>
<button>Hide them!</button>
```

In this example you will see we have three statements, all nested together. Moving from the inner-most statement out, we first have the action of actually hiding our paragraphs. This is executed as the callback of the statement it sits inside, meaning it is executed when the button element receives a click. Finally, we want to ensure that none of this occurs until the entire page is ready, as it is a response to a user interaction and not part of creating our page. To ensure this happens, all of this is nested inside a ready function attached to the entire page, which is referred to as document. This means nothing inside the $(document).ready… line will be available until after the page is done loading. Let us look at another example, where we change existing content instead of hiding it:

```
<script>
$(document).ready(function(){
   $("#btn").click(function(){
      $("#test").html("<b>We changed it!</b>");
   });
});
</script>
<p id="test">This is text we will change.</p>
<button id="btn">Set new HTML</button>
```

Like newer versions of CSS, we can traverse elements in our page by utilizing concepts like next and closest to move around from our starting point, without having to know exactly where our destination lies in the DOM. For example, if we were to call closest() on our $('#link') selector, it would traverse up through our page to find the preceding link. In our working example, we do not have one. In this case, the selector would return false, specifying that another link was not found. Otherwise, our selector would now represent that link, and any actions we took would apply to the new, preceding link that we had selected.

Using classes and IDs as our selectors is another best practice approach to using jQuery. While we could specify that we are looking for images that are in paragraphs that are in forms inside of a div tag, the resulting selector ($("div form p img"); is actually read in reverse. jQuery will process this by finding all images, eliminating those not immediately wrapped in a paragraph, eliminating from that list items which are not in a form, and then eliminating from what remains anything that is not immediately within a div.

Reading out the explanation is exhausting enough, let alone processing it. Although we could use the example above effectively, if we know the use case we want our selector to impact, we should simply add or implement an ID or class to those element(s) we wish to interact with. By sticking with a class or an ID, the selector can simply traverse the DOM looking for those identifiers. If you still need to use the combined selector approach, set it to a variable so you can refer to that variable in other places. This will save you the effort of finding all of those elements again.

The examples here are only a glimpse of the full power of jQuery. We are keeping it brief for a reason; until you are more comfortable with both JavaScript and CSS, immediately relying on a library can muddle the learning process. That being said, it is a powerful tool that you should embrace when ready to add more complex enhancements to your site.

LEARN MORE

Keywords, search terms: jQuery, jQuery libraries

50 jQuery Add-ons: http://tutorialzine.com/2013/04/50-amazing-jquery-plugins/

Full Documentation: http://api.jquery.com/

Section 3 Assessments

For each of these assignments, complete each step and submit all files (PHP, CSS, scripts, images, etc.) necessary by zipping and submitting your assignment folder.

Your First PHP

1. Comment your name and assignment number at the top of the file.
2. Create a variable that contains the current date and time.
3. Create a constant that contains the assignment title.
4. Make the assignment title the title of the page using the constant.
5. Output the date and time.
6. Output the PHP version, and server operating system (use system references).
7. Display the following string as shown:
   - "Chicken finger subs are the best!" said Clyde.
   - "I agree", said Bill, "but only when they are **extra hot**."
8. Calculate and display the following. Use variables for each value used in the equation:
   - 8 + 9 = 17
   - 24 % 8 = 0
   - 5 / 3 = 1.667

Forms and More

1. Create a website which presents the user with a registration form for a subscription service. Your form should request the following information:
   - First, last name
   - Occupation
   - Email address
   - Mailing address
   - Phone
   - Job Title
2. All information should be hidden (i.e., not be shown in the address bar).
3. Name, email, and mailing address fields should be required.
4. When completed, the form values are stored in a unique text file for each submission.
5. The user should see a confirmation that their submission was received.

What Time Is It?

1. Create an HTML page and complete the following with JavaScript only.
2. Output the current date and time to the screen.
3. Convert local time and date to UTC and display the result.
4. Add a button to your page that updates these times.

Let's Play A Game!

1. Create a page with a 3 by 3 grid to represent a tic-tac-toe board.
2. Using jQuery, assign an X or O (alternating back and forth) when a cell is clicked on.
3. Include a button to reset the board after a game.
4. Using canvas, put a colorful gradient of the words Tic-Tac-Toe at the top of the page.

Discussion / Written Response

1. How are tags in XML different from tags in HTML?
2. What is the difference between single and double quoted strings in PHP?
3. What is the difference between server side and client side scripting? What are good situations to use each?
4. What is the difference between GET and POST?
5. Describe the difference between notice, warning, and critical error messages in PHP.
6. Describe the difference between include, require, and require once.

Questions

TAKE THIS QUIZ ONLINE!

1. The array $array = ("One"=>1, "Two"=>2, "Three"=>3) is numeric.
    a. True
    b. False
2. Which equation equates to 14?
    a. 4 + 5 2 - 4
    b. (4 + 5) 2 – 4

   c. 4 + 5 (2 - 4)
   d. 4 + (5 2) – 4

3. The foreach() function in PHP is used when dealing with:
   a. Strings
   b. Arrays
   c. Objects
   d. Lists
4. Which PHP reserved array holds values passed in the URL?
   a. $_POST
   b. $_GET
   c. $_SESSION
   d. None of these
5. Which of the following is NOT a valid variable name?
   a. $variable
   b. $string
   c. $_string1
   d. $and-then
6. Which of the following is an incorrect definition?
   a. Apache = Web Server
   b. PHP = Object oriented language
   c. MySQL = Database Server
   d. HTML = Operating System
7. Which of the following PHP functions runs until a condition is met?
   a. foreach()
   b. while()
   c. during()
   d. None of these
8. Declaring strings using single quotes means PHP syntax in the string will be shown.
   a. True
   b. False
9. Which HTML element is used for JavaScript?
   a. <scripting>
   b. <javascript>
   c. <jscript>
   d. <script>
10. Where can we place JavaScript?

   a. <head>
   b. <body>
   c. A & B
   d. None of these

11. JavaScript and Java are the same thing.
   a. True
   b. False

12. DOM stands for
   a. Document Object Model
   b. Document Oriented Media
   c. Document Object Manager
   d. None of these

13. When a user views a page containing a JavaScript program, which machine actually executes the script?
   a. The user's browser
   b. The Web server
   c. Both
   d. None of the above

14. Which of the following cannot be done with JavaScript?
   a. Validating a form
   b. Sending a form's contents by email
   c. Storing the form's contents to a database file on the server
   d. None of the above

15. Which of the following is not a valid JavaScript variable name?
   a. 1stname
   b. _firstName
   c. FirstName
   d. None of these

16. What is the correct JavaScript syntax to write "Hello World"?
   a. System.out.println("Hello World")
   b. println ("Hello World")
   c. document.write("Hello World")
   d. response.write("Hello World")

17. jQuery uses CSS selectors to interact with page elements.
   a. True
   b. False

18. In jQuery, $('div') would select
    a. The first div element
    b. All div elements
    c. An element named div
19. Which jQuery function makes sure the contained code only runs when the page is done loading?
    a. $(body).onload()
    b. $(document).loaded()
    c. $document.ready()
    d. None of these
20. jQuery is an add-on library for JavaScript, not an independent language.
    a. True
    b. False

CHECK YOUR ANSWERS ON PAGE 284

Section 4:

Persistent Data Storage

Section Contents:

Database Types Data
Relationships MySQL
Data Types
Normalization MySQL
CRUD Actions
Advanced Queries

Learning Goals:

By the end of this section, you should be able to demonstrate:

- An understanding of basic database types
- How pieces of information can relate to each other
- The ability to normalize data into a structured query format
- The ability to create, populate, and interact with a MySQL database
- A basic understanding of the advanced capabilities of MySQL queries

Chapter 37

Database Types

While there are a number of databases available for use like MySQL, node.js, and Access, there is an additional list of the types of database structures each of these belong to. These types each represent a different organizational method of storing the information and denoting how elements within the data relate to each other. We will look at the three you are most likely to come across in the web development world, but this is still not an exhaustive representation of every approach available.

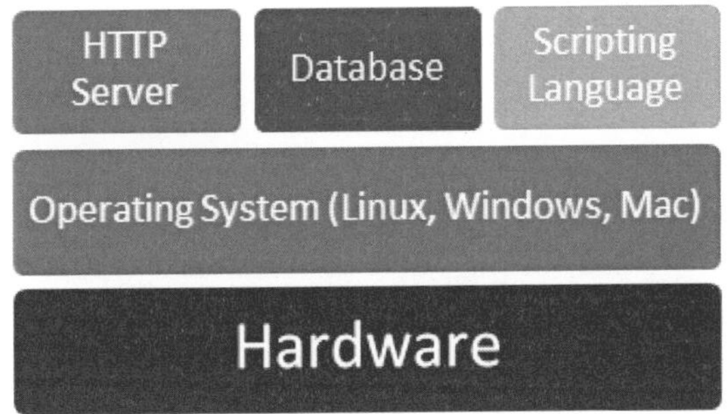

Flat File

Flat files are flat in that the entire database is stored in one file, usually separating data by one or more delimiters, or separating markers, that identify where elements and records start and end. If you have ever used Excel or another spreadsheet program, then you have already interacted with a flat file database. This structure is useful for smaller amounts of data, such are spreadsheets and personal collections of movies. Typically these are comma separated value files, .csv being a common extension. This refers to the fact that values in the file are separated by commas to identify where they start and end, with records marked by terminating characters like a new line, or by a different symbol like a colon or semi-colon.

The nature of all data being in one file makes the database easily portable, and somewhat human readable. However, information that would be repeated in the data would be written out fully in each record. Following our movie example, this could be the producer, studio, or actors. They have what we call a one-to-many relationship with other data in the database that cannot be tracked in this format.

Drawbacks to this format can affect your system in several ways. First, in our example, we would enter the studio name into each record for a movie made by that studio. If the person typing miss-typed an entry, it may not be found when users search the database, skewing search results through missing information. This often results in users creating new entries for a record that appears not to exist, causing duplication. Beyond search issues, every repetition is more space the database requires, especially when the value repeated is large. This was more of an issue when data was growing faster than storage capacity. Now, with exception to big data storage systems, the average user's storage space on an entry level PC typically surpasses the user's needs unless they are avid music or movie collectors. It is still important to consider when you are dealing with limited resources, such as mobile applications that are stored on smart phones that have memory limitations lower than that of desktops and servers.

Another issue with these files is the computational effort required to search the file, edit records, and insert new ones that are placed somewhere within the body of data as opposed to the start or end of the file.

Finally, flat files are not well suited for multiple, concurrent use by more than one party. Since all of the data is in one file, you are faced with two methods of interaction. The first approach is allowing anyone to access the file at the same time, usually by creating a local temporary copy on their system. While this allows multiple people the ability to use the file, if more than one party is allowed to make changes, we risk losing data. Say User 1 creates two new records while User 2 is editing one. If User 2 finished first and saves their changes, they are written back to the server. Then, User 1 sends their changes back, but their system is unaware of the changes made by User 2. When their changes are saved, User 2's changes are lost as User 1 overwrites the file. This can be prevented by checking last modified timestamps before allowing data to be written, but the user "refreshing" may have conflicts between their edits and the edits from another user, when the same record is changed.

The alternate approach to allowing multiple users is to block multiple users from making changes by only allowing one of them to have the file open at a time. This is done by creating a file lock, a marker on the file the operating system would see, that would block other users from using an open file. This approach does not support concurrent access to the data, and again even allowing read rights to other users would not show them changes in progress that another user has not completed and submitted. Another downside to this approach is what is called a race condition—where multiple systems are trying to access a file, but are unable to do so because another has the file locked, stalling all of the programs trying to access the data.

This was a key element in a large scale blackout of 2003 that took place in the Northeast United States and part of Canada. A summer heat wave created significant strain on the power system as demand for air conditioning increased, resulting in the emergency shutdown of a power station. This station happened to be editing its health status in a shared file between itself and other stations, a method used to allow other stations to adjust their operational levels in response to their neighbors. The purpose of this file was to act as a protection method, warning of potential spikes or drops in power at individual facilities. When the plant using the file shutdown, the file remained locked as the computer using it did not have time to send a close file command. Unable to properly close the file with the systems down, other stations were unaware of the problem until power demand at their facilities rapidly increased. As these stations could not access the file due to the lock, a warning could not be passed along. Since the power stations were under increasing strain with each failure, a cascading affect occurred throughout the entire system. Admittedly an extreme result of file lock failure, it is a very real world example of the results of using the wrong tools when designing a system.

Structured Query/Relational Database

Structured query databases can be viewed similar to flat files in that the presentation of a section of data can be viewed as its own table, similar to a single spreadsheet. The difference is that instead of one large file, the data is broken up based on user needs and by grouping related data together into different tables. You could picture this as a multi-page spreadsheet, with each page containing different information. For example, continuing with our movie example, one table would contain everything about the studio—name, opening date, tax code, and so on. The next table would contain everything about the movies—name, release date, description, production cost etc. Finally we might have a table for actors, producers, and everyone else involved. This table would have their information like birthday, hometown, and more.

What we do not have yet is a way to link these elements together. There is also a lot of information we *do not* want to include, because we can determine it from something else. For example, we do not want to store the actors age, or we would have to update the table every year on their birthday. Since we already have their birth date, we can have the server do the math based on the current date and their birth date to determine how old they are each time it is asked.

To relate an actor in our people table to a movie they were in from the movie table, as well as to the studio that made the movie in the studio table, we use a structured query. Structured query is a human readable (relatively) sentence-style language that uses a fixed vocabulary to describe what data we want and how to manipulate it. Part of this comes from adding extra tables. Since one actor can be in many movies, and each movie can have many actors, we have a many-to-many relationship between them. Due to this, we create an extra table where each row represents a record of an actor and a movie they were in. Instead of putting their full names into this table, we put the row number that identifies their information from their respective tables. This gives us a long, skinny table that is all numbers, called an "all-reference table," as it refers to other tables and does not contain any new information of its own. We will see this in action soon.

We can use our query language to ask the database to find all records in this skinny table where the movie ID matches the movie ID in the movie table, and also where the movie name is "Die Hard." The query will come back with a list of rows from our skinny table that have that value in the movie ID column. We can also match the actor IDs from a table that pairs actors with movies to records in the actor table in order to get their names. We could do this as two different steps or in one larger query. In using the query, we recreate what would have been one very long record in our flat file. The difference is we have done it with a smaller footprint, reduced mistyping errors, and only see exactly what we need to. We can also "lock" data in a query database at the record level, or a particular row in a database, when editing data, allowing other users access to the rest of the database.

While this style can be very fast and efficient in terms of storage size, interacting with the data through queries can be difficult as both one-to-many and many-to-many relationships are best represented through intermediary tables like we described above (one-to-one relationships are typically found within the same table, or as a value in one table directly referencing another table). In order to piece our records together, we need an understanding of the relationships between the data.

MySQL

Structured query language databases are a very popular data storage method in web development. While different approaches are emerging to address big data issues, the concepts you learn by studying structured query can help you organize data in any system.

MySQL, commonly pronounced as "my seequl" or "my s q l," is a relational database structure that is an open source implementation of the structured query language. The relational element arises from the file structure, which in this case refers to the fact that data is separated into multiple files based on how the elements of the data relate to one another in order to create a more efficient storage pattern that takes up less space.

In a traditional LAMP, MySQL plays the role of our data server, where we will store information that we want to be able to manipulate based on user interaction. Contents are records, like all the items available in Amazon's store. User searches and filters affect how much of the data is sent from the database to the web server, allowing the page to change at the user's request.

History

MySQL began when developers Monty Widenius and David Axmark attempted to use the mSQL database system to interact with their own tables they had created using low-level routines in ISAM. Their testing did not reveal the speeds or flexibility they wanted, so they created their own similar API, and dubbed it MySQL after co-founder Monty's daughter My.

After an internal release in 1995, MySQL was opened to the public with minor version updates spanning 3.19 to 3.23 from 1996 to 2000. Their next major version release, 4.0, arrived as beta in 2002 and reached production in 2003. Their next major release arrived as 5.0 in 2005 and included the addition of cursors, stored procedures, triggers, and views. These were all significant additions to the toolset.

In 2008, Sun Microsystems acquired what was then called MySQL AB with an agreement to continue development and release of the software as a free and open source item. When Sun was acquired by Oracle in 2010, MySQL was part of the package deal, under the same requirements. There have been some arguments over whether or not the spirit of the agreement between MySQL and Sun has been fully upheld by Oracle, including complaints from Widenius himself.

Structure

We organize data in MySQL by breaking it into different groups, called tables. Within these tables are rows and columns, in which each row is a record of data and each column identifies the nature of the information in that position. The intersection of a row and column is a cell, or one piece of information. Databases are collections of tables that represent a system. You can imagine a database server like a file cabinet. Each drawer represent a database in our server. Inside those drawers are folders that hold files. The folders are like our tables, each of which holds multiple records. In a file cabinet, our folders hold pieces of paper or records, just like the individual rows in a table. While this may seem confusing now, we will see it in action soon; this is the approach we will focus on for this section of the text.

NoSQL

NoSQL databases represent systems that maintain collections of information that do not specify relationships within or between each other. In reality, a more appropriate name would be NoRel or NoRelation as the focus is on allowing data to be more free form.

Most NoSQL system follow a key-value pairing system where each element of data is identified by a label. These labels are used as consistently as possible to establish common points of reference from file to file, but may not be present in each record. Records in these systems can be represented by individual files. In MongoDB, the file structure is a single XML formatted record in each file, or it can be ALL records as a single XML file. Searching for matches in a situation like this involves analyzing each record, or the whole file, for certain values.

These systems excel when high numbers of static records need to be stored. The more frequently data needs to be changed, the more you may find performance loss here. However, searching these static records can be significantly faster than relational systems, especially when the relational system is not properly normalized. This is actually an older approach to data storage that has been resurrected by modern technology's ability to capitalize on its benefits, and there are dozens of solutions vying for market dominance in this sector. Unless you are constructing a system with big data considerations or high volumes of static records, relational systems are still the better starting place for most systems.

LEARN MORE

Keywords, search terms: Database types, data structures, data storage

Node.js: http://nodejs.org/

The Acid Model: http://databases.about.com/od/specificproducts/a/acid.htm

Key-Value Stores, Marc Seeger: http://blog.marc-seeger.de/assets/papers/Ultra_Large_Sites_SS09-Seeger_Key_Value_Stores.pdf

Chapter 38

Data Relationships

Before we begin to design our database, we need to understand the different relationships that can exist between two pieces of information. For this example, we will start with two imaginary tables. The first will be names, and the second will be phone numbers. If we first consider a person with a cell phone that has no other numbers they can be reached at, we see a **one-to-one** relationship—the phone number for that cell phone is the only one associated with that person, and that person is the only one you reach when you call that number.

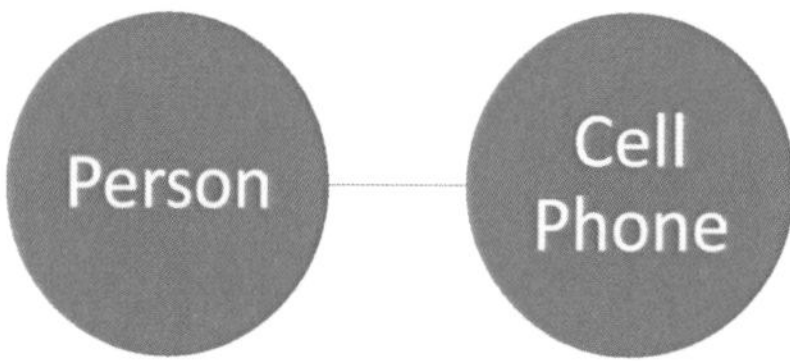

This does not cover all phone uses, though. Many of us still have phones at home or at work that are used by multiple people. In this case, the relationship between that phone and its users is **one-to-many**, as more than one person can be reached by using that phone number.

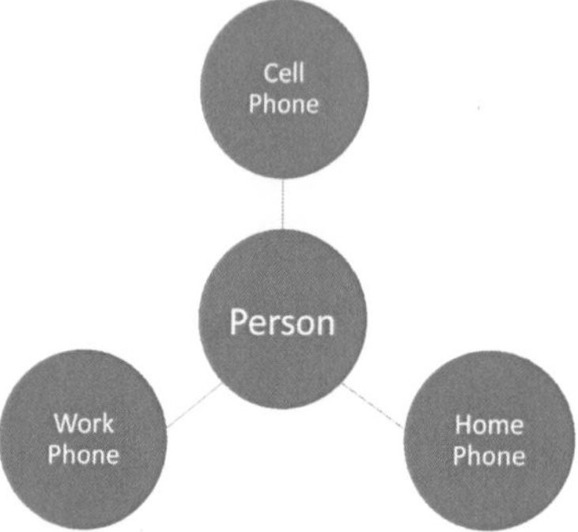

In reality, both of these are probably true for most people. This means that one number can represent many people (calling a house or business) and one person can be reached via multiple phone numbers. In this case, we have a **many-to-many** relationship where multiple values of the same table can relate to multiple values of another table. In this example, of all numbers (work, home, or cell) are stored in the same table, there can be multiple values connected to either side of a given number.

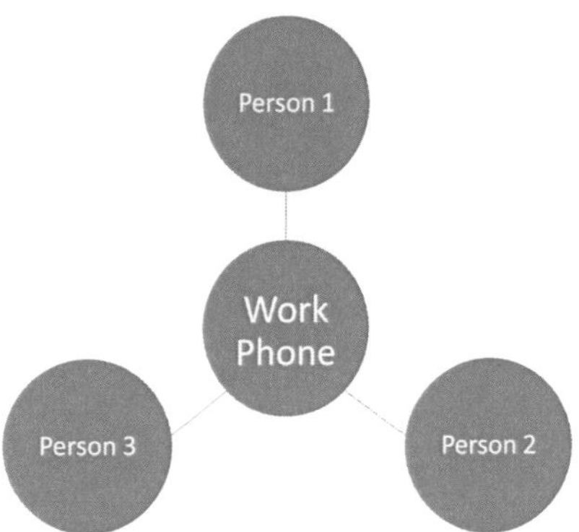

When we apply the theory of normalization to the database we are about to design, it is important to keep these relationships in mind as it indicates how we should structure our database. A one-to-one relationship can be resolved by keeping both pieces of information in the same table or by including a reference in either of the two tables to the other. For one-to-many relationships we need to keep the data in separate tables, and refer to the "one" item in our "many" table. Finally, for many-to-many relationships we do not have a good way to link directly between tables without violating normalization methods; instead we will create small connecting tables where each record represents a valid combination of the items from our two tables.

Primary, Foreign Keys

To find information in our database we need to be able to uniquely identify the record(s) we want to interact with. This can be done several ways. First, we can identify a piece of information from our table that makes each record unique, like a social security number identifies a US citizen. Sometimes, however, our record does not have one single piece of information that does this. Take a home address for example. To make an address unique, we need to take the street name, number, city, and zip code at a minimum. We can use this method to create a key that uses more than one column to identify a record, called a hybrid key.

Our last method is to let the database make a key for us, so every time we insert a record it receives a number unique for that table automatically. In this method, we let the database manage an auto-increment for that column. While it identifies a particular row, it does not contribute information that relates to the data it identifies. We will see examples of primary keys come into play as we normalize an example dataset, so for now you just need to keep the concept in mind.

Chapter 39

MySQL Data Types

The next few pages will likely be a little dry. Apologies now. However, whenever we create a table structure in MySQL we must identify the data type we intend to store in any given column, and depending on the type of data and other features we may want, this is just the beginning. Since one of our goals in the relational approach to database design is reducing overall size, it is also important to consider the *best fit* data type for what we want to store. Familiarizing yourself with the types available in MySQL will lend to your ability to design efficient table structures. The tables below are adopted from http://www.w3resource.com/mysql/mysql-data-types.php. They have been trimmed down in an attempt to not introduce an overwhelming amount of detail. You are encouraged to review the original version for more depth.

Table 14 MySQL Data Types

Integer Types

Type	Length in Bytes	Minimum Value(Signed/ Unsigned)	Maximum Value(Signed/ Unsigned)
TINYINT	1	-128 to 0	127 to 255
SMALLINT	2	-32768 to 0	32767 to 65535
MEDIUMINT	3	-8388608 to 0	8388607 to 16777215
INT	4	-2147483648 to 0	2147483647 to 4294967295
BIGINT	8	-9223372036854775808 to 0	9223372036854775807 to 18446744073709551615

Floating-Point Types

Types	Description
FLOAT	A precision from 0 to 23 results in a four-byte single-precision FLOAT column.
DOUBLE	A precision from 24 to 53 results in an eight-byte double-precision DOUBLE column.

Fixed-Point Types

Types	Description
DECIMAL	In the format DECIMAL(precision,scale). Maximum number of digits allowed are 65 before MySQL 5.03 and 64 after 5.03.
NUMERIC	Same as DECIMAL.

Bit Value Types

Types	Description
BIT	In the format b BIT(N), where N is an integer.

Numeric type Attributes

Types	Description
TYPE(N)	Where N is an integer and display width of the type is up to N digits.
ZEROFILL	The default padding of spaces is replaced with zeroes. So, for a column INT(3) ZEROFILL, 7 is displayed as 007.

DATETIME, DATE, and TIMESTAMP Types

Types	Description	Display Format	Range
DATETIME	Use when you need values containing both date and time information.	YYYY-MM-DD HH:MM:SS	'1000-01-01 00:00:00' to '9999-12-31 23:59:59'.
DATE	Use when you need only date information.	YYYY-MM-DD	'1000-01-01' to '9999-12-31'.
TIMESTAMP	Values are converted from the current time zone to UTC while storing, and converted back from UTC to the current time zone when retrieved.	YYYY-MM-DD HH:MM:SS	'1970-01-01 00:00:01' UTC to '2038-01-19 03:14:07' UTC.

String Types

Types	Description
CHAR	Contains non-binary strings. Length is fixed as you declare while creating a table. When stored, they are right-padded with spaces to the specified length.
VARCHAR	Contains non-binary strings. Columns are variable-length strings.

BINARY and VARBINARY Types

Types	Description	Range in bytes
BINARY	Contains binary strings.	0 to 25.

VARBINARY	Contains binary strings.	A value from 0 to 255 before MySQL 5.0.3, and 0 to 65,535 in 5.0.3 and later versions.

BLOB and TEXT Types

Types	Description	Categories	Range.
BLOB	Large binary object that containing a variable amount of data. Values are treated as binary strings. You do not need to specify length while creating a column.	TINYBLOB	Maximum length of 255 characters.
		MEDIUMBLOB	Maximum length of 16777215 characters.
		LONGBLOB	Maximum length of 4294967295 characters.
TEXT	Values are treated as character strings having a character set.	TINYBLOB	Maximum length of 255 characters.
		MEDIUMBLOB	Maximum length of 16777215 characters.
		LONGBLOB	Maximum length of 4294967295 characters.

ENUM Types

A string object whose value is chosen from a list of values given at the time of table creation. For example:

```
ENUM('small', 'medium', 'large')
```

SET Types

A string object having zero or more comma separated values (maximum 64). Values are chosen from a list of values given at the time of table creation.

Chapter 40

Normalization

Normalization is the process of structuring and refining the data we want to store in such a way that we eliminate repeated information and represent as much connection between records as possible. When a database meets particular rules or features of normalization, it is usually referred to as being in a particular normal form. The collection of rules progress from the least restrictive (first normal, or 1NF) through the most restrictive (fifth normal, or 5NF) and beyond. Databases can still be useful and efficient at any level depending on their use, and anything beyond third normal form is more of a rarity in real world practice.

Bear in mind, that normalization is a theory on data organization, not law. Your database can operate just fine without adhering to the following steps, but following the process of normalizing will make your life easier and improve the efficiency of your website. Not every set of circumstances will require all of these rules to be followed. This is especially true if they will make accessing your data more difficult for your particular application. These rules are designed to help you eliminate repeated data, are able to keep your overall database size as small as possible, and create integrity in your records.

Zero Normal Form

To begin, we need something to normalize. Through this section we will create a database to keep track of a music collection. First, we need a list of what we want to track. We will follow what is generally useful for a collection of music, like albums, artists, and songs. These categories give us a list of things we want to store, so let us come up with what a full record might contain:

Band Name	Album Title	Song Title	Song length	Producer Name
Release Year	Artist hometown	Concert Venue	Concert Date	Artist Name

To get a visual of what this table might look like, let us take a look at some sample data with many of these fields:

SONG TITLE	ARTIST	GENRE	SUB-GENRE	YEAR
Shannon	Henry Gross	Rock	Light Rock	1976
Lover's Will	Bonnie Raitt	Rock	Light Rock	1998
I Don't Wanna Live Without Your Love	Chaptercago	Rock	Light Rock	1988
Heart Attack	Olivia Newton-John	Pop	Adult Contemporary	1982
In A Dream	Badlands	Rock	Hard Rock	1991
With A Little Luck	Paul McCartney	Rock	Classic Rock	1978
It's A Miracle	Barry Manilow	Pop	Adult Contemporary	1975
It's Only Love	Bryan Adams / Tina Turner	Pop	Adult Contemporary	1984
Jazzman	Carole King	Pop	Adult Contemporary	1974
Jesse	Carly Simon	Pop	Adult Contemporary	1980
Just Like Jesse James	Chapterr	Pop	Adult Contemporary	1989
Little Miss Cannot Be Wrong	Spin Doctors	Pop	Adult Contemporary	1992
Lost In Love	Air Supply	Pop	Adult Contemporary	1980
Good Times	Sam Cooke	Hip-Hop	Soul	1964
Make It With You	Bread	Pop	Adult Contemporary	1970
Mandy	Barry Manilow	Pop	Adult Contemporary	1974
Miss Chaptertelaine	K.D. Lang	Pop	Adult Contemporary	1992
Never Gonna Fall In Love Again	Eric Carmen	Pop	Adult Contemporary	1976
People Get Ready	Rod Stewart	Pop	Adult Contemporary	1985
Try Honesty (Radio Version)	Billy Talent	Rock	Modern Rock	2007
Silver Threads And Golden Needles	Linda Ronstadt	Pop	Adult Contemporary	1974
So Far Away	Carole King	Pop	Adult Contemporary	1971
Fat Lip	Sum 41	Rock	Modern Rock	2001
Thank You For Being a Friend	Andrew Gold	Pop	Adult Contemporary	1978

As an example of non-normalized or "zero normal form" data, you can look to the data above where you see long, repeated fields. While this table is easy to read without a query or software, it quickly becomes unmanageable even in its readable format as 25 records turns into just a few hundred.

Let us take a summary look at our forms that will help us tackle this problem:

First Normal Form

1. Create separate tables for related information
2. Eliminate duplicated columns within tables
3. Create primary keys for each table

Second Normal Form

- Meet first normal form
- Move data that will repeat often into a reference table
- Connect reference tables with foreign keys

Third Normal Form

- Meet second normal form
- Eliminate columns that do not relate to their primary key

Fourth Normal Form

- Meet third normal form
- Has no multi-valued dependencies

When working with an existing data set like our example above, you can quickly move through normalization once you are familiar with the rules. By adjusting our table(s) until they meet each set of rules, our data becomes normalized. Since we are learning, we will formulate our database from scratch.

ADDITIONAL NOTES

As we draw up our design, each bolded word represents a table, and the names underneath represent our columns. We can simulate a record, or row, in our database by writing out sample values for each thing in our list.

First Normal Form

To get started, we will go through our draft list piece by piece. "Band Name" refers to the official name of the group or artist we are talking about. A good question to ask is does the column sounds like a concept, object, or idea that represents something, or would have properties, in our database. The concept of a band for us is important, and it will have properties made up of other columns we plan to have, like songs and albums. Since we can see this is a concept, it is a good candidate for a table, so we will start by creating a table for our bands. Just like we studied in the PHP section, it is good practice to keep a set of conventions when naming elements. With databases, it can be helpful to treat your tables as the plural form of what its rows will contain. In this case, we will name our table Bands. Under this name, we will list "Band Name" to the list of information in that table. A key element to think about every time we consider adding a field to a table is to make sure it represents only one piece of information. A band name meets our criteria of being only one piece of information, so we are on track.

Now our design notes might look more like this:

~~Band Name~~	Album Title	Song Titles	Song length	Producer Name
Release Year	Artist hometown	Concert Venue	Concert Date	Artist Names

Bands Band Name		

Our next element, Album Title, seems like it would relate to a band. At first, we might be tempted to put it in the band table because the album record we add belongs to the band. However, when we consider our data relationships, it becomes clear that we have a one to many situation; one band will (one-hit wonders aside) release more than one album. Since we always program to meet our highest possible level of relationship, the one-hit-wonders will exist perfectly fine even with only one album in our database. If you recall, we address one to many relationships by placing the two sides in separate tables and identifying in the "many" table which "one" the record is paired with. To do this, we will make an albums table just like we did for bands, and add a placeholder in our note to refer to the band table:

~~Band Name~~	~~Album Title~~	Song Titles	Song length	Producer Name
Release Year	Artist hometown	Concert Venue	Concert Date	Artist Names

Bands Band Name	**Albums** Album Name (reference to Band)	

Now we are on to "Song Titles." The songs are organized into albums, so we will add it in.

Albums

Album Name

Song Titles

Apply our tests and see if this works. Does this field represent one piece of information? Titles is plural as we have it written, but we cannot put more than one piece of information in a single cell. We will need to break that up into individual titles to resolve. To make that change in this table though, we would have to create a column for each track. In order to do that, we would need to know ahead of time the max number of tracks any album we enter will have. This is not only impractical, but violates our first normal form of not repeating columns. Through this we can see that we again have a one to many relationship on our hands as one album will have multiple tracks. To resolve this, once again we will break our multiple field out to its own table, where we can create a link back to our album table:

~~Band Name~~	~~Album Title~~	~~Song Titles~~	Song length	Producer Name
Release Year	Artist hometown	Concert Venue	Concert Date	Artist Names

Bands Band Name	**Albums** Album Name (reference to Band)	**Songs** Song Title (reference to Album)

We can already see a thread weaving its way through our tables. Even though these fields are no longer all in one record together, you can see how we can trace our way through by looking for the band we want in the albums table, and when we know the albums, we can find all the tracks the band has published. To continue with our design we will move to song length. This field sounds fitting in our songs table, and is only one piece of information, so we are off to a good start! We can also see that we would only have one song length per record as each record here is a song, so we comply with column count, too. We can put it there for now, and will see if it meets the rest of our tests as we move on.

~~Band Name~~	~~Album Title~~	~~Song Titles~~	~~Song length~~	Producer Name

Release Year	Artist hometown	Concert Venue	Concert Date	Artist Names

Bands Band Name	**Albums** Album Name (reference to Band)	**Songs** Song Title Song Length (reference to Album)

Now that we have an idea of first normal form, we will get the rest of our initial columns out of the way:

~~Band Name~~	~~Album Title~~	~~Song Titles~~	~~Song length~~	~~Producer Name~~
~~Release Year~~	~~Artist hometown~~	~~Concert Venue~~	~~Concert Date~~	~~Artist Names~~

Bands Band Name	**Albums** Album Name Release Year (reference to Band)	**Songs** Song Title Song Length (reference to Album)
Labels Producer Name	**Artists** Artist Name Hometown	**Concerts** Venue Date

Now that we have exhausted our initial list, we will consider the last element of 1NF, which is primary keys for each table. Many of our tables are not presenting us with good candidates, as band names, venues, albums, tracks, and even artists could share the same names as time goes on. To make things consistent, we will create auto incrementing IDs for each table. To follow best practices, we will use the singular version of the noun with ID after it to denote our primary keys. This identifies the row as a singular version of the concept our table name is a plural of:

Bands bandID Band Name	**Albums** albumID Album Name Release Year (reference to Band)	**Songs** songID Song Title Song Length (reference to Album)
Labels producerID Producer Name	**Artists** artistID Artist Name Hometown	**Concerts** venueID Venue Date

Second Normal Form

We have now reached first normal form. Now I must admit, I have been a bit sneaky. By introducing data relationships, and showing you how to apply the relationship when considering where to put columns, we have already addressed part of second normal form, so, technically, we are already beyond first normal form. The first piece of second normal form is creating tables anywhere where a value of a cell could apply to multiple records of that table. When we moved song title out of albums, we were fulfilling this requirement. Looking over our tables again, we can see that, as we have things now, this has been met.

The other element of second normal form is that connections between tables should be facilitated by foreign keys. We have already started that process by earmarking a couple tables with notes where we knew we needed connections. Now that we have our primary keys, we have the unique values we will need to use. For this pass, we will look at how our tables relate to each other and see if we need connections. This is another step where remembering how to solve our data relationships will be important. To start with the tables we earmarked, we will look at "Albums." Our reference calls for connecting it to "Bands," so we will add a foreign key in "Albums" that points to "Bands." To make things easy on us, we can use the same name in both tables so we know what it is for.

Bands	**Albums**	**Songs**
bandID Band Name	albumID Album Name Release Year bandID	songID Song Title Song Length (reference to Album)
Labels	**Artists**	**Concerts**
producerID Producer Name	artistID Artist Name Hometown	venueID Venue Date

We can do the same with our "Songs" table as well to reference our "Albums" table. Looking at our "Labels" table, it could be argued that since a band belongs to a label that we should connect them. However, the relationship between a band and a label can change over time as contracts come and go, which would give us a many-to-many relationship. Another place we can associate this information is in the album. Once an album is published, the label that produced it will not change, and multiple labels do not publish the same album. To resolve these, we need album in two places. First, we need a many-to-many relationship table for labels and bands, and a one-to-many link between albums and labels. We already know how to link on-to-many, so we will add a foreign key to producerID in or albums table. Then we will add a table that has an incrementing auto ID, a foreign key to labels, and foreign key to albums, and a timestamp:

Bands	**Albums**	**Songs**	
bandID Band Name	albumID Album Name Release Year bandID producerID	songID Song Title Song Length (reference to Album)	
Labels	**Artists**	**Concerts**	**Bands2Labels**
producerID Producer Name	artistID Artist Name Hometown	venueID Venue Date	id producerID bandID timestamp

By adding the timestamp column in our many-to-many table, we can sort by the date the records were added, assuming they were added chronologically. This means the newest record would represent who the band is signed with now, and we can look at all the records with a particular band to see who a band has worked with, and we can look at all the records for a label to see who they have signed.

If we wanted to round out this information more, we could add start and end timestamps that represent contracts with the label. With the additional of these fields we could create even more timelines.

Continuing on, we have our "Artists" table. We know performers can be solo or in groups, and can belong to different bands over time, so we have another many-to-many relationship. You will notice the name given to the table bridging our bands and labels relationship is labelled Bands2Labels. This of course is only one possible name we could use, but is an example of how to clearly identify the purpose of the table, as we are linking "bands to labels." Our last table to look at is "Concerts." We need a way to associate a particular concert with the band that performed. Since each row of this table is a particular concert we will add a foreign key in.

We now have foreign keys to link our tables together where needed, and do not have a situation where multiple records in a table would contain the same values. We have now reached second normal form.

Third Normal Form

Our next normal form requires that all of the fields in a table relate to the key (or are a key), or in other words the concept of that table. In our smaller tables this is immediately apparent to us—a band name relates directly to a band, and a producer name relates directly to a label. It can be remembered in a popular rewording to the well-known court room oath that references Edgar Codd, who created the concept of third normal form. My favorite variation is the following: "All columns in the table must relate to the key, the whole key, and nothing but the key, so help me Codd"(source unknown).

To see third normal form in action we will review our current design. We already considered bands and labels while describing this form, so we will mark them green as OK.

<table>
<tr><td>Bands
bandID
Band Name</td><td>Albums
albumID
Album Name
Release Year
bandID
producerID</td><td colspan="2">Songs
songID
Song Title
Song Length
(reference to Album)</td></tr>
<tr><td>Labels
producerID
Producer Name</td><td>Artists
artistID
Artist Name
Hometown</td><td>Concerts
venueID
Venue
Date</td><td>Bands2Labels
id
producerID
bandID
timestamp</td></tr>
</table>

When we review "Albums" and "Songs" we only have a couple fields to consider from each table as the rest are primary and foreign keys. Album names and release years both refer to albums, and the same holds true for song titles and length in the songs table. Bands2Lables is also easy to review as all of the elements are keys—it is an all-reference table.

<table>
<tr><td>Bands
bandID
Band Name</td><td>Albums
albumID
Album Name
Release Year
bandID
producerID</td><td colspan="2">Songs
songID
Song Title
Song Length
(reference to Album)</td></tr>
<tr><td>Labels
producerID
Producer Name</td><td>Artists
artistID
Artist Name
Hometown</td><td>Concerts
venueID
Venue
Date</td><td>Bands2Labels
id
producerID
bandID
timestamp</td></tr>
</table>

Next, consider the "Artists" table. Artist name, obviously, fits with artist. What about hometown? Certainly they relate—a person usually identifies one location as home—but the actual information that would reside in the cell (likely a city) does not just relate to an artist. Looking at our concert table for example, a venue would have a physical location in which it resides as well. This tells us that hometown needs to be moved somewhere else. Since we do not have a place in our database that speaks specifically to locations, we will have to add one. When we do this, we should also consider that in reality the hometown city name by itself is not sufficiently unique without a state and zip code reference as well, and we will need to change our existing hometown column to reference the new table:

<table>
<tr><td colspan="2">Bands
bandID
Band Name</td><td>Albums
albumID
Album Name
Release Year
bandID
producerID</td><td colspan="2">Songs
songID
Song Title
Song Length
(reference to Album)</td></tr>
<tr><td>Labels
producerID
Producer Name</td><td>Locations
locID
city
state
zip</td><td>Artists
artistID
Artist Name
locationID</td><td>Concerts
venueID
Venue
Date</td><td>Bands2Labels
id
producerID
bandID
timestamp</td></tr>
</table>

Almost there! When we consider the "Concerts" table, at first glance we appear to be in third normal form (because we are). While we are here though, we need to keep in mind that in each pass of normalization we need to consider the database as a whole and all of the other forms of normalization as we keep tweaking our tables. Here, while venue makes sense as a column, using venue as the primary key seems confusing, as we are identifying a particular concert, not a particular place. When we consider this, it may also become apparent that just knowing the name of a venue may not be enough to uniquely identify it either. Since we have created a location table, we can take advantage of it here as well:

<table>
<tr><td colspan="2">Bands
bandID
Band Name</td><td>Albums
albumID
Album Name
Release Year
bandID
producerID</td><td colspan="2">Songs
songID
Song Title
Song Length
(reference to Album)</td></tr>
<tr><td>Labels
producerID
Producer Name</td><td>Locations
locID
city
state
zip</td><td>Artists
artistID
Artist Name
locationID</td><td>Concerts
concertID
Venue
locID
Date</td><td>Bands2Labels
id
producerID
bandID
timestamp</td></tr>
</table>

Have we satisfied all forms? Well, not quite yet. We have adjusted our concerts table to better meet third normal form, but is it fully compliant or did we miss something? Imagine this table populated and you will notice that the venue field—the name of our location—would be repeated each time the venue was used. This violates second normal form. To solve this, we know we need to split the data out to its own table, so we need to see if anything else should go with it. The location ID we just created relates to the venue, not the event, so that should go too. The date is correct where it is, as it identifies a particular piece of information about the concert. Does this cover everything? We do not seem to have a means to identify who actually performed the concert at that venue on that date, do we? This is a key piece of information about a concert, and any given concert usually involves more than one performer. Not only do we need to add the field but we need to remember our data relationships and see that this is a many-to-many between artists and concerts. Multiple artists can perform at the same event, and with any luck a given artist will perform more than one concert. We can address all of these changes by creating a Venues table, a many-to-many reference table for concerts and performers, and adjusting our concerts table to meet these changes. Try writing it out yourself before looking at the next table!

<table>
<tr><td colspan="2">Bands
bandID
Band Name</td><td colspan="2">Albums
albumID
Album Name
Release Year
bandID
producerID</td><td>Songs
songID
Song Title
Song Length
(reference to Album)</td><td>Concerts2Artists
Id
artistID
concertID</td></tr>
<tr><td>Labels
producerID
Producer Name</td><td>Locations
locID
city
state
zip</td><td>Artists
artistID
Artist Name
locationID</td><td>Venues
venueID
Name
locID</td><td>Concerts
concertID
venueID
Date</td><td>Bands2Labels
id
producerID
bandID
timestamp</td></tr>
</table>

Now, all of the tables we had at the beginning of third normal form are complete. We need to review the three we created to make sure they, too, meet all three forms. In this example, they do.

Now that we have reached third normal form we can see how normalization helps us out. We could have a list of 2000 concerts in our system, and each of those records would just be numerical references to one record for each artist and concert. In doing this, we do not of repeat all of those details in every record.

Fourth Normal Form

While most systems (and most tutorials) usually stop at third normal form, we are going to explore a bit further. Fourth normal form is meant to address the fact that independent records should not be repeated in the same table. We began running into this when we looked for problems in complying with second normal form as we began to consider the data relationships between our fields. At the time, not only did we split out tables where we found one-to-many relationships, we also split out all-reference tables to account for the many-to-many relationships we found. This was easy to do at the time as we were focused on looking for those relationship types. That also means, however, that we have already met fourth normal form, by preventing many-to-many records from creating repeated values within our tables.

To keep fourth normal compliance in other systems, you will need to be mindful of places where user-submitted data could be repeated. For example, you may allow users to add links to their favorite sites. Certainly at some point more than one user will have entered the same value, and this would end up repeated in the table. To prevent this, you would store all links in a table and create a many-to-many reference with your user records. Each time a link is saved, you would check your links table for a match, update records if it exists, or add it to the table if it has never been used.

This process can be helpful when you expect very high volumes of records and/or need to be very mindful of the size, or footprint, of your database (for example, running the system on a smartphone).

Before we move on, we will make one more pass to clean up our design. Since we started with words as concepts, but want to honor best practices when we create our database, we will revise all of our tables to follow a consistent capitalization and pluralization pattern:

<table>
<tr><td colspan="2">Bands
bandID
bandName</td><td colspan="2">Albums
albumID
albumName
releaseDate
bandID
producerID</td><td>Songs
songID
title
length
albumID</td><td>Concerts2Artists
id
artistID
concertID</td></tr>
<tr><td>Labels
producerID
producer</td><td>Locations
locID
city
state
zip</td><td>Artists
artistID
artistName
locationID</td><td>Venues
venueID
venueName
locationID</td><td>Concerts
concertID
venueID
date</td><td>Bands2Labels
id
producerID
bandID
timestamp</td></tr>
</table>

Congratulations, you now have a normalized database! Flip back to look at our original design, and you will see a number of trends. First, the process was a bit extensive, and turned into far more tables than you likely expected. However, it also helped us identify more pieces of information that we thought we would want, and helped us isolate the information into single pieces (like splitting location in city, state, zip) which allows us to search by any one of those items.

LEARN MORE

Keywords, search terms: Normalization, boyce-cobb normal form

MySQL's Guide: http://ftp.nchu.edu.tw/MySQL/tech-resources/articles/intro-to-normalization.html

High Performance MySQL: http://my.safaribooksonline.com/book/-/9781449332471

Chapter 41

MySQL CRUD Actions

There are four basic actions that cover how we interact with the data and structures in our database. We can either create new data, read existing data, update something already in place, or delete it. These four actions are collectively referred to as CRUD, for Create Read Update and Delete, and represent the basic concepts behind data interaction. In MySQL, we will address these concepts through a collection of commands.

Opening SQL

From a Browser

If you are using an installation of WAMP, you will have access to PhpMyAdmin from your browser. This program includes a SQL tab where you can input commands to your server as well as use a graphic interface to interact with your databases. Typically you can get there by going to http://locahost/phpmyadmin or http://127.0.0.1/phpmyadmin (do not forget to add the port number if you changed yours from :80). Your credentials will be the same as described in the next section, and you will find a SQL tab that allows you to enter commands to follow along with our examples.

From a Command Prompt

Each MySQL installer includes a client access program to interact with your server. Due to the variety of operating systems and versions of MySQL, definitive directions for accessing your client program cannot be provided here, but can be found by searching online with the details of your particular system. In general, your programs list may contain a MySQL folder with a link to launch the client, or you can access it by using your system's terminal window. Once you have a terminal window open, you can log into MySQL by typing:

```
mysql -u root -p
```

This instructs your computer to start MySQL using the username (represented by –u) of root and asking it to prompt you for a password, represented by –p. Once you press enter, you will be prompted to enter the password. By default, MySQL uses root as the username. Your password could be root, password, or an empty password (type nothing at all) depending on your version. If you changed these values when you installed, use what you provided in place of this example.

Once logged in to your database, you can begin to take a look around to see what your server already contains. To see what is currently in your server, you can enter a simple command to ask for that list. In MySQL we need to end our statements with semi-colons just as we do with PHP. Our commands and interactions are structured to be sentence-like, which makes queries easier to understand. Let us take a look at what we have available:

```
Show databases;
```

In a new installation of MySQL, you should see a list similar to the following:

```
+--------------------+
|    Database        |
+--------------------+
| information_schema |
| mysql              |
+--------------------+
2 rows in set (0.00 sec)
```

Now that we have designed our database, it is time to describe it to the server, and get some data into it, so we have a fully functioning system. First we need to get into MySQL:

```
create database music;
```

After pressing enter you should see a response from the server that gives either a completed message or an error message, along with other information such as the amount of time it took to complete the instruction. If you receive an error that the database already exists, you can use a different name. If something happened and you are starting over, or know you can get rid of the existing database, you can get rid of it and all its data by typing:

```
drop database music;
```

Keep in mind this command deletes everything—the database and all tables and data stored in it. There is no "undo" option or garbage bin to recover from, so if you do not have a backup you will not be able to recover from this action. Once you have a database created, tell the server that is the one you want to interact with by typing:

```
use music;
```

You will notice we consistently use semi-colons after each instruction. Just like in PHP, this is how the server can tell where one instruction ends and the next begins.

Create

The first step in building our database is to create the tables from our design. Before we do so, we need to create the database we want to put those tables in. Be sure you have a music database created as we saw above. We will keep using the database we just designed. The create command for a table involves specifying that we mean to create a table (as opposed to a database), defining our table name, and then in parenthesis defining each column. This done with a comma separated collection of values that includes the name, type, null option, and other features of the column. Here we will look at the command necessary to create our first table:

Bands bandID bandName		**Albums** albumID albumName releaseDate bandID producerID		**Songs** songID title length albumID	**Concerts2Artists** id artistID concertID
Labels producerID producer	**Locations** locID city state zip	**Artists** artistID artistName locationID	**Venues** venueID venueName locationID	**Concerts** concertID venueID date	**Bands2Labels** id producerID bandID timestamp

```
Create table bands (bandID int not null auto_increment primary
key,
bandName varchar (40) not null
);
```

You will notice a few things about this statement. First, we only use commas to separate the entire definition of one column from another as opposed to separating each piece of information about a column. If you are using a command line interface, you can also use the enter key to format your statement as we did above, with one column on each line. This is due to the fact that the statement will not execute until the semicolon is present.

After we identified our first column as bandID, we identified it as an integer, referencing the data types we looked at earlier. We also stated that this column cannot be null, meaning it must have a value. We can apply this on any column that must be present in our table for a record to be considered useable. In this case, we want bandID to be entered for us by the database. Adding the auto_increment attribute will tell the database to assign each new record a value (we can also control the starting value if we ever wanted to start at something other than 1). Finally, we label this column as the primary key of our table, place a comma at the end of our definition, and move to the next column.

When we add our bandName to the table definition we needed to define far less. This time, we went with varchar (variable character) which means we expect the content to be text, but not necessarily long text like sentences or paragraphs. When we use varchar, we have to tell MySQL what the maximum number of characters is allowed in the field, so it knows how much space to reserve for each record. In this example, we have decided that our longest band name would be at most 40 characters. To complete this column we again specify that it cannot be null. In our example, it is the only field in the table outside of the id anyway. If we wanted to allow a null value, we could include the word null in place of not null, or just drop that piece altogether (MySQL will assume null is valid unless told otherwise).

After we execute this statement, we can use the command "show tables" to see what is in our database:

```
mysql> show tables;
+--------------------+
| Tables_in_music    |
+--------------------+
| bands              |
+--------------------+
```

```
1 row in set (0.00 sec)
```

To make sure everything was created as we intended, we can look more closely at the structure of the table we created with the command "show columns from":

```
mysql> show columns from bands;
+---------+-----------+----+-----+-------+--------------+
| Field   | Type      |Null| Key |Default| Extra        |
+---------+-----------+----+-----+-------+--------------+
| bandID  | int(11)   | NO | PRI | NULL  |auto_increment|
| bandName|varchar(40)| NO |     | NULL  |              |
+---------+-----------+----+-----+-------+--------------+
2 rows in set (0.02 sec)
```

Here we can see the structure of what we just created. Neither field can be null, bandID is our primary key, will auto increment, and neither field has a default value. If we want to assign a default value, we would include the word default followed by the value in quotation marks when defining our column.

We will create one more table here as a second example, and then you can continue creating the rest on your own in order to practice. Now we should create the Albums table so we can see a data field in use, which will cover all of the data types we will need in this database. Keep in mind that when we create tables with foreign keys in our example here, we are not going to define them as such at the database layer like we did when we defined our primary key. This is an available feature however, and allows MySQL to help us maintain data integrity by giving us an error if we try to insert a record where a foreign key value does not exist. As an example, if we tried to create a concert record but our reference to artist #5 did not exist in the artist table, MySQL would return an error instead of allowing the record to be created. You would have to create artist #5 first, then go back and try your previous statement again. Since this complicates the order of table creation and data insertion, we will ignore if for now until you are more comfortable, but know it is available and useful for production systems.

```
Create table albums( albumID int not null auto_increment pri-
mary key,
albumName varchar(70) not null,
releaseDate date,
bandID int not null,
producerID int
);
```

Once we have created all of our tables, we will need to put some data in them so we have something to interact with. To do this, we use the insert command. Using insert involves specifying the table we want to interact with, passing the list of fields we intend to fill, and then passing the values for those fields. The fields, as well as each set (or record) of values are contained in a comma separated list enclosed in parenthesis. Multiple records can be added at once, assuming each record is using the same set of fields, by adding another set of data in parenthesis. We can see this in action by creating our first band:

```
Insert into bands(bandName) values ("The Who");
```

If we want to pass more than one record, we just keep tagging on more sets:

```
Insert into bands(bandName) values ("Moxy Fruvous"), ("The
Doors"), ("Maroon 5");
```

Take note of the fact that we do *not* specify the bandID for these records. Before we can insert albums though, we need to know what each band's ID actually is. We will take a quick preview of the Read actions by using the following command to get that information:

```
Select * from bands;
```

This command should give you something like the following:

```
mysql> Select * from bands;
+--------+-------------+
| bandID | bandName    |
+--------+-------------+
| 1      | The Who     |
| 2      | Moxy Fruvous|
| 3      | The Doors   |
| 4      | Maroon 5    |
+--------+-------------+
4 rows in set (0.00 sec)
```

Now we can use these values to try an insert that uses multiple columns. Keep in mind that if you try to insert a record without including a required field you will still get an error even if you do not include it in the fields you wish to pass! We also need to format our date to meet what MySQL expect, or need to use a MySQL function to convert it to something valid. Here we will format it ourselves. The default format is YYYY-MM-DD meaning four digit year, two digit month, two digit day, all separated by dashes:

```
Insert into albums(albumName, bandID, releaseDate) values
("Tommy", 1, "1969-05-23"), ("Bargainville", 2, "1993-07-20"),
("Full Circle", 3, "1972-07-17");
```

As you can see in this example, complex values like strings and dates need to be wrapped in quotation marks so MySQL knows where they start and end, but we can leave basics like integers as they are.

Read

Now that we have some sample data, we will look at some basic techniques to see what we have. This is done with use of the select command, which comes with an assortment of filters and qualifiers. This is where the power of an SQL database comes into play as we manipulate, combine, and alter the information into what we want to see. We already saw one example of this when we needed to reference our bands table. The star that we used in "select * from bands" is a reserved character in MySQL that represents "all." What we effectively asked was "select everything in the bands table." We can drop the fields we do not want to see by specifying only the ones we want. For example, we can take a look at our albums table, but since we did not include producers yet and do not care about the record ID, we will just ask for certain columns:

```
Select albumName, bandID, releaseDate from albums;
+-----------+--------+-------------+
| albumName | bandID | releaseDate |
+-----------+--------+-------------+
| Tommy     | 1      | 1969-05-23  |
```

```
|Bargainville| 2        | 1993-07-20   |
|Full Circle | 3        | 1972-07-17   |
+------------+--------+-------------+
```

This gives us a more readable response. We will learn how to get the actual bandName soon, for now we will focus on how to change what we ask for. If we wanted to make this output more end-user friendly, we probably do not want to use the field names stored in the database. We can mask those by giving them an alias. We will also add some sorting in this example by applying the ascending sort (asc) in an order by clause to the album name (descending would be desc):

```
Select albumName as "Album", bandID as "Band", releaseDate as
"Release Date" from albums order by albumName asc;
+------------+--------+--------------+
| Album      | Band   | Release Date |
+------------+--------+--------------+
|Bargainville| 2      | 1993-07-20   |
| Full Circle| 3      | 1972-07-17   |
| Tommy      | 1      | 1969-05-23   |
+------------+--------+--------------+
```

We can also search for partial matches of text. Here we will use the "like" and "where" reserved words to further specify exactly what we want to see. You are probably noticing that most of our statements so far have been relatively human readable, meaning you can understand what is being done, just by reading the code. This is an intentional approach in structured query design as it makes it easier to design and debug more complex queries. Commas are used where more than one item is specified, however there is no comma after the last item in a list. You can see this where we do not include a comma after release date before moving on to specify the table we want in our "from" clause. You will also notice the use of % in the next example. This is another reserved character in MySQL, which represents a wild card, meaning anything found in that position is valid. In our example we will be searching for the word bargain, and because it is flanked on both sides by a % it will be considered a match anywhere in a string. If we only want things that start with bargain, we would only use the % after it.

```
Select albumName as "Album", bandID as "Band", releaseDate as
"Release Date" from albums where albumName like "%bargain%"
order by albumName asc;
+------------+--------+--------------+
| Album      | Band   | Release Date |
+------------+--------+--------------+
|Bargainville| 2      | 1993-07-20   |
+------------+--------+--------------+
```

You may have noticed that our search string had bargain lowercase, but MySQL still returned Bargainville even though it is capitalized. This case-insensitive search is the default on MySQL, but you can specify particular form of upper or lowercase if you want. If we want to match only a specific string, we can use = in place of like and %. In fact, we can use many of the operators we are already accustomed to when numbers are involved, such as greater than and less than.

We should add a few more records to see some more of the options we have at our disposal when selecting data:

```
Insert into albums(albumName, bandID, releaseDate) values
("Strange Days", 3, "1967-10-16"), ("Live Noise", 2,
"1998-05-19");
```

Now we have a couple bands with more than one album. We can actually infer more data than we are storing in the database by using MySQL functions to manipulate the data and results in real time. Try using the count() function to find out how many albums we have for each artist. We need to specify what we want to count (in this case, records, so we can just use *) and what piece of the record we want to group to be counted, in this case the bandID:

```
Select bandID, count(*) as "Albums" from albums group by
bandID;
+--------+--------+
| bandID | Albums |
+--------+--------+
| 1      | 1      |
| 2      | 2      |
| 3      | 2      |
+--------+--------+
```

We are not actually storing the total number of albums in any of our tables—MySQL is tracking the total number of each time a bandID occurs from the group by statement.

Maybe we want to answer a question, like which album was released most recently? If this were an excel document, we would just sort the table by the release date and look at the first record. We can do the same thing in MySQL by adding a limit in the number of records we want back. While we could certainly take the whole table result and read just the first row, when your data set gets larger you do not want to send your user more data than they want or need, because it is wasteful of resources and can degrade the user experience (as well as increase demands on your server).

```
Select * from albums order by releaseDate desc limit 1;
+---------+----------+------------+-------+-----------+
| albumID | albumName | releaseDate | bandID | producerID |
+---------+----------+------------+-------+-----------+
| 5       |Live Noise | 1998-05-19  | 2      | NULL       |
+---------+----------+------------+-------+-----------+
```

As a final example of some of the vocabulary available to us, we can also use the words "and" and "or" to add additional conditions to a statement:

```
Select * from albums where albumName like "%noise%" or album-
Name like "%circle%";
+---------+----------+------------+-------+-----------+
| albumID | albumName | releaseDate | bandID | producerID |
+---------+----------+------------+-------+-----------+
| 3       |Full Circle| 1972-07-17  | 3      | NULL       |
| 5       |Live Noise | 1998-05-19  | 2      | NULL       |
+---------+----------+------------+-------+-----------+
```

Keep in mind we are just touching the surface of the power of MySQL here. There are more reserved words, actions, abilities, and a whole library of functions that allow you to do even more.

Update

Now that we have practiced a bit of reading, we will try the next CRUD method, updating. Maybe instead of leaving the producerID as null we decide that we want it to say unknown by default. Since the producerID field is a foreign key reference, we cannot just change the value to text (we could use the Alter command to change the table structure, but this is out of our scope and would break our normalization). Since we only want to change the records where we do not have a producerID (even though in our case it is all of them) we need to specify that we want to change the column where the field is null. For update, we need to specify the table, define what we want our field set to, and the condition(s) required for the update to occur. Before we do this, we need a record in our Labels table where the producer name is "unknown." We will pretend it is our first record:

```
Update albums set producerID=1 where producerID is null;
```

Now, all of our records will show "unknown" when we begin to join tables. This keeps us from having to create extra code in our site to adjust output when the field would otherwise be empty.

If you want to change your values back, you can reset the whole column by setting the value without adding a where clause:

```
Update albums set producerID=null;
```

Delete

The final CRUD method, delete, is as final as it sounds. Use with extreme caution! There is no "undelete" or "undo" function at our disposal. The vast majority of the time, it is best practice to never allow your users to delete records. Instead, add flags to your records that will *hide* the data from ever appearing again, by adding a Boolean "disabled" column to each table or creating a disabled table that tracks records that should not be shown (just a couple examples, there are even more ways to do this!).

As partial protection to the fast-fingered typists, MySQL splits delete functions out to two keywords, delete and drop. Delete is reserved for row-level actions, while drop is reserved for table and database level actions. Dropping a table or database is as simple as typing "drop table [your table name here]" or "drop database [your database name here]." There will be no "are you sure" prompt either. If the value exists, it will be removed. In terms of deleting rows, the same holds true. We define the table we want to interact with, and the conditions that identify rows we want deleted. We will remove any albums with "live" in their name as an example:

```
Delete from albums where albumName like "%live%";
```

You should receive a response that says one row was affected, and if you review your whole table you will see that the Live Noise album is now gone.

LEARN MORE

Keywords, search terms: CRUD, structure query languages, SQL, MySQL

MySQL Functions List: http://dev.mysql.com/doc/refman/5.0/en/func-op-summary-ref.html

Beginner Tutorials: http://beginner-sql-tutorial.com/sql.htm

Chapter 42

Advanced Queries

To use relational databases to their fullest extent, we need to be able to connect our tables using our foreign keys in order to extract our full records. This is done by combining statements and joining tables together.

Joining

We can join tables a number of ways. The primary portion of the join is specified in our where clause, which is where we will specify which fields between the two tables are to be connected. The simplest join will return only the records from the two tables where the value is found in both tables. We will begin by getting all the values from our albums and bands tables so we can finally see the band name in our results:

```
Select * from bands, albums where album.bandID=bands.bandID;
```

You now probably have a messy looking table, but all our fields are there. Now, we can cut it back to just a simple list:

```
Select bands.bandName as "Band", albums.albumName as "Album",
releaseDate as "Released" from bands, albums where albums.
bandID=bands.bandID;
```

```
+--------------+---------------+------------+
| Band         | Album         | Released   |
+--------------+---------------+------------+
| The Who      | Tommy         | 1969-05-23 |
| Moxy Fruvous | Bargainville  | 1993-07-20 |
| The Doors    | Full Circle   | 1972-07-17 |
| The Doors    | Strange Days  | 1967-10-16 |
+--------------+---------------+------------+
```

You will notice we started to append the table name and a period before each field name. This helps clarify which field we are referring to when the same field name is used in more than one table. As a best practice, you may wish to always use this dot notation when selecting fields as it will help "future-proof" your queries if you expand or alter your database in the future, even if the field in question is unique to the database now.

You may also be noticing that we still have not seen Maroon 5 come up in any of these examples, even though they were created when we first set up our bands table. That is because the basic join (also called "inner join"), as stated above, only returns results where records exist in both joined tables. Since we never added an album for Maroon 5, they did not come back as a result. We can capture all results of either table, and still pair them when records are available, by using different approaches to our join called left join and right join. Each of these performs roughly how it sounds—a left join will include *all* records from the left table, plus additional values from the right table when they exist, and a right join will do the opposite, including all the records from the right table and adding data from the left when it exists. Next we will look at all "Bands," and any records they have, by using a left join. All we need to do is replace the comma between the tables in our "from" clause with the join method we want, and change the word "where" to "on":

```
Select bands.bandName as "Band", albums.albumName as "Album",
releaseDate as "Released" from bands left join albums on
albums.bandID=bands.bandID;
+--------------+--------------+------------+
| Band         | Album        | Released   |
+--------------+--------------+------------+
| The Who      | Tommy        | 1969-05-23 |
| Moxy Fruvous | Bargainville | 1993-07-20 |
| The Doors    | Full Circle  | 1972-07-17 |
| The Doors    | Strange Days | 1967-10-16 |
| Maroon 5     | NULL         | NULL       |
+--------------+--------------+------------+
```

There are more complex forms of join than just left, right, and inner. However, these three cover most use cases and a well-designed database will usually reduce or eliminate the need for overly complex queries.

We can continue to add tables, and joins, to our queries to get more and more comprehensive results. We can even nest queries within one another inside sets of parenthesis. The query is then executed from the inside out just like it would in an equation, where the resulting data from the nested query is available to the query it sits inside of. First, we can look at a more complicated query that tells us everything about a particular song. We will specify a song title, and build a query that would connect all the related tables. Since our database is limited, we will start by looking at our table structure. If you want to fully test this example, you will need to spend some time populating your tables further. Since we will have a song title, and the question is what else we can glean, we will use all the keys that make sense in combination with a song title. Within the song table, we have albumID. That is relevant, as it tells us the album(s) the song has been released on. Now that we have at least one albumID, we can get from our "Albums" table to the band table and producer table as well. Tracing to these does not reveal any additional keys we can use, so without extra nested queries this is our reach:

Bands	Albums	Songs	Concerts2Artists
bandID bandName	albumID albumName releaseDate bandID producerID	songID title length albumID	id artistID concertID

Labels	Locations	Artists	Venues	Concerts	Bands2Labels
producerID producer	locID city state zip	artistID artistName locationID	venueID venueName locationID	concertID venueID date	id producerID bandID timestamp

We are able to connect data from half of our database (ignoring our reference tables) just from having a song title. This query could look like the following:

```
Select bandName, albumName, releaseDate, title, length,
producer from bands, albums, songs, labels where songs.
albumID=albums.albumID and albums.bandID=bands.bandID and
albums.producerID=labels.producerID;
```

Each pairing of fields in our where clause creates another join between tables. As our queries become more complex, you may find they take longer to run. This is because more data has to be reviewed, and more connections found, to create the resulting table. This is also the point where optimization techniques like indexing (automatically building trees in the database) and other more advanced MySQL tools will come into play.

Nested Queries

We can take the results of one query into consideration in another by nesting queries within one another using parenthesis. This will frequently come into play when we do not have a starting value for a question we want to ask. For example if we wanted to find the artist with the largest album in terms of tracks, we would break the goal down into its elements. First, we need to find which album has the highest track count, since we do not have a known value to search for:

```
Select max(length) from songs;
```

This query looks at each record in the songs table and finds the one with the largest value. We could also have done this by sorting the table as descending on the tracks column, but since we are going to nest it we only want one value returned to keep things simpler. Our next step is to join the bandID value from albums to the id field in our bands table, in order to get our name:

```
Select bandName from bands, albums, songs where songs.length=
(select max(length) from songs) and songs.albumID=albums.
albumID and albums.bandID=bands.bandID;
```

Nested queries are also a great place to use a few more methods to search with, namely ANY, IN, SOME, ALL and EXISTS. ANY and SOME are equivalent, and IN works the same as ANY when your comparison is strict equality (just =). What this means is that when we interact with the results of a nested query, we can look at each record returned as a match against our where clause. Let us look at some mock examples:

Get the name of every artist who has an album with the word "free" anywhere in the title:

```
Select artistName from artists where artist.id = ANY (select
artist.id from albums where album.title like "% Free %");
Select artistName from artists where artist.id IN (select
artist.id from albums where album.title like "% Free %");
```

```
Select artistName from artists where artist.id = SOME (select
artist.id from albums where album.title like "% Free %");
```

To understand where these verbs become different, we could ask the question of which album(s) contain a certain set of songs. In this case, our nested select would include the songs we are interested in. Here, using the verb ANY would return all albums that have one or more of the songs listed on their albums. If we changed to ALL, then we would only get albums where all of the values returned by our nested query existed on the album.

LEARN MORE

Keywords, search terms: Nested queries, sql joins, indexing, mysql optimization

Jeff Atwood's Joins Examples: http://www.codinghorror.com/blog/2007/10/a-visual-explanation-of-sql-joins.html

MySQL's Nested Examples: http://dev.mysql.com/tech-resources/articles/subqueries_part_1.html

Section 4 Assessments

For these assignments, use mysqldump() to submit a database export file or submit written work as a single document file.

Database Design

Come up with a small database you would like to develop. Compile a list of fields and follow the process of normalization to create a data model with at least 5 tables that includes primary and foreign keys, and at least one table that is a many-to-many relationship.

Create a document that depicts your table structure and fields, identifies primary and foreign keys, and the connections between your tables.

Database Development

Using your database design from above, create the database using your system's command prompt. Create a text file that includes all of the commands you used to create your database as well as inserts for 3 full records in each table. Submit this file and a mysqldump of your actual completed database.

Database Interaction

Create queries that will interact with your database to complete the following:

1. Display one of your tables without including foreign keys
2. Joins two (or more) of your tables to show a complete record
3. Generates information about your records that is not stored in your database
4. Updates record(s) in a table to a new value

Submit your queries and the mysqldump file for your database.

Discussion / Written Response

1. Describe the three types of relationships between data and how to satisfy them in relational databases.
2. Describe the first three forms of normalization.
3. Describe the differences between flat file and structured query databases.
4. Describe the differences between SQL and NoSQL databases.
5. Describe when the different database types we examined are most useful.

Questions

TAKE THIS QUIZ ONLINE!

1. What does SQL stand for?
   a. Standard Query Linguistics
   b. Structured Query Language
   c. Strict Query Language
   d. None of the above
2. Which of these is used to retrieve information from a database?
   a. Get
   b. Fetch
   c. Select
   d. Find
3. Which of these commands would get the name column from a Persons table?
   a. Select name from Persons;
   b. Get persons.name
   c. Select persons.name
   d. Get name from Persons
4. Which of the following select records where the name fields starts with an A?
   a. Select * from Persons where name='a'
   b. Select * from Persons where name like "a%"
   c. Select * from Persons where name like "%a"
   d. None of these
5. Which of the following is the keyword used to sort results?
   a. Order By
   b. Sort By

c. Filter By
d. Ascending

6. Which of the following is used to find the number of records?
    a. Total()
    b. Count()
    c. Sum()
    d. None of these
7. Eliminating multiple identical columns from a table is which normalization?
    a. First
    b. Second
    c. Third
    d. Fourth
8. Eliminating repeated values from a table is which normalization?
    a. First
    b. Second
    c. Third
    d. Fourth
9. Ensuring no values are repeated in a database is which of the following?
    a. First
    b. Second
    c. Third
    d. Fourth
10. Ensuring all fields relate directly to the table they are in is which normalization?
    a. First
    b. Second
    c. Third
    d. Fourth
11. The CRUD actions are:
    a. Compose, Read, Update, Delete
    b. Create, Read, Update, Destroy
    c. Create, Read, Update, Delete
    d. Copy, Read, Update, Drop
12. Including all of the records in the first table of a join is done using:
    a. Join all
    b. Left join
    c. Right join

d. None of these

13. Queries can be placed inside of other queries.

    a. True

    b. False

14. Which of the following is used to remove a record from a table?

    a. Delete from

    b. Drop from

    c. Destroy

15. MySQL requires which of the following to run?

    a. Windows

    b. Linux

    c. Apple

    d. Any of these

CHECK YOUR ANSWERS ON PAGE 287

Section 5:

Tying it Together

Section Contents:

Learning Goals:

By the end of this section, you should be able to demonstrate:

1. The ability to create a site that incorporates multiple languages
2. The ability to extract information from a database and present it in a site
3. Basic security considerations to deter malicious attacks
4. The ability to interact with user data and alter a page as a result

Chapter 43

Security

Risk

It can be easy to both over and under consider the security of your website. New initiates tend to do everything possible to secure their code, which often results in overblown measures that can take considerable time to incorporate. This may only serve to protect something that may not require security in the first place. The dangers, then, are: getting tired of the complicated process, becoming complacent because nothing has happened, or neglecting to consider security in the first place. As a result, systems end up exposed.

Risk management is the practice of finding the sweet spot where the time and cost of implementing the measure is proportionate and acceptable to the perceived threat a compromise would create. Risk analysis is another of the many topics in this text that begs for much deeper study, and I would encourage everyone to read beyond what is here as it applies to everyone involved in a programming project.

In short, some things to consider about your system are its level of exposure, cost to acquire/replace its contents, importance of contents in relation to the company, and importance of the contents in relation to your clients. A number of industries are also bound to compliance measures based on certain types of information, or in order to achieve certain certifications.

Some questions to ask are things like:

1. Is this system only available on our network, or is it publically exposed?
2. Is this system only accessible through other security mechanisms like credentialing systems, SSL, etc.?
3. How much would it cost to replace the data the system holds?
4. Would it be possible to replace the data if it is lost?
5. Does the value of the data change if it is stolen or made publically available?
6. If the data is compromised, how would it affect our relationship with our customers?
7. Is any of the information required to be secured to a certain level?
8. Are we an industry (e.g., healthcare) that has to comply with a federal or other reporting guideline (e.g., HIPAA)

Answering these questions can be difficult, as you need to find quantifiable measures to questions that are better suited to qualitative analysis. An example of how to approach this is to determine risk values that address each topic. If data is irreplaceable, it might be an 8/10. If compromise poses no risk if stolen or exposed, it may be a 1/10. Using the same min/max range for each value allows us to add up our scores in order to get a summary value of the risk. This value can help you see the importance of your system better. From here, you can determine based on its value, particular values, or "red line" items that require specific minimums like federal requirements, exactly what security implementations you will need. You can also create estimates of what damages (data recovery costs, man hours to fix/replace the system, loss from lawsuits, etc.) might cost against that of implementing specific security measures as a cost/benefit ratio. For example, a mitigating effort of installing or developing a credentialing system might cost $5,000 dollars, but if the data is exposed a lawsuit might entitle the plaintiff to $80,000 dollars in damages. How much is spent to defend a system in relation to what the perceived losses might be will ultimately be determined by your executives and what the analysis reveals.

A common response to this issue is what if the system never gets attacked? Then the costs would be wasted! Alas, in many cases it can be hard to know or prove that risk management efforts actually stopped or prevented an attack. Time and money spent on security are difficult to defend, as their return on investment can rarely be proven. Was the system not compromised because of your efforts, or because no one tried? The typical reaction is to consider the survivability of the organization if the system is compromised or lost, and this is where strong metrics and analysis can save the day, the system, and maybe even your job.

Our example above of measuring each item on a fixed scale to determine a single threat value is just one mechanism. It is good for quick (relatively speaking) analysis and as a means of measuring multiple systems, or different possible versions of a system, against each other. More advanced techniques take more factors into consideration. For example, the NIST SP 800-30[1] analysis includes a threat-likelihood-impact matrix where values are assigned to each element (the amount of likeliness of a given threat compared to its impact), repeated for each threat. Placing things into the matrix helps to quantify the scenario.

To perform a full risk analysis, you will want to consider all possible sources of damage to your system. These include intentionally malicious or accidental actions of users both in and outside of your company (just because a user is authorized to access data does not mean it is being used correctly or as intended), natural or man-made disasters that would affect your system (floods = water; water + electronics = bad), or just general failure (power surge + electronics = bad). For the remainder here, we will only focus on the former as it directly applies to the topics we address in the rest of the text.

To delve deeper, look at some of the United States federal risk management initiatives.

- National Institute of Standards and Technology (NIST)[2]
- Department of Homeland Security (DHS)[3]
- The United States Computer Emergency Readiness Team (US-CERT)[4]

One parting note: No matter the size of your organization, even if you are the lone programmer, a risk analysis exercise should involve many minds, especially those of upper

1 http://csrc.nist.gov/publications/nistpubs/800-30/sp800-30.pdf
2 www.nist.gov
3 www.dhs.gov/topic/cybersecurity
4 www.us-cert.gov

management. Their determinations will weigh heavily on your activities, and their exposure to these exercises will increase their awareness overall.

Now that we have an idea of how to discover and quantify risks, we can look at some basic methods of protecting ourselves.

PHP

One of the easiest ways for a malicious user to attempt to take advantage of our database, or gain unauthorized access, is to use our own scripting language against us. Let us consider a basic example. Say you have a form that takes a username and password to log in a user. Even if you employ an encrypted password with hashing, a malicious person could still take advantage of your form. Since your form action and field names are available to anyone who views your page's source code, they could read your form to generate the following URL: http://yoursite.com/youractionpage.php?username=FAKEUSER&password=12345' or 1

Since they are using your form's variable names, your action page will, in this basic example, assume they are legitimate. The key element to note here is the apostrophe or 1 portion of the password field. If you are accepting user input without checking it first, like this:

```
mysqli_query("select * from users where username='$_
GET[username]' and password='".md5($_GET[password])."'");
```

Your populated query would actually read as follows:

```
select * from users where username='FAKEUSER' and pass-
word='12345' or 1
```

When evaluated, the malicious user is automatically logged in because the "or 1" makes the logic statement true, since "or true" will always be true, regardless of the first half of the statement. Your malicious user is now logged into your site! If you did not follow the "least needed privileges" theory (we will look at this next), they would then have access to anything in the database that the account is allowed to access—potentially even other databases.

To protect against this, we can use the sanitization[5] and validation[6] features of PHP to ensure our users' responses are valid.

For example, if we ask a user to enter their email, we can first remove anything that should not be in an email address:

```
$email = filter_var($_GET['email'], FILTER_SANITIZE_EMAIL);
```

And then make sure it is still in proper format:

```
if(filter_var($email, FILTER_VALIDATE_EMAIL)){echo "OK!";}
else{ echo "Please re-enter email!"; }
```

The above code would be OK for a regular email address, but anything missing an @, or a top level domain like .com, would ask for it to be re-entered. Our sanitization for an email address will remove all characters except letters, digits and !#$%&'*+-/=?^_`{|}~@.[]. You typically want to sanitize before validating. If your sanitization removes something that was actually a desired part of the input, the validation would then fail.

[5] php.net/manual/en/filter.filters.sanitize.php

[6] www.php.net/manual/en/filter.filters.validate.php

MySQL

The source (for us, at least) of the risk: the data itself. We are storing our data in MySQL, which our web pages interface with in order to build our interactive experience. When we store user credentials in our database, we need to consider the fact that since our website communicates with the database, there is an inherent weakness. This is true whether or not our database is on the same physical system, or lives in the same operating system, as the site itself. One of the basic mechanisms to protecting your site is to prevent unauthorized access. Part of this can be achieved by obfuscating our users' passwords when we store this. To do this, we can employ a couple of tactics called hashing and salting.

Hashing is the process of passing the password through a mathematical algorithm that turns the password into a much longer string of characters. The algorithm is designed to be one-way, meaning a hash cannot be passed to an algorithm that reveals the original text. The algorithm will produce the same hash every time for a given password (although occasionally duplicates may occur, a fault called a "hash collision"). The result is stored in the database in place of the user's actual password. Each time the user logs in, they type in their original password, your authentication system passes it through the algorithm, and you can compare the result to the stored value to make sure they match.

The use of a hash ensures that if someone is able to gain access to your database, they cannot simply copy the credentials and use them to their advantage, as the stored value is not the actual password they would use. A couple of popular methods that have been used to achieve this are MD5 and SHA-1, among others. I discourage the use of MD5, as its hashes are comparatively shorter than many others in use today, and enough data has been gathered about the algorithm that many password hashes can already be found just by using sites like md5decrypter.com.

Another issue of only relying on the original hashing algorithm is that other sites may be doing the same. If someothersite.com and your site are both using MD5 by itself, and someothersite.com is compromised, the attacker would have the usernames and passwords for their site. If any of your users also used someothersite.com, odds are some of them are probably using the same email address, username, and password. With all of this data, the attacker now has a set of usernames and passwords to try on your site. Since you are using the same hashing mechanism, the credentials used on both sites would work on yours as well.

The hashed value of the word password, for example, returns to us the value 5f4dc-c3b5aa765d61d8327deb882cf99. If you take this value and paste it into md5decrypter.com, you will see our original text (password) given back to us.

Never fear, however, as we can defend against this with a salt. Salting is the process of adding something extra to your user's password, like adding salt to food to make it better. This should ensure that even if a user has the same password on the other site, the one stored in our database is still different. This means a malicious person cannot use the encrypted password to get into our site.

If the salt for our user was #hsy5, our user's password that we would hash could be password#hsy5 or #hsy5password or even pass#hsy5word. When we hash password#hsy5, we get 5b48480a7171f41d2bf52093f4850281. Now, if someone tries to use known passwords, their hash for password will not work on our site. You can use salts by either creating a salt for every password, or using one that is coded directly into your script.

Keep in mind that if you are using a single salt for all values, make sure it is not running in a script the user would have access to, like a linked JavaScript value, or would appear in your HTML as a hidden value in a form. This gives them the missing key to circumvent the extra protection you added. By only having the salt in one script, malicious agents would need to gain access to your web server as well as your database, especially if this script is segregated from your database's home system. Storing a unique salt for each password means if one salt is discovered, not every account has been compromised. If the compromised account allows reading the salt table though, other accounts would eventually be accessible. Ultimately, using the best hashing algorithm available and both salting approaches would provide a high level of protection. How much you actually need to implement should be determined by completing a risk analysis.

Another strong self-protection method is to make sure your user accounts in your database are as locked down as possible. By this I mean abiding by a "least-needed security" approach. It is easy when developing to create a user account for your project with a simple password and wide open permissions to make development easier. Once you move your project live, however, you should take away all the permissions your users would not need and should not have. For example, your basic end users will likely not need the ability to alter or drop tables, so you should remove user access to those features. This means that if injection methods are used on your site, even if they succeed, the malicious threat still could not drop or alter your tables without also finding a vulnerability in your database.

To provide administrative users with an interface, you can set those pages to utilize a database user with higher credentials. The most sensitive operations (full database deletions, creating new administrators, etc.) should still be left in the hands of users who log into your database directly from a secured machine.

In MySQL, the full list of permissions elements are: *select, insert, update, delete, index, alter, create, drop*

Administrative privileges are: *create temp table, file, lock table, process, reload, replication, show dbs, shutdown super.*

We can quickly assign users the initial set of actions or the administrative set by using the keywords "usage" or "all" when assigning the account. Most sites can achieve everything necessary with the limited permissions of select, insert, update, and maybe delete. Keep in mind although overall this is quite restrictive, without proper precautions injection attempts could still use insert or update to infiltrate your site.

Depending on the element, security can be restricted to the user based on the levels of global (your entire database server, i.e., every database), database, table, or column. This granularity allows you to ensure users can only change what they need to.

Our database *de jour* for this text also allows us to require SSL connections, providing greater security between the user (an admin or our webserver) and the database. MySQL also allows us to limit the number of updates over a span of time, as well as the number of concurrent connections and queries per hour. Typically, we would want these values very high to support the highest volume of end users possible, but you may have a use case where you know these numbers should be in a certain range. For example, if your company has

50 employees, and only 40 need your site, then you could cap your concurrent users to 40. Anything beyond that could be an indicator of database problems or hacking.

Types of Hashes

There are a number of strong hashing algorithms available. Some of these are considered out-dated and are easily to reverse, like DES. Others are still widely in use even though databases of known encrypted/unencrypted values for many passwords are freely available, like md5. Sites like md5decrypter.com are examples of this weakness. For this reason, you will likely want to favor the newer approaches available to you at the time. As new encryption algorithms are created, the encrypted string lengths become much larger, making the computation power required to reverse them too time consuming (if even possible) for the current hardware available.

Credentials

Never say never, but never give root. Root, or the default user on your MySQL server, has the highest level of permissions in the system. This means a PHP script that uses the root account to establish a connection can do anything, even drop all databases. Because of the damage an accidental or malicious command can have on your data, any MySQL user account that your web server utilizes to interact with your data should be as limited as possible. The vast majority of applications can get by with simple CRUD actions (that is create, read update, and delete). In most implementations, I would go one step further and not even allow deleting, replacing it instead with an "inactive" flag for records to hide them from the user as if they were deleted. Depending on the system, your web users might need additional features like temporary tables, and these should be allowed only as needed. This means if the attacker tries to perform administrative type actions, and you are not preventing them, they will still be blocked as the user they are acting as will not allow it.

JavaScript

We always (Yes, always—laziness breeds poor security in our world) want to take a look at anything a user gives us before we interact with it. This is for two reasons: first, the user may have made a mistake. Maybe they mistyped an email address, or left a required field blank. Or, perhaps, the user is a malicious person or script attempting to do something other than what we intend with access to our site. It might be using our forms to spam others, gain access to our data, or make unsolicited changes to our site. We already discussed this under PHP but we can attack the problem with JavaScript too.

Taking this into account, before we use anything a user gave us, we need to make sure (as much as possible) that it is safe data to interact with. Usually we want to do as much of this as possible on the user (or client) side, so they do not need to click submit and wait for a response from the server to find out something is not quite right. To do this, we can use client-side scripting like JavaScript to make sure things are OK as we progress. As fields are changed, JavaScript can look at the content and make sure addresses are formatted correctly, required fields are filled in, etc. Coloring, highlighting, or providing messages to the user when problems occur. We can achieve this easily by tapping into jQuery's validation library:

```
<script src=(/lib/js/jquery.validate.js"></script>
<script>
   $(document).ready(function(){$("#commentForm").validate(
      cname : { required : true, minlength: 2 }
   );}
   );
</script>
```

This example would execute the validation once the form is loaded, showing that the cname field is required and the minimum length is two characters. Not only can jQuery help us display these requirements on the form itself, we can call the validator as fields are changed and/or when the form is submitted before leaving the page to enforce the rules we provided.

In terms of user experience, this is typically done in real time. As soon as a user leaves a field, the script makes sure it is OK, and provides confirmation of the fact (typically a green highlighting or "OK!" type of marker) or by not marking the field as bad (typically red, or prompting the user to re-enter the field).

Once the form is completed, JavaScript should ensure that the user's submission will be good on the first try (at least content-wise—we cannot confirm things like a username and password without talking to the server). This accounts for our number one concern: mistakes from the user. Even though we checked the submission, we want to repeat this process on the server-side in more depth. If the user is malicious they may be circumventing our page, or the user may have JavaScript disabled.

The server-side script should take into account the nefarious user. If someone tried to subvert our form, JavaScript probably caught it. If, however, we are using GET or they use a script to send data directly to our action page from our form (which they can easily find in our page source) then they can get around our JavaScript.

Execution Functions

Both PHP and JavaScript support features that allow the user to access and run other programs or scripts on the web server or local system. This can be useful when you want to interface with another application or system that the language does not have the ability to communicate with directly, but it exposes a huge security risk. Anything passed to these functions will be executed as if that user was sitting at the command prompt of your web server. The implications here are fairly obvious, as anything your server's "web user" account has permission for would be allowed. If you are passing a variable into the execute function, you have created a path directly to the heart of your system.

The best bet is to avoid using these entirely unless absolutely necessary. If you must, ensure that variables are not passed to the function if at all possible to prevent injection. Finally, if all else fails, sanitize and validate anything passed, limit your web server user role as much as possible, and keep your system as up to date as possible to deter hackers.

In PHP you will want to avoid the exec() function. JavaScript is a bit more removed, but some actions can create the ability, such as creating an ActiveX object:

```
<script>
   var wsh = new ActiveXObject('WScript.Shell');
   wsh.run('notepad.exe');
</script>
```

Segregated Systems

Your database server, ideally, would not live under the same operating system as your web server. This does not mean the same OS cannot be used on both systems, but that they are not residing on the same exact installation. This is important because if your system is exposed to, or faces, the Internet it is at a higher risk of compromise. Keeping the database within your network with a single controlled access point between the two means your data is not as compromised if the web server is.

LEARN MORE

Keywords, search terms: Web server security, risk management, secure programming

76 Tips for Securing Your Server: http://www.rackaid.com/resources/server-security-tips/

Apache's Security Tips: http://httpd.apache.org/docs/2.2/misc/security_tips.html

Symantec's Tips for MySQL: http://www.symantec.com/connect/articles/securing-mysql-step-step

Chapter 44

Integration Examples

The following code examples will demonstrate how the languages we have studied can be combined to create dynamic systems. In each of these examples two or more elements covered in the text will be combined. These examples are not intended to function fully based on the excerpts you will see, but are meant to demonstrate methods of integrating the languages.

Connecting to MySQL

In order to have our users interact with our database, we need to establish a bridge of communication between them. To do this, we will create a connection to our database and store it in a variable. Through PHP we have a variety of methods of creating this connection, among them are libraries called MySQL, MySQLi, and PDO. These libraries have different approaches to interacting with a database, and there are differences in what commands are available and how the connection is treated. While you will see many examples online that use the standard MySQL connector, I would warn you away from it. It is on its way to deprecation, and has little injection protection built in. The MySQLi library is the one we will focus on in our examples here as it is a better start for entry level programmers. Ultimately, once you are comfortable with integrating these languages, I would recommend moving to PDO. While it is not tailored for MySQL, it supports a wider range of SQL databases that will allow you to more easily change your backend system.

To begin, we will call a function to create our connection. The shortest avenue to do this is as follows:

```
$mysql = mysqli->connect("localhost","user","password","data
base");
```

By inserting your server's values in each set of quotes, the variable $mysql will become our line of communication to our MySQL database. When we created our connection by using a class method, our $mysql variable is now a MySQLi object. We could also have used procedural style with mysqli_connect. Assuming your database is the same system as your website, "localhost" or "127.0.0.1" should work just fine for you. Your username and password can be any account that exists in your SQL database. In a fresh installation, "root" as the user and "root," "password," or nothing—"" as a password will usually let you in, but as we saw in security, you should avoid this unless necessary and only on a low-risk machine. The declaration of the database we want to use is optional, but saves us from having to select one later or always declare our database in our queries.

In the spirit of this section, we will revise this example to make it more useful. By replacing our values with variables, we can keep our actual values apart from the rest of the code. Additionally, we can separate our connection out to its own file. By doing this, we can require() or include() it on any page that we need a connection. Then all we need to do when we use our database is remember to close the connection at the bottom of our page. An additional advantage is that we could also wrap our connection in a class of our own, allowing us to re-declare from our own class what functions are available. For now, we will keep it simpler:

```
$host = "localhost";
$user = "username";
$password = "password";
$dbase = "database";
$mysql = mysql->connect($host, $user, $password, $dbase);
```

If this code is its own file like database.php, we could use it in all of our sites, simply changing the values at the top to match the settings for the site it is in. To get information from our database, create or modify our databases, or create or change records, we use the same exact queries that we did from the command prompt. Our only difference is that we do it through a function, and store the response in a variable:

```
$results = $mysql->query("select * from albums");
```

The $results variable here, like our connection variable, is a reference. It is a pointer that lets us continue to communicate with the database and specifies what we are looking for, but is not the actual data. To get the data, we need to ask for each record. Since our example is very small, we will get all of the results at once, and build an array:

```
while($row = $results->fetch_assoc(){
   $data[]=$row;
}
```

This block of code uses the while statement to get every record available in our result set. Note that we used the variable with our result pointer to get the results, and not our connection itself. Inside our loop, we are simply taking the row (in this case, each album from our albums table) and adding it to a new array called data.

Secured Login

Logging into a web page involves receiving user input, sanitizing and validating their submission, appending any salts, hashing the submission, and sending it to the database for verification. If the database responds that the user's credentials match what is stored we can then continue and create a cookie and/or session so the user can interact with secured content.

Creating a User:

```
<?php
//create our salt
$salt=^%r8yuyg;
//store the filtered, salted, hashed version of the password
$passwordHash = sha1(filter_var($_POST['password'].$salt,
FILTER_SANITIZE_STRING));
```

```
//Add the user to the database
$sql = 'INSERT INTO user ($username, passwordHash) VALUES
(?,?)';
$result = $db->query($sql, array($_POST['username'],
$passwordHash));
?>
```

Logging them in:

```
<?php
//Prep their login credentials
$passwordHash = sha1(filter_var($_POST['password'].$salt,
FILTER_SANITIZE_STRING));
$sql = 'SELECT username FROM user WHERE username = ? AND pass-
wordHash = ?';
$result = $db->query($sql, array($_POST['username'],
$passwordHash));
//This time, look at the result to see if they exist
if ($result->numRows() < 1){
echo 'Sorry, your username or password was incorrect!';
}
else{
// Create the session
$session_start();
$_SESSION['active'] = true;
echo ('Welcome back!);
}
?>
```

Dynamic Canvas

By adding a loop in a canvas drawing of a circle, and using the random number function in the math library of JavaScript, we can instruct the browser to draw circles (in this example, 1000) of random shapes, sizes, and colors, all over our canvas. Each time the page is loaded or refreshed in the browser, the circles will be redrawn, and since we are using random values, this means our image will change each time.

```
<canvas id="myCanvas" width="600" height="600"></canvas>
<script>
   var canvas = document.getElementById("canvas");
   var ctx = canvas.getContext("2d");
   var w = canvas.width, h = canvas.height; //Set variables of
   the width, height of the canvas
   var i = 0;
   do {
   ctx.fillStyle = "rgb(" + Math.round(255*Math.random()) + ","
   // Creates an R value
      + Math.round(255*Math.random()) + "," // … and for G
      + Math.round(255*Math.random()) + ")"; // … and for B
```

```
    ctx.beginPath();
    ctx.arc(w*Math.random(), h*Math.random(), // creates our
    random size
       50*Math.random(),
       0, Math.PI*2, true); // Uses Pi*2 to make the arc a
          circle
    ctx.closePath();
    ctx.fill();
    } while (++i != 1000); // Loops this do 999 more times
</script>
```

Table of Results

If we only need to display the information to the user on the screen, or do not plan on manipulating the data or using the data elsewhere on our page, creating the array of results can be a wasteful use of memory. Instead, we will modify our while loop to create a table of our results:

```
<table width="75%">
   <tr><th>Title</th><th>Artist</th><th>Year</th><tr>
   <?php
      while($row = $results->fetch_assoc(){
      echo "<tr><td>$row[title]</td><td>$row[artist]</
         td><td>$row[year]</td></tr>";
      }
   ?>
</table>
```

This approach only stores one record at a time in our $row variable and is much more conservative, especially when using larger data sets. You will notice we nested our PHP within regular html in this example. Take a look at what our whole page might look like, assuming we also created our database.php file:

```
<?php
   require("database.php"); // Now that this file is loaded, we
   can use $mysql on this page
   $query = "select title, artist, year from albums";
   $results = $mysql->query($query);
?>
<table width="75%">
   <tr><th>Title</th><th>Artist</th><th>Year</th><tr>
   <?php
      while($row = $results->fetch_assoc(){
      echo "<tr><td>$row[title]</td><td>$row[artist]</
         td><td>$row[year]</td></tr>";
      }
   ?>
</table>
```

At this point, we now have all of the data we need from the database, and since we will not need the database anymore for this example, we can close our connection by adding the following after our table:

```
<?php mysql->close($mysql); ?>
```

Repopulating Forms

If a user has submitted a form or is editing existing data, we can use these values to re-populate our form so the user does not have to type them in again. This is done by echoing the value inside the quotes in the value attribute of the form element. For example, if our name was in the URI as page.php?name=myName, we could make it the value of the input field with:

```
<form action='page.php' method='get'>
<input type='text' value='<?php echo $_GET['name']; ?>' />
</form>
```

By suppressing errors with error_reporting, using this technique, and with a little logic, we can combine all of the elements of providing the form, validating the submission, and taking action on what the form is for, all from one single page.

With some careful planning, we can provide our user with a form, check their submission, and store their information, all from one page. First we need to create some pseudo-code of the flow of logic so we can dictate what we want to do, and under what conditions:

```
<?php
    if(form has not been submitted){
        show user the blank form
    }
    else{
        check the form for errors
    if (there are errors){
        show user their form and data
    }
    }
?>
```

By following the logical order of events, the above pseudo-code represents what would be a perfectly functional page. With a couple of tweaks, however, we can make some improvements. First, in this example, we would have to create the same form twice—once blank, and again with placeholders for what the user submitted. While we could use copy/paste and then modify the second copy, this will greatly inflate the overall size of our page. We can also simplify our logic by reversing the order of events in our code. First, we will see if the form has been submitted. If it has, we will check for errors. If there are none, we will complete the submission. After that, we will simply display the form with placeholders for user submitted data if there are errors or the form has not been submitted. This will cover both cases in one place and replaces our if/else and nested if with three if statements:

```
<?php
    if(form as been submitted){
        check it for errors.
```

```
        create a status flag declaring if there are errors or not
    }
    if(the status flag is set to "ok"){ // The form must have
    been submitted, and there are no errors
        submit the user info to the database
        send any confirmation emails
        display a success message
        set the status flag to show the form is complete
    }
    if(the status flag is anything other than "ok" or does not
    exist){ //either there were errors, or the form has not
    been submitted
        show the form with placeholders for submitted data
    }
?>
```

To make this form more flexible, we can declare an array of field names in our first if statement that lists what elements in our table are required or need to be validated. Once we have done this, we can check each submitted field to see if it needs to be checked, pass it through the appropriate tests, and create a list of feedback. There are a number of ways to approach this. Here we will create an array of responses as our error flag. If there are no errors, we will simply set it to "OK." We will create a hidden field with a known value that will be included every time the form is submitted. This will help deter outside scripts from using our form, as they would need to know to include the hidden field (which we will check for in our logic) in order for our script to respond. In our example, we will make a short registration form:

```
if($_GET[hiddenDate]==now() [check]){
$check = array('firstName', 'lastName', 'email', 'email2'); //
We will require these fields
    foreach($check as $field){ [make sure & is in php section]
    [include "for each thing in" way to remember
        if($field in $_GET) [verify]{
        //sanitize variable
        if(length < 3){ //establishes that our required fields
            should be at least 3 characters long
        $_GET[$field]="; //clear the user submitted value as it
            does not qualify
        $errors[]="$field is required and must be at least 3
            characters long";
        }
    }
}
    if($_GET['email'] != $_GET['email2']){ // Make sure the
    user entered the same email twice
        $errors[]="Both email fields must match";
        $_GET['email'=''; $_GET['email2']='';
 }
 else{ // email wasn't entered and/or fields matched
```

```
    if(!empty($_GET['email'])){ // Eliminate the possibility
    that email is simply empty
        if(validate($_GET['email'], EMAIL)==false{$errors[]=
          "Invalid email address" [check]; // We only need to
          validate one, since they are the same
        $_GET['email']=''; $_GET['email2'];
     }
  }
    if(!isset($errors)){ // if nothing tripped an error, the
    array was never created
       $errors='ok'; // Set the flag to 'ok' (or 1, or whatever
          else you like) so next section fires
     }
}
```

We have now checked all of the required fields from our form. We may have had more fields, but for whatever reason are not concerned enough about their contents to require or validate them. You may be wondering why we are validating in PHP since JavaScript can do this before the form is submitted in real time. There are two reasons (re)validating with PHP can help you. First, is the more obvious case in which the end user's browser, firewall network policy, etc. has disabled JavaScript. While your form would still function, you would end up with possibly invalid data. Second is that any bots that find your form and attempt to use it maliciously are likely to read your form's destination and send data directly to your processing script, also circumventing your validation. This allows you to add sanitization through PHP in addition to other safety precautions to further harden your site.

Next we will take a look at some options of what we can do once the form has been checked and is OK. Ultimately, there are two main tasks for you here. The first, is do whatever it is you want to do with what the user gave you—email the results, store them in a database, process a registration or login, use them to search data or affect output, etc. The second, is to provide feedback that demonstrates to the user how their action affected the system. It could be search results, a "successful" notice like "Thank You for Registering!" or the result of their interaction, like them being logged into the system.

```
if($check=='ok'){ // email ourselves a copy of what they sub-
mitted and tell them they are done
mail("us@oursite.com","$_GET[firstName] created and account.",
print_r($_GET,true),"From: noreply@oursite.com");
echo "Thank you for registering!";
}
```

Finally, our last logical test will be true if the user has not submitted anything or if there were errors. By creating this section as follows, we can support both cases at the same time:

```
if($errors!='ok'){ //there were errors or the form is not
submitted ?>
foreach($errors as $error){echo "$error</br>";}
   <form action='<?php echo $_SERVER['PHP_SELF']; ?>'
   method='get' name='registration'>
      <input type='text' name='firstName' value='<?php echo
         $_GET['firstName']; ?>' /><br/>
```

```
        <input type='text' name='lastName' value='<?php echo
           $_GET['lastName']; ?>' /><br/>
        <input type='text' name='email' value='<?php echo $_
           GET['email']; ?>' /><br/>
        <input type='text' name='email2' value='<?php echo
           $_GET['email2']; ?>' /><br/>
        <input type='submit' name='Register' value='submit' />
    </form>
<?php } ?>
```

In our last section, the foreach in the second line will print any errors that were added to the array. Since we have reached this point, $errors either is an array and our entries will print to the screen, or it was never set, and will not show anything on the screen if we are suppressing notices. If you want to avoid the notice generated when the form has not been submitted, we could wrap line 2 with an If statement:

```
if(!empty($errors)){foreach($errors as $error){echo "$error</
br>";}}
```

In our form you will see we re-entered PHP inside of the value attribute of each input. By echoing the value of the input in our get array, if there is one, we will re-populate our form with what the user entered. Since the first section of our code already checked these values if the form was submitted, any bad entries will have already been reset to nothing, helping the user see what needs to be re-entered.

This effectively completes our one page form, validation, and response. We could add jQuery validation on top of our form elements to improve the user experience as well by validating during the form completion process, but bear in mind this is a progressive enhancement, meaning we should assume JavaScript is off, and that anything we use that works improves upon an already working system.

Drag and Drop

Certain tags in HTML5 now support the ability to be treated as drag and droppable items. Items that support the ability allow for attributes including draggable, ondragenter, ondragover, ondragstart, ondragend, and ondrop. When we want to define the actions that take place when one of these conditions is met, we need to call a JavaScript function, that we define ourselves. We will look at our example by creating it in layers, first defining the structure with HTML, then adding our CSS apply our visual, and finally we will add our JavaScript to give it full functionality.

The first piece of our structure is to define the places in our page where moveable objects are allowed to be. These will typically represent the start and end areas that we are allowed to move objects to and from, like a product page to a shopping cart icon, or just two big empty areas. We will create a simple two location page for now. To define our two areas that are drag and drop friendly, we define our divs as we are accustomed to doing and simply add the references to actions that are allowed, or that we want to instigate actions or changes in our visual cues:

```
<div id="startingLocation" ondragenter="return
dragenter(event)" ondragover="return hover(event)"
ondrop="return drop(event)"> </div>
<div id="endingLocation" ondragenter="return dragenter(event)"
ondragover="return hover(event)" ondrop="return drop(event)">
</div>
```

Next, we will add the objects we want to interact with. They need a place to live when the page loads, so we will put them in the startingLocation div.

```
<div id="startingLocation" ondragenter="return
dragenter(event)" ondragover="return hover(event)"
ondrop="return drop(event)">
   <div id="item1" draggable="true" ondragstart="return
   start(event)" ondragend="return end(event)">Item #1</div>
   <div id="item2" draggable="true" ondragstart="return
   start(event)" ondragend="return end(event)">Item #2</div>
   <div id="item3" draggable="true" ondragstart="return
   start(event)" ondragend="return end(event)">Item #3</div>
</div>
```

While this now gives us a drag and drop foundation, it is not exactly user friendly yet. If you save and test what we have, you will find a very blank screen that is probably rather difficult to interact with as we cannot tell where the different objects start and end, and even at that we have no actions. To address this, we need to add some CSS to our file:

```
<style type="text/css">
#startingLocation, #endingLocation{
      Float:left;
      Width:200px;
      Height:200px;
      Margin:10px;
}
#startingLocation{
      Background-color:red;
}
#endingLocation{
      Background-color:green;
}
#item1, #item2, #item3{
      Width:60px;
      Height:60px;
      Padding:5px;
      Margin:10px;
}
</style>
```

To give us functionality, we need to add JavaScript to dictate what happens when items are moved around on the screen. We need to provide the start function permission to move items, dictate what information it needs to bring with the dragged object, and what to display when the object is in motion:

```
<script type="text/javascript">
```

```
function start(event){
    //Give the draggable object permission to move
    event.dataTransfer.effectAllowed='move';
    //Grabs the dragged items ID for reference
    event.dataTranser.setData("id",event.target.
    getAttribute('id'));
    // Sets our drag image with no offset
    event.dataTransfer.setDragImage(event.target, 0, 0);
    return true;
}
</script>
```

Next, we need to define what happens to our objects when they are held over an area that takes drops. To do this, we will add the definition of the hover() function we referred to when we created our HTML:

```
function hover(){
    //reads the ID we provided of the dragged item
    var iddraggable = event.dataTransfer.getData("id");
    // reads the ID of the object we are hovering over
    var id = event.target.getAttribute('id');
    //All items can be dropped into endingLocation
    if(id=='endingLocation') return false; else return true;
}
```

If we wanted to declare that only our first two draggable items are allowed into the endingLocation box, we would change our if statement to specify which items are allowed:

```
If(id=='endingLocation')&& (iddraggable== 'item1' ||
iddraggable=='item2') return false;
```

Next we need to complete the act of moving our item to its new location. We will add one more function we have already made reference to in our HTML, drop():

```
function drop(){
    var iddraggable event.dataTransfer.getData('id');
    event.target.appendChild(document.
    getElementById(iddraggable);
    event.stopPropagation();
    return false;
}
```

Finally, we need to clean up. Now that our item is dropped, we do not need to worry about its value any longer:

```
function end(){
    event.dataTransfer.clearData('id');
    return true;
}
```

If we were going to use our drag and drop system as a shopping cart, we would want to flesh out more actions in our end function. We would add code to add the item to the session or cookie record of our shopping cart, and could trigger other actions like updating our cart total on the screen or prompting for a number of that item we want in our cart.

Chapter 45

Finishing Touches

Search Engine Optimization (SEO)

Search engine optimization is the process of making your site the best possible candidate for favorable listing placement in search engine results. The factors that weigh in on a site's scoring and ranking and constantly growing and evolving, and encompass far greater than just the correspondence between a searched word or phrase against the page content in your site.

Covering all aspects of SEO is a task in and of itself just for one search engine. Accounting for the differences between Google, Yahoo, Bing, and all the others would be a text in and of itself and would be out of date before the printer finished the first page.

True optimization is an almost daily task, involving monitoring changes in algorithms, refining the site as content changes, and using systems like Google's Ad Sense for commercial placements on search results pages. Even at that, portions of today's SEO algorithms are out of your control, in that they take into account things that are out of your control like previous traffic, outside links, and more. Start with these basics first to get a good start:

1. Make sure you are mobile optimized
2. Use meta tags and <h> tags to emphasize important content
3. Use those same keywords as page titles
4. Do not include too many keywords in your meta tags
5. Update your content regularly
6. Integrate with social media for exposure

Analytics

A close cousin to the tasks of optimizing your site for search engines is optimizing it for your target audience. There is no better way to do this than to understand who your audience is, which you can find in your website logs. You can learn surprising things with analytics, which has spurred many of the extreme large data sets now in existence, and resulted in some of the more controversial features of websites like tailoring ads to your interests or recent searches.

Within your web server's logs, you might find that your visitors are coming from countries you had not anticipated—signs that may induce you to add additional language support, improving their experience. You might find that your users are trying to use mobile devices that you were not quite supporting, or that they are using a resolution higher than you thought, allowing you to redesign your site to provide more content or a smaller interface.

Tracking where a user goes, what they look at, how long they look at it. In fact, every action they take can provide insight. Aggregating this data across a volume of users over time give you the means to discover things you (and perhaps even your users) are not aware of.

You can see these data sets in use when you see features like "Other users also viewed this show" or "You recently looked at this item." Following up on trends by interviewing users has also shown companies how to covert more leads. To address users leaving with items in their shopping cart before purchasing, some companies discovered through surveys that most of those users decided against a purchase because of shipping costs, or uncertainty over taxes and surcharges. This allowed them to make changes to their site, providing more information sooner to address concerns, and allowed for particular marketing techniques. Instead of making all shipping free, a number of companies will trigger automatic follow-up emails when digital shopping carts are abandoned, or orders are immediately canceled, by offering free shipping or additional coupons or discounts to convince the shopper to complete the sale, improving their conversion rate.

To begin with analytics, you can start by taking a look at the raw logs your server creates. Since our example throughout the book has been using a LAMP, your log location is probably in /etc/httpd/logs. A file search for the word logs will likely reveal the correct folder for your particular installation. Depending on your server configuration this folder may have one or more files that track things like people accessing files on your site (everything from pages to images and anything else a user can see or use) as well as errors that were encountered or reported by elements of your server involved in rendering pages.

These files by themselves are not easy to interpret in aggregate form until you have spent time working with them or are seeking answers that are small amounts of the record like the last error or searching for a particular file. Instead, most people who interact with logs prefer to use an outside program that reads the files and helps them see trends over time so they can extrapolate more information than the raw file provides by itself. A free, open source solution (for personal use) that you can use to this end is AWStats, which compiles your logs into a variety of charts, graphs, and tables that focus on a number of aspects of your site like where visitors are coming from, what browser they used, what pages are most popular, and more.

For more specialized information, many sites create databases that track everything about their site, a user's entire experience, and apply everything else they know about a user to determine larger questions like how best to get the customer to return to the site again or what coupons to offer them like the shopping cart example above.

Privacy Statement

You may wish to include (and abide by) a privacy statement for your users. Spell out exactly what type of information you collect about them, how long it is stored, whether or not you will share or sell their information to another party, and so on. This is also a good place to spell out or link to a location where they can request that their information be removed as well.

This type of statement will allow users to determine if they are comfortable using your site and gives transparency into how you will treat their data.

Terms of Use

In much the same vein as a privacy statement you may also wish to include a terms of use that clarifies to the user the extent to which they are allowed to use your site and its information. We are all familiar with the epic novel terms of use documents that are frequently included with software and hardware purchases these days, but there is a growing movement to embrace a more non-lawyer friendly set of these types of documents.

Which one you decide to use is up to you, and there a great deal of examples in the wild. This is one area in which you may still want to include a lawyer, attorney, or your company's legal department before posting.

Chapter 46

Now What?

By this point you are hopefully comfortable with the fundamentals of web design, and have the ability to balance and integrate at least those languages covered within in order to optimize your site and provide a positive, useful experience for your end users. You have, as some might say, just enough knowledge to be dangerous. There is still far more to learn. Each topic we covered in this text was a tip of the iceberg. The languages we covered, methods and approaches, design techniques, histories and all go into much greater depth.

This text took effort to give you an understanding of each topic, but in many implementations each of these topics is addressed by different parties. Fortune 500 companies typically have one or more employees addressing focused topics such as networking, database development, front-end programming, etc. The consumer research and design aspects alone have created entire departments. Who your team is composed of and how many of you there are become determined by the size of the project, the size of your company, the particular needs and complexities of the project in questions, as well as time line and budget. Similarly sized, timed, and budgeted projects may have distinctly difference staffing simply because one is a financial system requiring input from accountants and lawyers and the other is a museum, requiring input from librarians and art historians.

Now it is time to get some real projects under your belt. After a few full implementations, you will learn which aspects are of most interest or come most naturally to you. Once you have these identified, you have found your niche. Then it is time to go deeper, learning the facets and minutia of one or more of the topics we covered. The references section is a treasure trove of excellent resources to go deeper into any of the topics covered here.

Glossary of Terms

Bot

A bot is a script designed to perform a repeated operation, like reading websites to find email addresses, indexing site pages for search engines, and more. They are used for both malevolent and benevolent purposes. You may also see bot defined as a computer attempting to mimic human behavior like fake friend message requests and text messages, as well as to represent a computer controlled player in a game, however in the web world we stick with the first definition.

FOSS

Free, Open Source Software. This abbreviation is used to identify open source projects that are free in terms of cost and the ability to access the code, as opposed to open source projects that may require a licensing purchase or other fiscal investment.

Hacker

A hacker is a generic term for a person who attempts to gain unauthorized access to a controlled system. Historically, the first hackers performed these activities out of curiosity. Today this term has become associated with hackers whose goal is to cause malicious damage for personal gain.

FTP

File Transfer Protocol. An alternative communication method to HTTP and part of the Internet Protocol suite, this transmission standard focuses on moving files between computers.

Interpreter

The interpreter is the program that receives our written code and translates it to the required output format. In this text, for example, the PHP interpreter takes our code and transforms our requests and commands into the full HTML output that is then provided to the browser. The browser, too, works as an interpreter, translating the HTML into the visual page that we see.

IRC

Internet Relay Chat can be equated to the Internet equivalent of text messaging. Message from two or more parties are displayed for all parties to view in linear format in a space referred to as a chat room.

MIME Type

Multipurpose Internet Mail Extensions. MIME types are used to identify sections of an email that contain different files like images or attachments.

RFID

Radio Frequency Identification. These objects are electronic tags, or markers, that can be placed inside or attached to items to help identify their location. They are read by special readers, typically placed at points of interest (e.g., in shipping bays at a warehouse) to help track items in motion. They can be powered by battery (active tags) or can absorb energy from the electromagnetic field generated by the reader (passive tags) in order to transmit the information encoded on them.

Pixel

The smallest point on a screen that can be assigned a color value by the display.

Platform

A synonym for your operating system. Typically used when referring to more than one operating system, or when the discussion is not contingent on a particular operating system.

SCADA

Supervisory Control and Data Acquisition. This is the controlling equipment that monitors and sets configuration settings for physical equipment, usually found in places like machine shops, utilities, and factories.

Syntax Highlighting

The ability for a document processor, development environment, or other software to identify and distinguish different aspects of written code in one or more language, applying color coding or other features to assist the programmer.

UDP

User Datagram Protocol. Similar communication method to HTTP, but differs in how it communicates by avoiding error checking and correction in favor of improved transmission speed.

UNIX

UNIX is an operating system created by Bell Labs (AT&T) employees in 1969 that focuses on multi-user and multi-tasking abilities.

WebKit

WebKit is an open source web browser engine. WebKit is also the name of the Mac OS X system framework version of the engine that is used by Safari, Dashboard, Mail, and many other OS X applications.

XML

Extensible Markup Language. This flexible, user-defined markup format allows data to be labelled and transmitted in a more system-independent format.

Index

Section 1 Questions

1. Which IP address convention uses both numbers and letters?
    a. IPV4 [IPV4 uses 4 blocks of numbers]
    b. IPV6 [Correct!]
2. Which of the following is not in the OSI 7 layer framework?
    a. Application [Layer 7]
    b. Network [Layer 3]
    c. Migration [Correct!]
    d. Data Link [Layer 2]
3. What name has the acronym PHP not represented over time?
    a. Hypertext Pre-Processer [This is used now]
    b. Personal Home Page [This was the original name]
    c. Pre-HTML Processing [Correct!]
4. Which of the following is true?
    a. Open source software is always free in cost [It is not always free]
    b. Users can edit the source code at their pleasure [Correct!]
    c. Users can change and sell their version of the product [You may not be able to profit from your changes]
5. Is open source software always free?
    a. Yes [Not all open source products are free]
    b. No [Correct!]
6. Which of these is not a benefit of virtualization?
    a. Reduced hardware footprint [Placing multiple systems onto one set of hardware is possible]
    b. Reduced operating costs [Utilities are lowered by using less physical hardware]
    c. Increased speeds when using systems [Correct! Virtualization does not always mean improved performance]
7. Which of these best describes cloud computing?
    a. Using servers that are in orbit [These don't exist for commercial use]
    b. Hosting services on virtualized, Internet connected hardware [Correct!]
    c. Sharing a file online [Not everything online is part of a cloud]
8. The predecessor of the internet was
    a. CompuServe [Like AOL, CompuServe was a means of accessing the Internet]
    b. Arpanet [Correct!]

c. DARPA [This government agency participated in its development]

d. Al Gore [Despite popular misconception, this is not true]

9. Cloud computing is

   a. Shared services available online [Correct!]

   b. Portable jump drives [These are not Internet devices]

   c. Outsourcing [You can create your own clouds]

   d. Portable servers [Portability does not define something as a cloud]

10. Which of these is not available as a service?

   a. Software [Incorrect]

   b. Operating systems [Incorrect]

   c. Hardware [Incorrect]

   d. None of the above [Correct!]

11. Web warfare has already emerged as a tactic in conflicts between nations.

   a. True [Correct!]

   b. False [See the Russia-Georgia conflict]

12. Botnets are

   a. Local networks [Only the compromised systems are part of a botnet]

   b. Groups of compromised computers [Correct!]

   c. Viruses [Viruses may help create the networks, but the collection of systems are not a virus]

   d. All of the above [Incorrect]

13. Which of the following is not part of a standard WAMP server?

   a. HTTP server [Incorrect]

   b. Scripting engine [Incorrect]

   c. Database [Incorrect]

   d. FTP [Correct!]

14. Linux is a(n)

   a. Operating system [Correct!]

   b. HTTP server [Incorrect]

   c. Server [It may be used to create a server, but does not have to be one]

   d. All of the above [Incorrect]

15. MySQL is a(n)

   a. HTTP server [Incorrect]

   b. Database [Correct!]

   c. Server [Incorrect]

   d. None of the above [Incorrect]

16. PHP is a(n)
    a. Web server [Incorrect]
    b. Scripting language [Correct!]
    c. Operating system [Incorrect]
    d. Database [Incorrect]
17. Open source is always
    a. Free to be modified [Correct!]
    b. Free in cost [Incorrect]
    c. Shareable [Incorrect]
    d. All of the above [Incorrect]
18. Apache is a:
    a. Web server [Correct!]
    b. Scripting language [Incorrect]
    c. Database [Incorrect]
    d. None of the above [Incorrect]
19. FTP stands for ____________.
    a. File Transfer Protocol [Correct!]
    b. Files To Push [Incorrect]
    c. File Transmission Pipe [Incorrect]
20. HTTP stands for ___________.
    a. Hyper Text Translation Program [Incorrect]
    b. Hyper Text Transfer Protocol [Correct!]
    c. Hyper Transfer Text Program [Incorrect]
21. The SQL part of MySQL stands for _________.
    a. Super Question Language [Incorrect]
    b. Structured Question Language [Incorrect]
    c. Structured Query Language [Correct!]
22. An IPV4 address is made up of __ blocks of numbers.
    a. 3 [Incorrect]
    b. 4 [Correct!]
    c. 5 [Incorrect]
    d. 6 [Incorrect]
23. An IPV6 address uses both letters and numbers.
    a. True [Correct!]
    b. False [Incorrect]
24. URL stands for ______.

a. Universal Resource Locator [Correct!]
b. Unordered Resource Location [Incorrect]
c. Unsorted Relational Language [Incorrect]

RETURN

Section 2 Questions

1. What does HTML stand for?
    a. Hyperlinks and Text Markup Language [Incorrect]
    b. Hyper Text Markup Language [Correct!]
    c. Home Tool Markup Language [Incorrect]
    d. Hyper Text Manipulation Language [Incorrect]
2. Choose the correct HTML tag for the largest heading.
    a. <heading> [This is not a valid tag]
    b. <h1> [Correct!]
    c. <header> [This is a document section]
    d. <h6> [This is the smallest heading]
3. Which of these is a properly formatted link?
    a. <a link="www.google.com">Link</a> [Incorrect]
    b. <a href="www.google.com"/> [Incorrect]
    c. <link location="www.google.com">Link</a> [Incorrect]
    d. <a href="www.google.com">Link</a> [Correct!]
4. How can you open a link in a new tab/browser window?
    a. <a href="url" target="_blank"> [Correct!]
    b. <a href="url" target="new"> [Incorrect]
    c. <a href="url" new> [Incorrect]
5. Which doctype is correct for HTML5?
    a. <!DOCTYPE HTML5> [Incorrect]
    b. <!DOCTYPE html> [Correct!]
    c. <!DOCTYPE HTML PUBLIC "-//W3C//DTD HTML 5.0//EN" "http://www.w3.org/TR/html5/strict.dtd"> [Incorrect]
6. What is the correct HTML for making a drop-down list?
    a. <select> [Correct!]
    b. <input type="dropdown"> [Incorrect]
    c. <input type="list"> [Incorrect]
    d. <list> [Incorrect]
7. Which of the following is correct?
    a. HTML is used for exchanging data, XML is not. [Incorrect]
    b. XML is used for exchanging data, HTML is not. [Correct!]
    c. HTML can have user defined tags, XML cannot. [Incorrect]
    d. Both b and c above. [Incorrect]

8. What is the correct HTML5 element for playing video files?

    a. <movie> [Incorrect]
    b. <video> [Correct!]
    c. <source> [Incorrect]
    d. None of the above [Incorrect]

9. What is the correct HTML for inserting an image?

    a. <img src="image.gif" alt="MyImage"> [Correct!]
    b. <image src="image.gif" alt="MyImage"> [Incorrect]
    c. <img href="image.gif" alt="MyImage"> [Incorrect]
    d. <img alt="MyImage">image.gif</img> [Incorrect]

10. The <canvas> element in HTML5 is used to:

    a. Display database records [This is possible, but not the main purpose]
    b. Manipulate data in MySQL [Incorrect]
    c. Create draggable elements [This is possible, but not the main purpose]
    d. Draw graphics [Correct!]

11. In HTML5, which attribute is used to specify that an input field must be filled out?

    a. Formvalidate [Incorrect]
    b. Validate [Incorrect]
    c. placeholder [Incorrect]
    d. required [Correct!]

12. Which HTML5 element is used to display a measurement within a fixed range?

    a. <gauge> [Incorrect]
    b. <range> [Correct!]
    c. <measure> [Incorrect]
    d. <meter> [Incorrect]

13. What does CSS stand for?

    a. Cross-site scripting [Incorrect]
    b. Cascading Style Sheets [Correct!]
    c. Creative style sheets [Incorrect]
    d. Compiled site styles [Incorrect]

14. Given the following, what value does the left margin have?: margin: 10px 5px 20px 15px;

    a. 10px [This is the top]
    b. 5px [This is the right side]
    c. 20px [This is the bottom]
    d. 15px [Correct!]

15. Which style rule overrides the other?
    a. Class [Incorrect]
    b. Id [Correct!]
16. What property creates space between HTML elements?
    a. Margin [Correct!]
    b. Padding [This is inside an element]
    c. Spacing [This is between text]
    d. Float [Incorrect]
17. What property creates space within an element?
    a. Margin [This is between elements]
    b. Padding [Correct!]
    c. Spacing [This is between text]
    d. Float [Incorrect]
18. Which set of tags are used to define CSS within the page?
    a. <style type="css"></style> [Correct!]
    b. <class type="text/css"></class> [Incorrect]
    c. <inline css></inline> [Incorrect]
    d. None of the above [Incorrect]
19. Which of these is the correct way to define a hover state for an anchor tag?
    a. :onHover [Correct!]
    b. :mouseOver [Incorrect]
    c. :hover [Incorrect]
    d. None of These [Incorrect]
20. Which property of a position rule will force content to a position regardless of other elements?
    a. Fixed [Incorrect]
    b. Absolute [Correct!]
    c. Relative [Incorrect]
    d. Strict [Incorrect]
21. Responsive styling allows us to support many devices with one style sheet.
    a. True [Correct!]
    b. False [Incorrect]
22. Which of the following is the best fit for defining styles on small mobile devices?
    a. @media only screen and (max-width: 479p) [Correct!]
    b. @media only screen and (max-width: 769p) [This is best for tablets]

c. @media only screen and (max-width: 120p) [This is very small!]

RETURN

Section 3 Questions

1. The array $array = ("One"=>1, "Two"=>2, "Three"=>3) is numeric
    a. True [Incorrect]
    b. False [Correct!]
2. Which equation equates to 14?
    a. 4 + 5 2 - 4 [10]
    b. (4 + 5) 2 – 4 [Correct!]
    c. 4 + 5 (2 - 4) [-6]
    d. 4 + (5 2) – 4 [10]
3. The foreach() function in PHP is used when dealing with:
    a. Strings [Incorrect]
    b. Arrays [Correct!]
    c. Objects [Incorrect]
    d. Lists [Incorrect]
4. Which PHP reserved array holds values passed in the URL?
    a. $_POST [Incorrect]
    b. $_GET [Correct!]
    c. $_SESSION [Incorrect]
    d. None of these [Incorrect]
5. Which of the following is NOT a valid variable name?
    a. $variable [Incorrect]
    b. $string [Incorrect]
    c. $_string1 [Incorrect]
    d. $and-then [Correct!]
6. Which of the following is an incorrect definition?
    a. Apache = Web Server [Incorrect]
    b. PHP = Object oriented language [Incorrect]
    c. MySQL = Database Server [Incorrect]
    d. HTML = Operating System [Correct!]
7. Which of the following PHP functions runs until a condition is met?
    a. foreach() [Incorrect]
    b. while() [Correct!]
    c. during() [Incorrect]
    d. None of these [Incorrect]
8. Declaring strings using single quotes means PHP syntax in the string will be shown.

a. True [Correct!]
b. False [Incorrect]

9. Which HTML element is used for JavaScript?
   a. <scripting> [Incorrect]
   b. <javascript> [Incorrect]
   c. <jscript> [Incorrect]
   d. <script> [Correct!]
10. Where can we place JavaScript?
   a. <head> [This is one place]
   b. <body> [This is one place]
   c. A & B [Correct!]
   d. None of these [Incorrect]
11. JavaScript and Java are the same thing.
   a. True [Incorrect]
   b. False [Correct!]
12. DOM stands for
   a. Document Object Model [Correct!]
   b. Document Oriented Media [Incorrect]
   c. Document Object Manager [Incorrect]
   d. None of these [Incorrect]
13. When a user views a page containing a JavaScript program, which machine actually executes the script?
   a. The user's browser [Correct!]
   b. The Web server [Incorrect]
   c. Both [Incorrect]
   d. None of the above [Incorrect]
14. Which of the following cannot be done with JavaScript?
   a. Validating a form [Incorrect]
   b. Sending a form's contents by email [Correct!]
   c. Storing the form's contents to a database file on the server [Incorrect]
   d. None of the above [Incorrect]
15. Which of the following is not a valid JavaScript variable name?
   a. 1stname [Correct!]
   b. _firstName [Incorrect]
   c. FirstName [Incorrect]
   d. None of these [Incorrect]

16. What is the correct JavaScript syntax to write "Hello World"?

    a. System.out.println("Hello World") [Incorrect]
    b. println ("Hello World") [Incorrect]
    c. document.write("Hello World") [Correct!]
    d. response.write("Hello World") [Incorrect]

17. jQuery uses CSS selectors to interact with page elements.

    a. True [Correct!]
    b. False [Incorrect]

18. In jQuery, $('div') would select

    a. The first div element [Incorrect]
    b. All div elements [Correct!]
    c. An element named div [Incorrect]

19. Which jQuery function makes sure the contained code only runs when the page is done loading?

    a. $(body).onload() [Incorrect]
    b. $(document).loaded() [Incorrect]
    c. $document.ready() [Correct!]
    d. None of these [Incorrect]

20. jQuery is an add-on library for JavaScript, not an independent language.

    a. True [Correct!]
    b. False [Incorrect]

RETURN

Section 4 Questions

1. What does SQL stand for?
    a. Standard Query Linguistics [Incorrect]
    b. Structured Query Language [Correct!]
    c. Strict Query Language [Incorrect]
    d. None of the above [Incorrect]
2. Which of these is used to retrieve information from a database?
    a. Get [Incorrect]
    b. Fetch [Incorrect]
    c. Select [Correct!]
    d. Find [Incorrect]
3. Which of these commands would get the name column from a Persons table?
    a. Select name from Persons; [Correct!]
    b. Get persons.name [Incorrect]
    c. Select persons.name [Incorrect]
    d. Get name from Persons [Incorrect]
4. Which of the following select records where the name fields starts with an A?
    a. Select * from Persons where name='a' [This will get names that are only a]
    b. Select * from Persons where name like "a%" [Correct!]
    c. Select * from Persons where name like "%a" [This will select things that end in a]
    d. None of these [Incorrect]
5. Which of the following is the keyword used to sort results?
    a. Order By [Correct!]
    b. Sort By [Incorrect]
    c. Filter By [Incorrect]
    d. Ascending [Incorrect]
6. Which of the following is used to find the number of records?
    a. Total() [Incorrect]
    b. Count() [Correct!]
    c. Sum() [Incorrect]
    d. None of these [Incorrect]
7. Eliminating multiple identical columns from a table is which normalization?
    a. First [Correct!]
    b. Second [Incorrect]

c. Third [Incorrect]
d. Fourth [Incorrect]

8. Eliminating repeated values from a table is which normalization?
   a. First [Incorrect]
   b. Second [Correct!]
   c. Third [Incorrect]
   d. Fourth [Incorrect]
9. Ensuring no values are repeated in a database is which of the following?
   a. First [Incorrect]
   b. Second [Incorrect]
   c. Third [Correct!]
   d. Fourth [Incorrect]
10. Ensuring all fields relate directly to the table they are in is which normalization?
   a. First [Incorrect]
   b. Second [Incorrect]
   c. Third [Correct!]
   d. Fourth [Incorrect]
11. The CRUD actions are:
   a. Compose, Read, Update, Delete [Incorrect]
   b. Create, Read, Update, Destroy [Incorrect]
   c. Create, Read, Update, Delete [Correct!]
   d. Copy, Read, Update, Drop [Incorrect]
12. Including all of the records in the first table of a join is done using:
   a. Join all [Incorrect]
   b. Left join [Correct!]
   c. Right join [Incorrect]
   d. None of these [Incorrect]
13. Queries can be placed inside of other queries.
   a. True [Correct!]
   b. False [Incorrect]
14. Which of the following is used to remove a record from a table?
   a. Delete from [Correct!]
   b. Drop from [Incorrect]
   c. Destroy [Incorrect]
15. MySQL requires which of the following to run?
   a. Windows [Incorrect]

b. Linux [Incorrect]
c. Apple [Incorrect]
d. Any of these [Correct!]

RETURN

Made in the USA
San Bernardino, CA
27 August 2018